D1034031

HARRY MIDDLETON

T H E

BRIGHT
COUNTRY

A Fisherman's Return to
Trout, Wild Water, and Himself

SIMON & SCHUSTER
New York London Toronto Sydney Tokyo Singapore

SIMON & SCHUSTER
Simon & Schuster Building
Rockefeller Center
1230 Avenue of the Americas
New York, New York 10020

Designed by Pei Loi Koay
Manufactured in the United States of America

1 3 5 7 9 10 8 6 4 2

Library of Congress Cataloging-in-Publication Data

Middleton, Harry.
The bright country : a fisherman's return to trout,
wild water, and himself / Harry Middleton.
p.   cm.
1. Middleton, Harry—Mental health. 2. Depressed
persons—United States—Biography. 3. Depressed
persons—Rehabilitation—Case studies.
4. Trout fishing—Therapeutic use.
I. Title.
RC537.M52   1993
362.1'968527'0092—dc20   93-23988 CIP
ISBN 0-671-75859-4

ACKNOWLEDGMENTS

I have thanked those few people whose friendship, help, and advice helped me through the writing of this book the way they should be thanked, personally and privately. There are several exceptions. I would like to thank Trish Lande and Carolyn Krupp, Rosemary Misurelli, the directors, members, and staff at Yaddo for their kind and generous invitation. I truly wish things for me had been different, so that I could have come. The invitation alone, however, was a great honor, one I will always remember warmly. Too, wherever she might be, I would like to thank Lilly Yoshida for reasons she alone will understand.

Otherwise, this book, like everything else I have written, is my doing. It was not funded by any grants or stipends, any awards or fellowships, public or private, though God knows I tried.

This one is for Bob Bender and Annie Dillard

To everyone back in Never-Never Land, back in paradise,
OLLIE-OLLIE-OXEN-FREE

CONTENTS

I approached near unto Hell, even to the gates of
Proserpina, and after that I was ravished throughout
all the elements, and I returned to my proper place:
about midnight I saw the sun brightly shine.

—APULEIUS

What's madness but nobility of soul
At odds with circumstance? The day's on fire
I know the purity of pure despair.
My shadow pinned against a sweating wall,
That place among the rocks—is it a cave,
Or winding path? The edge is what I have.

—THEODORE ROETHKE

PREFACE

This is a book about a great many things that are common, even peculiar, to human beings. Things like paradise and unemployment, friendship and loneliness, joy and laughter. There is a common theme running through this story, my story, all these details and years and moments. The common theme is a disease, the disease I suffered from for years and years, a disease Dr. Lilly Mutzpah told me I had probably been born with, that was, for me, genetic, as common in my family as hazel eyes and blond hair. I had no idea. Being shy and quiet, moody and blue had always seemed perfectly normal to me.

The disease is depression.

This is a story of time, too, of the years passing steadily by. Time is like that: it just goes on and on. Life is like that, too. There are no clear beginnings and endings. And the only map is the pulse of time, the years passing. The years that pass by in this book are from 1989 until tonight, this cool, October night in 1992 as I write these words, the first words of this book, which I am writing last.

The year that haunts this story more than any other is 1990.

It was some year, at least for me.

That was the year I met Swami Bill and his main squeeze, Kiwi LaReaux. That was the year the blind brown trout rose from the deep green pool of the Middle Fork of the South Platte River. Its sightless eyes were pools of color and light and shadow. I kept finding remnants of my own memory in its dead eyes.

Nineteen ninety was also the year I lost my job.

I was fired.

Being fired these days, of course, is hardly extraordinary. Indeed, it happens all the time. It's as common as the cold, headaches, having the blues, or paradise.

Losing my job caused whatever pink-cheeked chemicals there were left in my brain to sizzle and pop, go bad, go sour.

I had had the blues before. Who hasn't? I even had a name for my blues: the meat bucket blues. They had always come and gone.

Not this time. They got worse and worse.

And I would later learn, after ending up in Denver, Colorado, where I found work and eventually turned up in Dr. Lilly Mutzpah's office, that my worsening blues were a full-blown disease.

Depression.

Depression is something else that is as common as the cold, as being fired, as paradise.

This is the story of what the depression that bubbled in my blood and scorched through my brain burned, turned to ash, and what it left.

Dr. Mutzpah had good news for me. My disease could be treated, controlled, cured. There were medicines to repair all the burnt wiring and circuits in my brain, medicines that would ease the pain, douse the depression's black flames, make all my synapses healthy and good-natured and cheerful again.

I saw Dr. Mutzpah every Thursday for as long as I was in Denver.

After work each Friday, I would drive over Kenosha Pass,

spending every weekend and holiday, every spare day, up along the Middle Fork of the South Platte River that coils through South Park, a great valley of earth and sky, mountains, sunlight, and bright, moving water.

While I walked along the river, fished for its trout, as I spent more and more time in the high mountain meadows of South Park, I started poking through the ashes in my brainpan, sorting through what was left there—frayed desires, blackened wishes, half-melted dreams.

A blind brown trout rose in one of the river's deep, blue-green pools. Its blind eyes looked to me like great pools of gathered light and color and shadow. In those shimmering pools I discovered and rediscovered moments of time, memories, whole and fragmented, embroidered in patterns of color and sunlight, wind, and water, so that in time they seemed as complete and inseparable as that whole bright country: mountains and river and sky.

The blind brown trout haunted me for months. So did the river and the mountains and the high meadow. That's because among the ashes in my scorched brainpan was my old addiction, my wonderfully terrible and ruinous addiction to trout and to the wild country that trout demand.

All of which keep showing up in my books, again and again, not because they are books about fishing or trout or the high mountain country, but because of my calamitous addiction to such things and such places. Actually, my skills as a fly-fisherman are modest. I am no better at it than I am at life in general. Perhaps that is why it fascinates me so, though. Trout don't give a damn about my amateur status. And a hooked trout, as I have often said, can haul you anywhere, even to the edge of the universe.

As an average American writer, I have been asked to give and have given one interview.

Here it is, the whole thing.

INTERVIEWER: "Mr. Middleton, what have fish got to do with it?"
ME: "For Chrissakes, that's what I'd like to know."

What I keep discovering, of course, is that trout and wild rivers, mountains and sunlight, wind and shadows and the press of time upon the earth have everything to do with it.

At least for me.

It is well after midnight here on this hardluck Alabama mountain top. There is a wonderfully cool wind coming through my room's open window. The wind is blowing hard from the north and west, out of Tennessee and Arkansas.

County garbage truck No. 2 ended its nightly run hours ago. I am up here in my room where I am supposed to be scribbling away, but I am getting little done because I keep staring out the window at the October night sky and thinking of the high country beyond the topaz blue western horizon, that great, bright country of mountains and rivers and high meadows.

If I were there now, at sundown, it would be time for Swami Bill's harmless and innocent Sweet Hour of Prayer.

It is easy to imagine the heartbreakingly beautiful Kiwi LaReaux, Bill's main squeeze, smiling shyly, as always, the soft autumn light glistening like threads of gold in her lush red hair, flashing like tiny suns in her deep green eyes.

She would be repeating the homilies and creeds of Bill's church in progress, saying after each, "Pass it on . . . Pass it on."

I would be standing nearby, staring, as I always did, at the light in her hair, the light in her eyes, thinking of the river, its fast, cold water, how it had eased the depression that had moved through my brain and blood like a black tide, thinking of that blind brown trout in the deep pool of the river and how the light reflected off its eyes seemed to wrinkle with the history of the world, seemed to hold every moment of time, even the remnants of my own burnt-out memory.

All of this story is true, by the way, though I have changed some names, fiddled with appearances, altered some locations. I can only say, again, what I said to Juan Ortez, age fifteen, of Angel Fire, New Mexico. I got a letter from Juan Ortez this year. He wrote to tell me that everyone in his ninth-grade English class had to write a report on something called "creative nonfiction." Poor young Juan Ortez had had the bad luck to be assigned my books.

"Help me out on this thing," Juan Ortez wrote. "How much of all this stuff is imagined?"

It is a fair question. This is what I wrote back to Juan Ortez, age fifteen, of Angel Fire, New Mexico.

Dear Juan,

Sorry to hear you drew me for your English assignment. As for your question, all I can say is that in the end, not nearly as much as I had hoped. Not nearly as much.

The newest album by John Gorka is on the cassette player. It arrived today in a package from Mi Oh, the drop-dead lovely hostess of the Now & Zen Restaurant in Denver. Like Kiwi LaReaux, Swami Bill and the stuffed parrot on his shoulder, the blind brown trout, the Colorado high country, unemployment, Dr. Truth, and depression, Mi Oh is part of this story. She is determined to widen my musical appreciation, broaden my mind. Unlike the music of Helmet, the Lemonheads, Nine Inch Nails, the Butthole Surfers, and Nirvana, musical groups that Mi Oh has also introduced me to, the music of John Gorka does not make my teeth hurt. Indeed, I have become a dedicated fan of John Gorka.

I can't get enough, just as I can't seem to get enough of Mississippi Delta bluesmen, Loudon Wainwright III, mountain rivers, high country, wildness, trout, the night sky, the press of life.

Harry Middleton
Jonah's Ridge, Alabama
October 6, 1992

LIQUID MEMORIES

O remember
In your narrowing dark hours
That more things move
Than blood in the heart.

—LOUISE BOGAN

Please, pour yourself a drink, open a window, curl up in your favorite chair, listen to the rattle of the wind, to the unyielding press of time. Time has a language all its own. To me, it is more like a song, as simple as a nursery rhyme that pulses in the blood, whispers in every muscle and bone. The rhythm of things as they are.

Ebb and flow. The rhythm of things that come and go, come and go.

I always keep my room's window open, whatever the season or the weather. Tonight, there is a cool wind rattling among the hickory trees along the ridge of this eroded, Alabama mountain where I live.

As I write these lines, it is well after midnight. The hours on the back side of midnight, the hours when the blue and red dawn rises, are mine, and I sit here every night filling page after page of the notebooks I get by the dozen at the Piggly Wiggly supermarket down the mountain.

Like donuts, the notebooks are cheaper by the dozen. I save twelve cents buying them that way, a penny per notebook. It adds up. Everything adds up.

I cannot seem to scrub the smell of county garbage truck No. 2 off my skin. It is the same way with each one of us on the crew, all four of us. We all smell of piss and green mayonnaise, bubble gum, stale beer, and rancid meat. I have been on the crew of county garbage truck No. 2 for two years now.

There used to be five of us until Woody Moos got fired for stealing a smoked turkey last Thanksgiving. He plucked the smoked turkey off a lady's barbecue pit. He was supposed to be getting the garbage cans. He smelled the turkey being slowly smoked over coals and hickory chips and could not resist. Moos tucked the smoked turkey under his neon yellow rain slicker and hopped back on the truck. He was smiling innocently through a mist of delicious pale blue smoke.

While Moos was stealing the smoked turkey, tucking it under his neon yellow rain slicker, I was at the house next door, hauling their big green plastic garbage cans up to the back of the truck and letting myself daydream about mountains and cold, fast mountain streams and rising trout.

It does not matter that I have not been back to the high country, that I have not heard or seen or fished the cold, fast waters of a mountain stream in nearly two years. I am always thinking and dreaming about mountains and rivers and wild fish. Indeed, I have given up trying not to think about them. I confess that I have a terrible, implacable, ruinous addiction to wild water, to mountains and the high country, to trout. It is an addiction I have tried to kick again and again. Again and again I have failed, and the addiction has only gotten pleasantly and wonderfully worse.

As I went about being fired from my job as a full-time magazine writer on a lovely June afternoon in 1990, I found myself thinking about wild water, about mountains and high country

meadows soaked in brilliant sunlight. I kept thinking of wild country and wild fish because it helped ease the pain.

That trout and wild trout rivers should have filled my aching brain as my friend went about telling me to pack up my things and get out, was not so unusual, really.

I was fired by a friend. My friend was the CEO of the company for which I worked. That morning, a balmy June morning, I had been in my friend's office giving him a fly-fishing lesson. I gave him a short piece of rod, fitted with a cork grip at one end. At the other end I had tied twelve feet of neon orange yarn, so he could practice the basics of fly casting right there in his office, or wherever he went. We laughed and talked about trout and the angling life and laughed some more as we cast the willowy piece of neon orange yarn at pieces of executive furniture that we pretended were trout. Trout rose from under his massive desk, from the shelves of his bookcases, from between the chairs and the couches. And we laughed and laughed, as though we were long-lost boyhood friends, as though we were a couple of Lost Boys having the time of our lives in Never-Never Land.

Even later, after I had lost my job and so much else besides, after the depression that had been smoldering in my head burst into a black maelstrom, melting all the chemical wiring in my brain, and got worse and worse, finally dumping me in an unfurnished room in downtown Denver, Colorado, the singed folds of my memory still fed on dreams of remembered wild country, of mountains and high mountain valleys, of green meadows bisected by wide, bright rivers, trout on the rise.

The depression that burned through my brain left as much as it took. Among the ashes in my burnt-out brain was my old addiction to wildness, to mountains and wild rivers and trout.

Lucky me.

Lucky, indeed.

Working on county garbage truck No. 2 has taught me that I do not actually have to go fishing to satisfy my addiction. All the mountains and rivers and trout of yesteryear are still wrinkling around in my memory. They survived depression's black maelstrom, too. Everything is still there, deep in my brain, even that bright country of Colorado's Mosquito and Sawatch mountains, the great high meadows of South Park, the waters of the Middle Fork of the South Platte River flashing silver blue at dawn and twilight, and the blind brown trout that rose out of the green waters of the deep pool below Spinney Mountain. Its sightless eyes took me in and out of time, drenched me in life's continuum, hauled me even to the edge of the universe.

From May through the first week of September, the crew of county garbage truck No. 2 cleans up the Hoover Metropolitan Stadium after each Barons baseball game. The Birmingham Barons are a minor league baseball team, part of the White Sox organization.

We pick up after the games, after the crowds have gone, after the teams have left in the dark blue hours between midnight and dawn, after the stadium has been locked up. We clean the bathrooms. We pick up the parking lot. Two men pick up the stands. I am one of them. We do it by hand, picking up a section at a time, filling bag after bag after bag. Then we haul the bags to the truck, take them to the stadium dumpster up on the hill, toss them in, crush them. The summer nights are heavy and hot. A slick film of humidity covers every surface. We wear shorts and strip to the waist, tie bandanas about our heads to keep the sweat from filling our eyes as we move through the stands and box seats, reaching underneath, feeling for trash, no longer curious and only vaguely aware of what goes soft in our hands.

The stadium seats ten thousand, though there have been crowds of thirteen thousand, maybe more. Last season, Woody Moos was the second pickup man. After the final game of the season, Moos told me that he figured we had picked up a half million pieces of trash.

"Some field of dreams, eh?" said Woody Moos.

"Some field of dreams."

We get a fifteen-minute break every three hours. We all gather around home plate because the drinking fountains in the dugouts spurt out ice-cold water. We cannot get enough. We drink and drink, and use our T-shirts as rags to wipe the sweat off, along with dribbles and spurts of ketchup and mustard, bits of uneaten hot dogs and hamburgers, wilted knots of salad, smears of nachos, hardened shreds of spit tobacco, splashes of Coke and beer, dollops of unused pizza dough.

We all smell just like the stadium smells—of piss and vomit, of stale beer, spit tobacco and bubble gum, and meat going bad.

By the time we gather around home plate, we have filled and hauled off more than a hundred large plastic garbage bags and emptied the stadium's forty trash barrels. The barrels are always easy because the fans rarely use them. Why should they? Barrels, said Moos, are for tennis courts and golf courses. Baseball stadiums are places where you are supposed to hawk and spit, wad and fling, throw and stomp, tear and rip, puke and roar, register your anger and your joy by splattering gooey glops of nacho cheese on the seats in front of you, your neighbor, on top of the dugouts. It is high celebration, baseball reduced to the poetic metaphors of drunken brawls and food fights. Cleaning up is somebody else's job. *Our* job, part of what the crew of county garbage truck No. 2 does.

We are the county's tax dollars at work.

It is hard work. I do not mind. I am, as the saying goes, lucky to have the job.

Lucky, indeed.

When I lost my job, as my friend the CEO went about firing me, as he smiled and laughed and assured me things would be fine, that I could walk out the door and have my pick of writing jobs, I was quietly thanking whatever gods there are for my calloused hands and strong back.

Gathered about home plate, the crew of county garbage truck No. 2 gulps down the ice water from the fountains in the dugouts. We rarely talk. We lie in the cool green grass, listen to the stadium troll down in the belly of the stadium watching pornographic movies as he washes and dries the team's uniforms and jock straps. We call him the stadium troll because no one has ever seen him. Sometimes we see his shadow moving slowly through the stands. We can hear him picking through the trash, looking for lost change and half-eaten candy. When he is down in the locker rooms washing and drying and watching pornographic movies, we always know when the good parts of the movies come along, because the stadium troll begins screaming uncontrollably, "Oh, play ball! Oh, yes, play ball, goddamit!

"Oh, my-my-my goodness, PLAY BALL!"

Woody Moos was always wondering about the stadium troll. He put him in the same category as the hunchback of Notre Dame. Woody Moos told me he expected to turn on his television one morning and learn that the stadium troll had kidnapped Velvet Snatch, the beautiful porno queen, taken her high up among the banks of lights at the top of the stadium. He would be wearing Babe Ruff's grimy, frayed dog suit. Babe Ruff is the Barons' mascot. There would be the press of a swelling crowd, Moos said, spinning his tale to its end, and reporters shouting questions, and the stadium troll, clutching the delicious Ms. Snatch about the waist, would be dancing among the lights, swinging a bat, smacking bubble gum and chewing tobacco and yodeling, "Sanctuary! Sanctuary!"

As Moos talked I would lie in the cool green grass, waiting for that moment of bliss when the field's sprinklers come on, and stare up at the deep summer night, at the great sprawl of night, of stars and fiery moon, of blue shadows and earthglow, and let myself drift to the edge of the horizon and remember that bright country to the west, that high country of mountains and meadows and fast rivers, that endless spread of domed blue sky and bright water, the sound of the river splashing over the smooth

backs of eroded stones, trout rising. And remember that light dripping from the blind trout's eyes, that smear of light and form and shadow in which there were no boundaries, in which the whole bright country was joined and inseparable and, like the dome of sky, seemed to go on forever.

I began this book talking about fish, about fly-fishing. The few bookstore owners I have met tell me my books are curious offerings, that they are never quite certain where to shelve them. Usually, they end up among the outdoor books. Given my awful addiction to wild trout and the waters they inhabit, waters that still speak in tongues of time, that is as good a place for them as any.

As for fly-fishing, all I can say about it is that I am no better at it than I am at life, which may explain why it fascinates me so. Of late, I have read more than a few authors peddling fly-fishing as an art. When it comes to fly fishing, I am certain of nothing and especially its standing among the arts. Whenever I am asked about fly-fishing, I always give the same answer. I tell people that one way they can sample the myriad emotions that overwhelm the typical fly-fisherman is to go home, haul a large tub of ice water into the house and place it as far from the fireplace as they can. There should be a good fire going in the fireplace. Then, while standing barefoot in the tub of ice water, they should take fly rod in hand and practice casting hundred-dollar bills into the fireplace. While this exercise may not give them much of a feel for fly-fishing as art, it will, I think, permit them to share in some of the wonders of fly-fishing, especially the wonder of why fly-fishermen keep at it.

With little effort fly-fishing can become a powerful and impressive obsession, the best part of which is not so much the angling, but rather where fly-fishing takes me. As a junkie for wild country and rivers and fish, I am certain of one other thing about fly-fishing. There is something wonderfully simple about it, a rhythm, a rhyme, some beat of heart and blood and bone beyond the normal geography of language.

Among the ashes left in my brain after depression's black firestorm had burned through was this relentless mercurial rhyme. Every attempt I have made to put this rhyme in words is clumsy and awkward. So I keep saying what it sounds like, feels like to me as it bounces along my spine whenever I am along a wild stretch of river—the rhyme of things that come and go. As simple and profound as a child's nursery rhyme.

Because I am always looking and listening, sitting down on riverbanks and not fishing, or not caring so much whether I catch fish or not, I have to admit that, happily, I know little about the mechanics of fly-fishing. Among average fly-fishermen like me, too much thought about mechanics and angling technology leads to trouble and fatigue, and it tends to dull the uncluttered enjoyment of just fishing—the push and pull of a river, colored shadows dancing among the black ridges of distant mountains, the endless ranges of sunlight washing across the land, flashing off the river, the sudden wonder and relentless mystery of rising trout, the rhythm of moving water, which rises as suddenly as trout and is like some childhood song suddenly and wonderfully recalled and heard again, as the fast water, the bright water, rushes over shoals of smooth, colored stones.

Things come and go.

Like so many addicts, I simply can't help myself.

The geography of my life wrinkles with water, with rivers, and with fish. Always there has been water: dark seas and bright rivers, blue oceans and mountain streams hissing down deep canyons of layered dark stones that are time's boneyards. Long

before I took up fly-fishing and became a junkie hooked on rivers and fish, there was still water. Even my memories seem liquid, rivers of light, streams of feeling and sensation, oceans of experience rising and falling, endlessly breaking against the shores of consciousness, wrinkling in and out of awareness.

I never said that water was kind or merciful, that it was anything but what it is, what life is, coldly indifferent. According to my mother, water never scared me. Apparently, it just kept tempting me. I could not resist. My mother was always reminding me that I came close to drowning three times. Once in the lovely, warm, green-blue waters of the Mediterranean Sea, once in the dark, cold waters of the China Sea, and once in the perfect blue water of the Gulf Stream. I was always trying to go too far, dive too deep. Exhaustion whispered in my ear. Or so it seemed. To the boy I was, moving water seemed to have a voice. It seems that way still, to the man I have become. Its voice was as beautiful as Chopin's music, perfectly convincing. It told me struggle was futile, that it was time to give up, let go, so I did. Even so, the water, for some reason, has always found me distasteful and spit me out. And I kept going back. I cannot get enough. I had it bad for rivers and mountains, for wild stretches of water, even before I knew of such places, had ever seen them. I was hooked on moving water, fast water, cold, wonderfully mysterious water the way some people are junkies for certain drugs or alcohol.

Swami Bill is in this book. I met him in Colorado, where he runs the Holistic Trailer Park, Ashram & Coin Laundry in Boulder with his main squeeze, Kiwi LaReaux.

Swami Bill and Kiwi LaReaux are themselves part of a troubled river, the river of humanity.

All through this story, the river of humanity keeps spitting people out and swallowing them up.

People like Odell Euclid and William Marley Bubo. And Dr. Truth. And my mother. And my friend the CEO of Southern

Progress who fired me on a beautiful Alabama afternoon in June. My friend the CEO never actually told me I was fired. To make sure I understood what my friend the CEO meant, the creative director of the company showed up in my office, or in what used to be my office, after my friend the CEO had finished with me. His lips quavering with resplendent creativity, the creative director told me that he knew that subconsciously I had always wanted to be fired. He was smiling broadly as he talked. He looked happy and content. I had no idea that the creative director was also in charge of divining what the company's employees subconsciously wanted, and I was saddened that in all my years with Southern Progress he had never shared any of my other subconscious yearnings with me.

On the day that I lost my job, waves of depression hummed and sizzled in my gray-pink brain like downed electrical wires. I would later learn that depression is a disease and that I had probably had the disease all my life. This came as news to me. Being shy and pensive had always seemed perfectly normal to me.

Dr. Mutzpah gave me good news, though. Depression can be treated, can be cured. She prescribed little purple pills that made the soured chemicals in my brain smile again, repaired the faulty wiring in my head, brought a smile to my moody molecules, left them jazzing about again in this mobile home of flesh that is me.

On a cold Thursday afternoon, while Denver was dressed in blowing swirls of delicate snow, Dr. Mutzpah would advise me to get out of town.

Which I did, heading for the high country beyond Kenosha Pass. I ended up along the banks of the Middle Fork of the South Platte River. I did not know it yet, but there was a blind brown trout in one of the great arching bends of the river that would get under my skin, haunt me for months, keep me coming back to the river again and again.

There would be a moment that would leak out of time, a moment when I would see the brown trout rise out of a deep pocket of dark water, see it wrinkle up toward the surface. I would see nothing but its eyes, eyes that were blind, eyes that looked thick

and gummy as curdled milk, eyes that looked like the smear of distant galaxies drifting in an endless press of blackness, eyes that did not reflect light but held it like bowls of glass until the light overflowed, moving like tides: rivers of light mingling with the moving river.

I kept going back to the river, walking its banks, casting my line over its moving bright water, hoping to hook wild trout, wanting to see that blind trout again, to drift into the river of light that fell from its blind eyes and flashed like bands of colored lightning through the fast, cold water, swallowing stones and trees, fields of honey-colored grasses, whole mountains.

Those endless folds of mountains pressed against the sky like swells of colored stone, the river's bright silver blue waters and the brown trout's dead eyes would swallow something else.

Me.

And they would spit me out again, too.

Depression and loss and the blind trout and everything else are part of the story, this story, my story, the story of how I got from there to here. I will go ahead and tell you how this story ends: it doesn't. It does what life does, offers no conclusions, no clear endings.

My grandfather and great uncle had a failed farm in the Ozark Mountains of Arkansas, up along Starlight Creek. Come late summer, when the sun rose white-hot and boiled across a cloudless sky, when the day's heat shimmered in thick visible sheets off the hillsides and felt like acid against the skin, my grandfather would walk from the fields down to the edge of the creek, sink two gray metal pails into the creek, carry them back into the suffocating heat of the open fields, and pour the cold creek water over our heads. Icy water, wild water that smelled of rot and stones and trout. I remember the feel of it as it gushed down off my hat brim and onto my burning face, my crusted eyes, my cracked lips, onto my sunburned shoulders and chest and arms, a thin mist of steam rising off my open shirt. I remember just standing there in the field, under that baking sun, my eyes closed, my cortex cool and free of thought, free of everything but the feel of the cold creek water. It seemed more than mere water. To me that liquid seemed enchanted, full of the creek's chilly shadows, its wild chaos of light, the feel of its cool, smooth dark stones, its endless mystery.

The blind brown trout in the waters of the Middle Fork of the South Platte River and the mountains and the high country meadows of South Park would have the same effect on me. Trout and river would come to fill my head, my days. As it turned out, the blind brown trout and the river, that whole bright country, would be what washed over me, carried me away, got me from there to here.

Water.

It has always been water, moving water, water still marked by wildness, water that is active rather than passive. Wild water scrubs away layers of dead skin, stirs my dreams and the legacy of blood and bone, the legacy of earth and sky, sunlight and wind, water and fire, the rush of the universe, the drift of time.

THE MEAT BUCKET BLUES

Ducunt volentem fata, nolentem trahunt.
The fates lead him who will. Him who won't, they drag.

—SENECA

◣▬▬▶ The morning seemed liquid, seemed to drip down the dark flanks of the mountains west of Denver, the peaks of the Front Range. At the base of the mountains, the light gathered in sparkling pools. The pools were the color of crusted blood and seemed to boil like an alchemicus of melted stones. The land glowed in deep, lush, Hadean light.

On the seventh floor of the rust-colored building at the corner of Seventeenth Street and Stout, somewhere near Denver's fuliginous heart, I noticed that Dr. Lilly Mutzpah had kind blue eyes.

Dr. Mutzpah greeted me in the small, quiet, calming, marmoreal white alcove adjacent to her office. There were twin couches, soft and accepting, and a fox brown coffee table festooned with brightly colored magazines, the latest editions of *The New Yorker, Esquire, Vanity Fair.*

The alcove's single window was stained glass—panes of chrome red, cyan blue, mikado yellow. In the corner stood a milk white Art-Deco floor lamp, its head a great open-throated chrysanthemum that seemed to be forever probing toward the seductive light.

Dr. Mutzpah spoke, filling the nervous silence with her small voice. She thought I might be curious about her name.

"My father had his heart set on Dante, my mother on Shelley. They settled on Lilly. You know parents, Mr. Middleton. They want us to be fascinating right down to our names."

Dr. Mutzpah smiled, then the silence rushed back in, filling the room like shadow.

Dr. Mutzpah straightened the corners of the magazines, giving them a more soothing appearance.

"Now, Mr. Middleton, tell me, what brings you here?" she said.

I returned her smile weakly, tentatively.

"I can't seem to remember," I said, "whether Humpty-Dumpty fell or was pushed."

Dr. Mutzpah's pale blue eyes absorbed the morning sunlight and flecks of burnt copper glowed in all that shimmering blue.

"As good a question as there is," said Dr. Mutzpah.

Her office was a geography of extremes, whites and blacks, lamplight delicately coating peaceful, swan white walls. Hanging on the walls was a collection of Inuit paintings, totems, and crafts.

I fell into a huge chair that rose out of the polished darkwood floor like an outstretched hand. The hand was gloved in smooth, sloe black leather.

"I like the mornings," said Dr. Mutzpah, sitting in a smaller chair next to the lamp that coiled up the smooth wall like some tropical vine. Minor eruptions of soft light came off the ceiling like halos of lit roman candles.

"I mean the light this time of morning is simply lovely, isn't it?," she said.

I noticed a greatly enlarged salmon fly—a tapestry of reds and blues, silver and red, handsomely framed in dark wood on the wall behind her. The great, gaudy, fraudulent insect, some angler's image of perfect temptation, was highlighted by a small spotlight attached to the frame.

I kept staring at it, and every fish I have known and collected in my memory stirred. I sank deeper in the chair and smiled.

On the morning I noticed Dr. Lilly Mutzpah's kind blue eyes, I had greeted the morning huddled in my blue sleeping bag on the floor of my room off Colorado Boulevard, clutching a can of half-eaten bean dip and a bag of tostadas. I had not slept for five days.

Crawling lizardlike out of the sleeping bag, I retrieved the Denver yellow pages and the telephone, came across Dr. Lilly Mutzpah's name and number listed under "Physicians," subheading "Psychiatrists."

Dr. Mutzpah is one of those who have devoted their lives to helping the befuddled and disconnected, the confused and dysfunctional, the sullen and silly, the hopeless, the manic and the depressed.

I noticed from the address listed under the good doctor's office that her office was close to the offices of the magazine where I worked.

How reassuring, I thought, crawling back into my sleeping bag, that mental health should be so near at hand. That's when I noticed the morning sunlight flashing among the mountains piled against the horizon. Suddenly the sunlight flooded over the gnarled, fractured peaks, and in an instant the land was purged of night's cold shadows and became luminescent.

As I dialed Dr. Mutzpah's number, the morning light poured through the room's open window and across the frayed, mottled, pus green carpeting. On the wall it sculpted daring arabesques of bold yellows and oranges, swirling eddies of blues, a chorea of madder reds among the rising dust motes and scattered bits of tostada. A tendril of light wrinkled across my arm, leaving a warmth which sank easily down through layers of exhausted skin, settling comfortably at the base of my spine.

I put a Robert Johnson tape in the cassette player sitting on the floor next to my sleeping bag and heap of half-read books. The sound came low and plaintive, the feel of the Mississippi Delta and its rhythms, like backbones cracking. Broken-down, hard-luck music: songs of life bruised and battered yet hanging on.

As the music and the morning took hold, I toasted both with my last ice-cold bottle of root beer, then stumbled into the bathroom down the hall, which had no door and smelled of urine and whiskey and cheap after-shave. In eight days I had managed but two hours' sleep. My eyes looked like pools of boiled plasma and felt as though they had been marinated for weeks in Tabasco sauce. My lips were swollen, marked by deep cracks the color of mashed mango, and the skin on my face felt as though it had been sutured to my skull with heavy wire. My nerves sizzled and buzzed like static electricity in a brooding, menacing thunderstorm. Tiny pockets of drawn flesh at the corners of my eyes twitched.

Dr. Mutzpah's shiny dark hair was pulled back tight against her head, held in place by a small clip as white as polished bone. Her ears were small, perfectly shaped, unpierced. Her lips appeared always to be on the verge of a seductive pout. Alluring dark shadows swanned across the surface of her olive-colored, translucent skin.

The tremendous black chair in Dr. Mutzpah's office cradled me softly. Closing my eyes, I felt as though I had been embraced by fingers of thick black silk. The shadows dancing across Dr. Mutzpah's smooth skin made me smile because they reminded me of trout: the shadows of fish in some cool, fast mountain river, rising toward pale sunlight flashing off the surface of the water, drifting in radiant colored mists among thick stands of trees, cool grasses, warm stones. I had not thought of trout in a long time, and the sudden release of memory left me giddy, made me dizzy as a drunk warming to the whispered lies of cheap wine.

For a moment there in Dr. Mutzpah's office in downtown Denver, time wrinkled, took the shape of the shadows that moved like rising trout over the good doctor's beautiful skin. Stasis wrapped the moment, marked it. There was equilibrium, balance, a harmony in which things seemed forever new and undiminished. The future seemed wide open.

A good moment. I hated to see it go, but go it did, slipping back into the flow of time as my stomach gave way to a burst of gastric epiphany. I remembered I had not eaten anything for days but bean dip and greasy tostadas, root beer and ice water. My digestive system had become a neurasthenic beast, wailing and moaning, a gurgling pool of gnawing acids and edgy enzymes trying to suck nutrition out of the stringy flesh of fatigue and despair.

Dr. Mutzpah kept scribbling in her small notebook. Even the pupils of her eyes seemed inviolate blue. While she wrote, I let my imagination cast for the shadows on her skin that wouldn't stop looking like trout rising at evening. Often, it seems the better part of angling resides in mind and imagination, endures in muscle and nerve and bone, forever a measure of feeling, not only what is past and inexorable, but what is immediate, relentlessly urgent. I leaned back even farther in the enormous black chair. It was like sinking into crushed velvet. I dozed.

When I woke, Dr. Mutzpah handed me a stack of yellow and blue appointment slips.

Over the next week, I lurched, crawled, cantered, loped, and sidled, crablike, into and out of a dizzying array of doctors' offices, all of them painted some benign shade of beige.

A neurologist giggled as I hopped blindfolded about the examining room in my underwear trying to sing "God Bless America" while touching the index finger of my left hand to the tip of my nose.

A nosologist graphed the deeper meanings of my scars, coughs, and dull blue tattoo. An otologist filled my ears with light, gave me a shot of cortisone to adjust my faulty equilibrium, while a moody serologist grimaced as he checked the color and viscosity of my serums. A tocologist checked my chart, shook my hand, was certain I wasn't pregnant. A bald-headed podiatrist with cold hands and a fixed grin tickled the bottoms of my feet with exotic bird feathers and straight pins, and a cheerless chiropractor, believing my woes to be the result of poor posture, cracked my neck and realigned my spine.

A bored mycologist found my lungs free of any aggravating and therefore interesting fungi. As a light as thin and frail as cut

roses flooded through the office window, a mopey, chinless endocrinologist sighed darkly at the state of my endocrines. They were normal.

That same afternoon a nurse named Kilgore with black eyes and hair the color of ripe tangerines took my pulse and let me know with obvious personal regret that I did not have glandular plague, Unterricht's disease, epilepsia gravior, blennorrhea, podagra, Heberden's rheumatism, irritable bowel syndrome, milk leg, yaws, pinkeye, consumption, angina pectoris, hives, tetter, or calenture. She said the results from the bacteriologist showed I was well scrubbed, covered with only harmless and helpful colonies of bacteria.

Kilgore spoke with breathless enthusiasm, the words falling from her moist red lips as perfectly as cultured pearls, as she told me that the parasitologist had found a whopping case of malaria in my blood.

Thoroughly pinched, poked, probed, questioned, filmed, photographed, examined, and sampled, I returned to Dr. Mutzpah's office. My backbone gave way like a stalk of boiled broccoli as I dropped into her great black chair, that sacristy of softness and black leather compassion. I used my feet to inch the chair out of the shadows, turn it into the diminishing September sunlight receding across the polished floor.

I could feel Dr. Mutzpah's voice on my skin. It was like a small wind, as cool and fragile as porcelain. It was a wind with a message. I listened. Dr. Mutzpah leaned close, moving out of the window's light into the room's shadow, and told me that my despair was a disease and that the disease had a name: depression.

Like so many, many others, I had been laid low by what is becoming the most common condition of modern times.

The word had the presence of heavy machinery; it filled the room, pressed menacingly against the walls and windows, mixed with the light and shadow so that the room seemed encased in a cerulean camphor.

My despair had a name.

I smiled and looked out the window. The sunlight felt warm on my face. Blue mountains rose against the distant horizon, and I thought of mountain rivers, imagined the dark shadows of fish rising in cold, fast water, rising over black stones, moving cautiously toward wide spirals of bright sunlight drifting just above the river's surface like the remnants of a gold fog.

Where the mountain peaks were stacked high into the sky, the sunlight thickened, deepened, became a wild blue-black sea, and the mountains rose out of the sea like islands. Rising and falling, the light pressed against ragged, dark stone cliffs. It illuminated the entire sky, even beyond the horizon.

The malaria in my blood was deposited there by a female mosquito off the Honduran coast where I had been sent by the magazine to write a story about uncharted saltwater flats bristling with crowded schools of bad-tempered permit. When I was not angling for permit, I was snorkeling nameless, heartbreakingly blue-green lagoons tucked away among the Hog Islands, Cayos Cochinos, which seemed to rise out of the blue sea like a prayer cairn of blue-green islands, sand and wind, sunlight, water, volcanic stone, coral reefs, and shimmering layers of life.

The Hog Islands are part of the Honduran Bay Islands. After arriving on the big island of Roatan, I took a bush plane out to the smaller islands. The plane landed on a deserted slice of beach on Cochino Pequeño, Little Hog Island. A freshly painted ponga waited to carry me across the narrow channel to the big island, Cochino Grande.

For days I gorged myself on the islands' endless bounty of bananas and pineapple, fresh fish and lobster tails as thick as my forearm, all washed down with bottled water and warm beer that was flown in weekly from Roatan. It was a regimen that in a week's time left me in a diarrheic stupor, folded painfully in a rope hammock under the cool, green shade of swaying palm

trees, drifting in and out of sweet delirium, waking in the moon-drenched Caribbean night, the wind soft and smelling of the sea, ripe with the glottal creaking of sailboats moored in the deep bay, rocking gently beneath an indigo moon full above the dark swells, endlessly rising and falling. On such a night a nondescript Hondoran female mosquito bit me, left a whelp on my arm and a load of malaria in my blood.

The hammock smelled of sweat and fear, my fear: of bananas, pineapple, fresh fish and lobsters, warm beer. Late afternoon was a perfection of colors—blues and greens, clear skies and bright water, everything fresh and pungent.

William Bubo wiped my lips with a piece of T-shirt drenched in raw pineapple juice, helped me from the hammock to his wooden canoe. A few strokes carried us away from the beach and into deeper water.

The sail on William Bubo's dugout canoe was a neon yellow shower curtain. The curtain had been jettisoned by a passing cruise ship. The ship was full of American divers hoping to sink their troubles in the curative, magical blue waters off the coast of Belize. The yellow shower curtain had been thrown overboard along with a bucket of rancid hambuger meat, empty champagne bottles, colored party hats, thousands of bright orange Cheese Doodles—all that remained of "Caribbean Magic" night aboard the cruise ship.

Bubo found the yellow, mildew-stained shower curtain and fashioned it into a handsome sail. The sail made him a fisherman of consequence among the other fisherman of his village on Monitor Cay, across from Punta Cana Brava on Cochino Grande.

When he was not fishing, Bubo kept the yellow shower curtain in his hut, in a corner of the packed sand floor under a shelter of palm leaves and wood, wrapped in old T-shirts tourists were always giving him.

Bubo knew his luck with the sea and with the fish had been good, and he honored the yellow shower curtain as if it were a minor god, one that had freed his cracked and calloused hands from the wooden paddle and let the canoe ride the sea's wind. With the yellow sail, Bubo could reach the deeper, dark blue water beyond the islands, out where the great reef suddenly disappeared as though it had fallen off the edge of the earth, where the truly big fish hunted and fed, moved in the dark water, their eyes cold and black.

Bubo believed the yellow sail would bring him good fortune, bring him a good fish, a significant fish, a noble fish to feed him, nourish him, fill him with the sea's strength and wisdom and magic, a fish that would bring him enough wealth perhaps to buy a soft mat to sleep on, another hundred yards of good fishing line, a dozen more big steel hooks.

Bubo fished every day the weather allowed. He would push his canoe off the beach and into the sea as the sun set, paddle hard until he was beyond the polychrome shadows of the big island and into the deep water. Then he would raise the yellow sail, just at twilight as the sky melted into a whorl of milky blues marbled with eddies of damson and saffron light.

He would let the canoe drift as the first stars appeared, while he secured his heavy fishing line to a nail driven deep in the stern of the wooden canoe, near the simple wooden rudder. He had already baited the big silver hook with a thick, fresh chunk of bonito belly. Then he simply let the hook and line go slowly over the side until he knew the hook had sunk down more than fifty feet into the sea.

The palms of Bubo's brown hands were the color of faded quince and crisscrossed with deep scars where the handline had cut through layers of callus into soft, salmon-colored flesh. The scars reminded me of the dark fish that rose in my dreams: their white bellies looked like the dim nimbuses of fallen gods.

On our third night together Bubo passed the handline to me and I wrapped it like anchor rode about my right hand and elbow, keeping the lengths even, tight, free of tangles. The fever in my brain kept sending me in and out of time, but I could always feel the salt spray on my face, feel the empyreal night wind against my skin, see that yellow shower curtain pressed hard against sea and sky, a bloated, shiny yellow light, like some alien sun. The fever washed through me with the relentless energy of breaking waves, submerged me, so that I was a man drowning in life's debris, in memory. The only pain came from struggling, so I let go and sank down to where the dark fish swam.

And danced deliriously in my malarial dreams until I felt the fish's great weight on the line as it tore at the white, dripping chunk of bonito belly into which William Bubo had buried the hook, finally swallowing it whole, then going deep, the big steel hook digging into the sides of its hard throat. Line uncoiled quickly over the side of the canoe, a lonely scraping sound in the night. Line and more line, until I could feel the fish, all of it, every wild molecule, ripping at the muscle and bone of my back, arms, hands. The fish took it all, every inch, the line coming off my elbow and hand, in violent jerks, yanking me forward, pitching me on top of Bubo, dumping me against the yellow sail. The length of line still wrapped about my hand dripped with porphyrin red blood that went carbon black the instant it mixed with the sea.

The fish went deeper, deeper, traveling not steadily but in bursts of speed and jerks of raw, violent power. Bubo worked his way around me, took hold of the line, so that both of us pulled against the fish as it hauled the canoe, the yellow sail, and us beyond sight of the islands, through a rising gray fog, out to the edge of the great reef, toward the bone black edges of the horizon.

Some fish: a fish the imagination welcomes, feeds on. It snapped the line sometime during the night, never surfacing. I hauled the slack, gnawed line in. Even so, the big fish lived on in exhausted bone and muscle, spent nerve, images that filled my head, boiled along with my fever. Without a name, the fish became all presence, essence, an undiminished and indomitable scaled and finned Polyphemus, a potency of sinew and grace, something unspeakably intense, unrelenting, enduring, and overwhelming.

I spent half a week more in the hammock strung between

shady palm trees on Cochino Grande Island, malarial shakes trembling through my brain like some clawed harmattan, while scalding, incinerating fevers sheathed every muscle, joint, and length of bone. The hammock swung me in and out of time, a traveler freed of limits and boundaries, geographies, journey and destination. One rattling chill put me back in William Bubo's dugout canoe, the great fish pulling the canoe mercilessly beyond sight of land, out into its world of dark water, the canoe's yellow shower curtain sail suddenly looking as feeble as a dying star in a distant galaxy. Another wrinkle of fever would find me crawling unsteadily about the wonderfully cool tiles of a bathroom floor, crouching between sink and bathtub like some antediluvian beast, sweat stinging my eyes, dripping from my chin and chest, giving the tile floor a lardaceous shine.

The bathroom floor turned out to be the one in room 404 of a Holiday Inn west of St. Louis, Missouri. I was well on my way to Colorado. You can never tell when the malaria will come. It begins with a sudden chill, as though dry ice were being injected below the skin; the body quivers terribly like a sheet of corrugated tin roofing assaulted by high winds. When that first chill comes, I can almost hear the bones rattling against one another. When the fever takes firm hold, it is as though the inside of my skull were being scrubbed with a wire brush. Time bends and twists, deposits me here and there like some disaffected time traveler. When the fever comes there's no telling where my throbbing brain will transport me—back in the arms of the hammock on the beach of Cochino Grande off the Honduran coast—swaying in a balmy wind, looking out beyond the island to the sea, looking for that burst of yellow against pure blue that will mark William Bubo's dugout canoe, the yellow shower curtain he used for a sail. Or on the cool tile floor of a bathroom in a Holiday Inn, or simply falling off the bed in some darkened room. Usually, just before the fever breaks, as the chills and shaking stop and recede, it feels as though my brain is nothing but a sweaty cloud of particles and waves adrift among arbitrary stars, a colossus of wheeling, indifferent galaxies that to my fevered inner eye resemble spinning, elegant, double-edged, gleaming spiral arms of steel. Somewhere in there, just before sleep drags me off into the more rational regions of darkness, I feel as though I am dissolving into pure light. This sensation comes after all the wracking, sweat-drenched colonic spasms, bones feeling as though they have been struck for hours with rubber hammers, the folds of the brain quavering like a vat of Jell-O. Then it comes: that feeling of dissolving into a wisp of light, a quality of light described, before Newton's genius gave the world corpuscular rays of light, as "luminiferous ether." Even the fever-induced sensation of being reduced to a ray of light seems a kind and wonderful fate.

Staring at the mountains from Dr. Lilly Mutzpah's office made me think of the malaria in my blood and how its fever could compress me into a trace of light.

I went right on looking at the mountains in the near distance and not listening to whatever it was Dr. Mutzpah was saying. Instead, I was imagining the rush of fast, cold mountain rivers eroding down through massifs of stone, water in relentless motion, probing its way to the distant sea. The sunlight that poured into Dr. Mutzpah's office that day was a delicate coral pink, fragile enough, it seemed, to be shattered by the force of a single breath. I had seen such a light before, when I was a boy living in other mountains. Those days, too, were marked by water, by the sun, and by trout rising at the edge of the shoals and deep pools of Starlight Creek, and I remember jumping in the icy waters of Karen's Pool down by Elias Wonder's cabin and rising up, bursting into the warm sunlight as though I was evolution's newest creation, mutable and imperfect, impetuous, perishable, fugacious, but alive, a fortunate anomaly swimming naked in deep, wild pools of river water. I felt as though I was a single membrane, all sensation, raw and expectant, rubbing up against life—life not only as process, but that which endures, abides.

There is in me, among so many longings, a yearning for the essence of things, of mountain and sky, sunlight and shadow, wild fish rippling in deep, dark waters still touched by wildness, moving in time's inexorable flow, life as it comes and goes.

Years ago when I was young, very young, I walked off alone into the Utah badlands, thinking that after a week out there in that unforgiving white-hot heat, with the honest companionship of rattlesnakes, scorpions, and vultures, a raw vision would boil in my brain, come to me in some muddle of scorched light and burnt shadow, especially if I fasted and drank no more water than the high desert itself. I limped back to town three days later, sunburnt, dehydrated, looking like two hundred pounds of jerked beef, a savant of fata morgana, heat, and edible desert fare. There were no visions, or at least no new ones. The desert is spare, even with its visions. As it turned out, I walked out of that hard country with exactly what I had walked in with, with this: life is more than adaptation and survival, it is connection and collaboration, symbiosis. There is common ground, unions of mind and universe, observer and observed, wave and particle, mandalas of motion and time, and everywhere the quintessence of light.

Dr. Mutzpah got me to agree to an EEG, an electroencephalogram. A brain technician wearing a faded orange sweatshirt and wrinkled black combat boots dabbed cream on my head and attached twenty-two separate electrodes. A bushel of wires blossomed out of my head, so that I looked like some futuristic marionette. The brain technician took me by the hand, led me to a cheap lounge chair in a darkened room, told me to sit, lean back, relax. I was to close my eyes until he told me to open them and leave them open until he told me to close them. He warned me about the lamp arched over my head, that it would come on in bursts of light.

"It's nothin'," said the brain technician, "just a lot of flashing lights, that's all. Keep calm and keep quiet. We don't want to pull the wires loose and have to do it again."

He checked the electrodes, re-attaching those that felt loose.

"Close your eyes," he said. "Go ahead and sleep if you want. The old brain'll talk whether you're up or not."

I heard him leave and sit down in the room behind the glass. For a moment it was like being inside of some cheap video game, with me as the game and the brain technician the player at the controls. I thought about trying to throw the entire test by sending him vague, uninteresting signals, a single message over and over again.

This was the lullaby I sang again and again to myself and to the bored brain technician through the wires: *Ho-hum.*

Ho-hum.

Ho-hum.

Then I fell asleep and fell into a dream I often have, the one where I sink slowly, ever so slowly, down through whirling black water. My right hand is the last to go under. I can feel a cold wind against my fingers. There is no struggling to regain the surface. Looking up through the water I can see a smudge of sunlight, still hear the muffled chatter of birds in the trees. The dark water presses and I follow willingly, sinking into the sea's endless black membrane.

The dream transports me instantly to a beach of black sand. I am running on the beach. The black sand is hot and edged, like a shoal of black thumbtacks. The sun is high overhead, washing the beach in hard, intense light, a light with no memory of man. Precambrian morning. Cretaceous dusk. Devonian afternoon. Ah, take me back to the Age of Fishes.

Beyond the beach, mountains rise in a cold blue sky. The sea is pounding hard against the shore and I am thrashing my arms wildly over my head. My mouth is open but nothing comes out.

Tattered shadows come down the mountains, slouching toward the water, the horizon now as red as a ruptured blister, and every shadow shudders, trembles like dying leaves on a winter wind.

Over the wind's hissing is the stentorian rattle of the sea, a resonating chaos of sea pounding against a shore of eroded black stone, of light and shapes mixed with the reedy cries of circling shorebirds. From beneath the stones comes what seems like a tympani of insects clicking, scuttling, scratching, and the deep, whispering groan of roots probing among the stones, seeking anchor, some momentary hold on the oily neck of time and place.

The light slips through shades of black. Grizzled clouds settle in the high valleys and there is rain, a staccato sputtering among the trees and in the black sand.

Everywhere the sound of things, the yap and yowl, snap and throb of things. A groan of natural harmonics rolling down that black beach while clouds of red light flare above the horizon, and suddenly from my open mouth some rude, raw utterances—language older than memory. Prayers, perhaps: canticles, motets, hymns, prosodons, requiems, chants mouthed in strange tongues as cauled shadows slip into the pounding waves. On my hands are images I recognize. I have seen them before, images left by ancient man on the walls of the Dordogne caves. Beyond me, shadows of great fish rise in the dark sea, so many that the surface of the water seems to boil as they break the surface. The water dripping from their muscled flanks flashes in the brutal light like liquid firestorms.

The great swarms of black fish in my dream look blue against the dark sea and there is, in their movements, their rising and falling, the comfort of old mythologies, time's forgotten legacy, pure energy. I watch from the black beach and cannot speak. Language fails. That is nothing new. It is always failing. There are worlds words have yet to grasp, cannot express, gods they cannot embrace, places they can experience and explore but never name. On the horizon, veins of light wrinkle through the sky: distant signal fires burning at the edge of the universe.

Everything sinks easily into the light. What had been dismembered is unified. Palingenesis. Consciousness seems no more than a drop of ocean water evaporating on parched lips.

Suddenly, I am a boy, thigh-deep in a mountain stream, casting a line, fishing. The water is fast and cold and tugs at my legs. There is a cool wind high in the trees and I am smiling.

"Eyes open," said the brain technician, and the dream ended.

The first time I had the dream I woke to find myself knotted in sweat-soaked sheets, trembling with fever, my muscles caught in the jerks and quavering of some involuntary, nervous tarantella.

The brain technician let me see the results of the test. On a long ribbon of thin graph paper was a portrait of my brain's dim electrical hum. And the dream? It was just so many squiggly lines, electrical peaks and valleys.

Peaks and valleys.

Astonishment is one of the chief by-products of life. For what seemed an hour I had been deep in an incandescent dream, a journey deep through the folds of my brain away from chaos and toward unity, some strange essence of wholeness, a dream that had whispered to me that every living cell holds the mind of the gods and the history of life, a dream of ripeness. Apotheosis. I mentioned some of my dream to the brain technician. He told me not to worry too much about dreams. That they were all only so much vague electrical activity and squiggly lines.

Squiggly lines.

In the dream, by the way, I get to find Eden. As it turns out, the joke is on me, on every human being. Eden is not above the earth, under the earth, beyond the earth; it *is* the earth: sunlight and water, earth and stones, life as it is, that which burns but is never consumed. Mana. Wakonda. Shakit. Trout. The essence of things, like some cloud of intoxicating, tempting pheromones that remind us, in the end, that we carry in our cells and memory and blood the paradises we exhaust a lifetime searching for.

The brain technician did not know it, but the last set of squiggly lines on this graph was the dream's end, was me again on that black beach. And the sea was calm, and there was a blue moon on the rise, and in the distance was Marley Bubo's big handmade canoe, its sail, that yellow plastic shower curtain, pressed full with a favoring wind and illuminated by a fading nimbus of refulgent sunlight.

God bless that Honduran mosquito and its load of malaria, that fever burning with misery and magic.

The first time the dream of the black fish boiled up in my brain was in Biloxi, Mississippi, where I woke up to find Muldoon's tattoo stitched into the still stinging blood-smeared flesh of my left arm.

"Ganesha who?" asked the old woman mopping the floor around me with a concoction that smelled of lye and pine.

"Ganesha?"

"Yessur. You been sayin' it for an hour. Spooky-like. I nearly called 9-1-1 to getcha some help." The woman had great brown eyes and short-cropped gray hair tucked beneath a red bandana. She swirled the ragged mop in great circles across the floor.

Evidently, I had been praying. Ganesha, with an unctuous body, four flailing limbs, and the face of a genial elephant, is a Hindu god, one who supposedly considers the supplications of those besieged with overwhelming impediments, obstacles, handicaps and encumbrances.

I was sprawled out on the cool floor of the Shrimp's Tail Restaurant, the vile residue of fever clawing at my skull and Muldoon's tattoo freshly stenciled on my arm. Sharing the floor with me were overturned chairs, a plate of shrimp and empty root beer bottles. All of this seemed like enough trouble to bring on prayer and lots of it, especially since I recalled that I was supposed to be in Key West spending my days stalking bright saltwater flats, fly rod in hand, writing a story about the Keys' elusive bonefish, and my nights dining heroically on fresh red snapper,

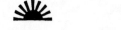
triggerfish filets bathed delicately in lime and melted butter, and freshly boiled shrimp dipped generously in Tabasco sauce and wine, all of it washed down with gallons of fresh iced tea.

Instead, I was staring at Muldoon's tattoo, which looks like this:

Muldoon was Sergeant Muldoon. He had anemic blond hair and gentle brown eyes, a wide, permanent grin, and a voice like ice cracking.

Years ago and far away, in the long dead Republic of South Vietnam, outside a nameless village at the edge of a lush green jungle, Sergeant Muldoon and the other pink-faced boy soldiers of his squad machine-gunned the people of the village.

It was war. People had been dying all day. Most of them checked out with lonely, twisted smiles on their lips and nothing to say. Muldoon and his men had been pinned down by heavy motor fire from the beautiful hills that rose in the lush green jungle behind the village. Finally, someone called in air strikes. Two five-hundred-pound bombs filled with napalm—jellied gasoline—landed short, tumbled innocently into the village. It was like someone tossing a lit match into a fireworks factory. Everything and everyone lit up instantly. Clouds of fire sucked the oxygen from the air; the sky became a billowing tapestry of reds and blacks. Fires hissed and popped.

A young girl came out of the noxious cloud, at the edge of the village. She wore a halo of orange flames and moved dreamlike, like a spectre. There were others behind her, all on fire. Human

Roman candles. The singed air smelled of burnt flesh.

Standing in one of the village's bountiful gardens, heavy with new fruit, Muldoon opened fire. You could see reflections of the burning village in his gentle brown eyes.

Muldoon kept screaming and screaming.

"Show them mercy! . . . mercy! . . . mercy!"

"Depression." Whenever she said the word, Dr. Mutzpah sighed, as though even mentioning the word might send a black wind through my mind, a black tremble among my nerves, a black chill through my emotions. After hearing about my mother and her mother and Uncle Albert, Dr. Mutzpah told me that she believed my variety of depression was the inherited strain, a melancholy so black that it is actually passed on from generation to generation.

Luck and depression make for a dark oxymoron, but the two do dance on occasion. They held hands for me. The depression dissolved after it was enveloped by the right medication, though finding the right one took time. Dr. Mutzpah and I passed the time talking.

For months, late each Thursday afternoon, Dr. Mutzpah and I talked. I never told her about Muldoon or how his tattoo showed up on my arm. Perhaps I should have. Perhaps she could have settled it, interpreted the torment of Muldoon's screams: murder or purest compassion?

Cool rains turned to ice and we talked. The ice changed to snow and we talked. And I must confess that I often found the doctor's company and conversation as soothing and helpful as the medication.

What did I tell her? Everything, almost. Except for Muldoon and the village and his tattoo. Save for that, everything. I had spent the last year losing things—like my mother (to brain cancer), my job (and with it at least one version of the future), friends, family, desires, love, the dead, the living, promises, dreams, hope, my favorite fly rod (which disappeared in the rush for bags and luggage at the airfield on Roatan, in Honduras). And on and on.

Evidently, depression feeds on loss the way cancer feeds on fresh tissue, slowly and without notice until it has you by the gut and by the throat and you sink past the boundaries of "normal" human despair and regret, acceptable moodiness, appropriate dejection, suitable dismay, reasonable melancholy.

The depression sloshing about in my blood, swelling, growing, left me a sagging lump of tired muscle and bone, insensate nerves, a dulled brain. As the year wore on, I sidled through my days with a fixed sardonic smile pinched on my face, a sure sign, I imagined, looking in the mirror every morning, of either strychnine poisoning or dystonia. My great-uncle Albert had such days, especially near the end of his life when the tumor in his brain was growing like bacteria in a petri dish. He would sit for days in his room at the top of the stairs, moaning into his pillow. He couldn't stand light of any kind. I remember jamming old clothes under the door, around the window, trying to keep the light from leaking into his room, and he would be sitting on his bed drooling like a baby, yowling like a feral dog. Once he held me close and began speaking in a perfect British accent, reciting scenes from Shakespeare's *King Lear*. While he turned into King Lear and held me close, Albert told me that it was miraculous and pitiful that a man should survive, even for a moment, the death of his life.

Dr. Mutzpah wanted more tests—a PET (positron emission tomography) and an MRI (nuclear magnetic resonance imaging). She longed for detailed photographs of the bruised brain inside my skull, all those one hundred billion quivering cells. Somewhere in there, in that moist gray blob of tissue and sizzling chemicals and bristling nerve cells, something was out of sorts, down in the dumps, fed up, worn out, bleakly discouraged and malfunctioning.

Dr. Mutzpah told me that the number of possible connections in the average brain is perhaps greater than the number of atoms in the universe. The brain feasts on connections, hungers for them.

"Considering all that tangled chemical wiring, it's amazing anything works at all," said Dr. Mutzpah. "Connections give out all the time." She was trying hard to be reassuring, cheerful.

I rubbed my forehead. Bad connections. Blown circuits. Discouraged neurotransmitters fed up with trying to make sense of life an impulse at a time.

There would be no more tests, however. In a matter of weeks my insurance decided it could no longer insure that I was not potentially a protracted and ruinous medical risk and therefore a certain financial loss.

American medical technology gleamed in the distance, its acclaimed benefits shining beyond my grasp and my means.

Each Thursday afternoon, Dr. Mutzpah bravely took my blood pressure, checked my reedy pulse, charted my undulant moods on a piece of graph paper, shook her delicate moon-shaped face tenderly from side to side. We would sit, talk. She would reassure me by telling me that what had gotten hold of me was much more than a case of the blues. And so it was. She wanted to know how it felt. Depression is different for every one of the millions of human beings who are laid low by it. For me, it was a paralysis of the soul, a catalepsy of the spirit, a skull full of cackling crows, a storm of black, whirring wings.

Depression is often a disease with a cyclothymic character: periods of almost delusional joy are followed by tormenting abulia, not so much catatonic stupor as an emotional cage of immeasurable fear and doubt and confusing, exquisitely silly obsessions, like spending hours on the telephone in disconnected reverie, my good friends the Gold Cards at my side, trying to buy contentment and equilibrium—a week in Tibet, two weeks in Africa, a month's fishing in New Zealand, expensive fly rods, watches that promised not only to measure time but to embrace it. There was little, I learned, that could not be ordered by mail, delivered to my door, often by the next day.

On such days I buzzed with a kind of frenzied energy, an energy that knew no exhaustion. I was as indefatigable and hyperkinetic as a fistful of comic book superheroes. If someone had told me that gallons of secret ingredient Z-49 ran through my bristling, exuberant veins, I would hardly have doubted it.

One month I was as robust and menacing as a choir of experimental rats, the next a plenary exhaustion covered me like a caul, leaving me pallid, colicky, racked by chills and postpredacious gluttony as I gorged on menudo covered with fresh scallions, sweetbreads, imported beluga, fried alligator dipped in incendiary salsa, conch chowder and jalapeños, sacks of spicy boudin, endless plates of speckled trout. Fish. Had to have fish. Brain food. I could taste wild rivers and glowing sunlight in the fresh, white meat.

And vials of vitamin E to keep the brain cells vital, kicking, glowing.

Then on some dreary morning marked by a bloated sunrise, I would slink back to my dimly lit room, plunged into the arms of anorexic guilt, swear loyalty to abstinence, becoming, there on the cool bathroom tiles, at once a reformed rechabite and a risen encratite in an apron stained with tomato sauce, shunning everything caloric, living for days on water, potage aux herbes, lichen gruel, bits of wild morel and burdock tubers, bowls of tepid jaundice tea.

"There, there," said Dr. Mutzpah every Thursday afternoon as I went on telling her about the depression in my brain and blood and bones, and as she went about leading me through the geography and etiology of the disease, an infinitely complex labyrinth, thick as paste, of misery and malaise.

Leaving her office every Thursday afternoon, I would flee to the library, where I sat by a great floor-to-ceiling window reading everything I could find on depression—medical books and journals, novels of gloom, the poetry of loss. What was I looking for in all those words of torment, all that chilled flesh and emotional fear, in all those descriptions of a black and bloated hell? I was looking for comon ground, common threads and themes, similar experiences, feelings, symptoms. I would read and read until the Denver Public Library closed. Outside, in the deep night, the dim streetlights left a shallow green shine on the roads and I would drive back to my room feeling either vaguely adrift, as though gravity had failed, or moored in a harbor of intractable, inescapable dread. All of this is part of depression's common ground. It's all there: compost of bleached bones, blackening skulls, fried nerves, soured and rotting Edens, desiccated souls. It seems nearly all those struck and wasted by the disease feel couched in an unspeakable darkness, a netherworld so bleak as to be beyond the power of language to understand it, grasp it, explain its black winds, the knotted fingers of pain clamped firmly about the brain.

After a time, depression sours everything, every feeling, every emotion. Life loses its sweet taste. Simple things like food and drink gnashed like tinfoil against my tongue and teeth.

After Dr. Mutzpah found the right medication, the one that made my chemicals put on a happy face, after the depression began to ease, recede, dissolve, I was surprised it had left me so much, even my old addictions to wildness and trout. That the depression left me this was not a matter of divine forgiveness or a spiritual victory of good over evil. It was just plain good luck.

Lucky me.

One of the things the depression burned to ash, along with my job and at least one version of the future, my future, was the sound of the depression when it was at its worst, when I ended up in Denver, in an unfurnished room, crawling out of the blue sleeping bag, searching the pools of morning light on the room's floor for the telephone and the Denver yellow pages. What was the sound? Bells. Thousands and thousands of them, all of them cast iron with great stainless steel clappers, and all of them clanging on and on, as the pain in my skull washed through my brain, dripped slowly down my spine, into my limbs, into my gut. The bells I heard were the bells of churches, especially the little church across the street from the Querencia Hotel in the Big Bend country, the church near Questa, New Mexico.

My mother heard bells, too.

Small world.

She heard bells as the galaxy of tumors in her brain went about killing her. The bells she heard tolled on and on.

She told me, by the way, that the bells were not just tolling for her. They were tolling for everyone.

Dr. Mutzpah and I went on talking and talking.

Even as it became apparent that I had perhaps suffered from depression for years, perhaps all my life, in some dim, diluted form, the true catastrophic nature of the disease did not manifest itself until I lost my job.

"Tell me about it," said Dr. Mutzpah gently, smoothing her dark hair with small, delicate hands. As she spoke, I watched tiny shadows move like drifting clouds over her lovely, smooth, olive-colored, translucent skin.

This is what I told her. I had been a senior editor with the Southern Progress Corporation in Birmingham, Alabama, a wholly owned subsidiary of Time Warner Inc. Southern Progress publishes mainly regional magazines, including *Southern Living,* touted as the largest regional magazine on the planet. I wrote for all the company's magazines, but my passion was the "Outdoor South" column I wrote each month for *Southern Living.* When the company started a new magazine called *Southpoint,* I wrote for it as well. *Southpoint's* birth was a difficult one, filled with complications and defects. The magazine languished for nine issues, then died. It suffered from a common malady among magazines—too much image and no personality. There were massive circulation problems, editorial hubris, a two-headed staff, writers and editors and managers split between two cities, an undefined readership that remained a blur, always just out of focus and therefore out of reach.

Time Warner's five-year commitment to the new magazine ended in less than a year. The first issue appeared in August 1989, the last in May 1990. No open casket. No graveside service. No flowers. No mourning. It was a magazine that didn't work. Happens all the time.

Things come and go, come and go.

On the morning of June 21 I gave a fly-fishing lesson to my friend Don Logan, who was then the CEO of the Southern Progress Corporation. For fifteen minutes or so his spacious, handsome, fifth-floor office became trout water, fast and bright, with wonderfully arrogant trout hanging in the tricky current that eddied around chairs, couches, the curves of his great brown desk. When it comes to fly-fishing, and especially casting, I claim little knowledge or skill of any value, but the lesson seemed rewarding, at least to me. We both did well, hooking chairs and books and other pieces of executive office furniture that we imagined were rising trout.

My friend the CEO and I kept casting that morning in his office while he talked excitedly about a fishing trip to Alaska he was planning. I had gotten together some information on guides and lodges for him.

It was a Friday—a warm and sleepy summer's day. My friend the CEO and I laughed between casts. I can remember the feel of the warm sunlight coming through his office's smoke gray windows, a light already cooled by the dense shade of the thick pines and hardwoods that surround the building.

It was a splendid light, one of subtle textures, one heady with intimations, one that made it easy to imagine the high country of the Blue Ridge Mountains to the east and north in northern Georgia and the Great Smoky Mountains just beyond them, and all the cold mountain rivers full of trout flowing down those mountains. My friend the CEO and I talked as we cast, talked about angling,

about fly-fishing and the wild trout and rivers of Alaska.

Late that afternoon Don Logan's secretary called. He wanted to see me.

I had been staring out my office window, fishing for a new shade of green, and welcomed the interruption. I pushed away from my desk smiling, hoping the message meant another cast or two, more talk of Alaska and trout and rivers.

Mr. Logan closed his door behind me. A closed door late on a Friday afternoon is a bad sign. A chill seized my spine, scratched at my bones and nerves, raising gooseflesh. Atavistic hairs bristled at the back of my neck. The scars on my hands and arms puckered and went from blushing pink to crushed violet to deep purple.

My friend the CEO indicated that I should take a seat on the soft gray couch. The day's bright white sunlight had softened, become the silky green light of a fading late afternoon. Even so, I could still feel the day's full measure of heat through my light summer shirt, hard against my shoulders like heated iron. There were patterns of sunlight on the office's lush carpeting—rays and shafts, beams and veins of dissolving summer light. Thin beads of glistening sweat appeared on my forehead, on my upper lip, on the palms of my hands. I noticed that my fingertips had turned a lovely pale blue. I saw the little fly rod I had left with Mr. Logan that morning on the corner of his desk.

The whole thing took less than eight minutes. I was fired. He never said the word. He implied, I inferred. My friend the CEO took the news especially well. He kept smiling. He told me I was the best writer in the company, the hardest worker, and that I had eight days to pack up and get out. He asked me to pack up my things over the weekend. That way, he said, my departure would cause as little excitement and disturbance as possible among the other employees. Southern Progress likes all of its employees to think of each other, to think of the company, as one big happy family. That Friday in Don Logan's office, I learned that I had never been part of the family at all, that I had always been just another hired hand.

"A year from now," said my friend the CEO, "you will look back and see this as the best thing that ever happened to you."

That was the last thing my friend the CEO said to me. I walked back to my office, to what used to be my office, stared out the window, watched the day burn down, watched the night rise from the folds of the worn dark hills in the near distance, watched as a tide of darkening shadows flooded the moonless night. Great tendrils of white clouds wrinkled across the sky, pressed by a warm, humid wind that blew out of Mississippi and smelled of rain. It was a lovely southern night indeed.

Did I tell you the last thing I said to my friend the CEO?

All I could say was this:

"I guess this means no Rolex?" Anyone lasting twenty years at Southern Progress gets a Rolex. There's no telling what retirement might bring. For one editor, it brought a race horse. Think of that!

Being fired, by the way, is nothing unusual, hardly extraordinary. It happens to more than eleven thousand Americans each day, every day. It's as common as the flu, taxes, unemployment, death, and depression.

Woody Moos would later tell me that being fired was a kind of death.

"I oughta know," he said above the metallic roar of county garbage truck No. 2. "I've died eleven times in the past year. Dying ain't so bad. You get used to it after a while."

Woody Moos smelled of sour milk, rotten meat, and orange peels. All of us who work on county garbage truck No. 2 smell of sour milk, rotten meat, and orange peels.

Moos and I worked together on county garbage truck No. 2. It was steady work. We were lucky to have any job at all.

I am still a member of the crew of garbage truck No. 2. Times are hard.

Even in flush times, work as a writer and editor is hard to come by. In hard times, there is no work at all.

Like me, Woody Moos has all kinds of college degrees, liberal arts degrees, fine art degrees, graduate degrees. Moos told me once that if we gathered up all of our liberal arts degrees and took them down to the recycling center in downtown Birmingham, handed them over, we would not get enough loose change for them to buy a cup of coffee.

Every Sunday, Woody Moos and I go to the county library to scour the want ads in newspapers and trade magazines. By the time we answer the few ads we find, they are months old. The letters we write are never answered. Why should they be? Moos told me that he keeps filling out applications and answering employment listings because doing so reminds him that he is still alive.

Moos and I are lucky. We have callused hands and strong backs.

I am still there on the back of county garbage truck No. 2, just as I am still shelving groceries at the Piggly Wiggly supermarket down the mountain and sweeping the floors in the shoe factory in the valley.

Three jobs. And I am lucky to have them. If my luck holds, perhaps there will be four. I could use another.

Each evening, county garbage truck No. 2 picks us up down the mountain, in front of the Piggly Wiggly supermarket. The truck always comes at sunset, huffing and puffing, a belching and gurgling metal digestive tract on wheels encased in vapor of suppurating rot and diesel fumes. As it squeals to a stop, Woody Moos appears, emerges from the inky fog drifting among the tangle of oak trees across from the Piggly Wiggly, comes out of that fog like an apparition stitched together by some lesser god. Moos skips across the damp, dark highway wearing what he always wore—red spandex bicycling pants, pressed white shirt and mauve bowtie, soiled sweat socks and steel-toed chukka boots.

On truly cold days he added a tricolored ski mask, brocade vest, seedy green muffler, and yellow rain slicker.

In his former life, Woody Moos had been a professor of medieval history. He was fired. Night after night on the back of county garbage truck No. 2, I heard Moos sobbing gently into the smelly folds of his grimy green muffler.

Our lunch hour comes before midnight. It was always an hour of exhausted silence until the day Moos looked up from gobbling down his fried egg sandwich and spoke, spewing bits of egg and bread and onion on Hamadullah, who has driven county garbage truck No. 2 for ten years.

"Go fuck yourself, Moos!" said Hamadullah sincerely, brushing spewed egg off his faded green army jacket.

"Did you know my ex-wife, Hamadullah?" Moos giggled darkly. "That's what she used to say to me every time I tried to make love to her."

Hamadullah liked watching Moos in the truck's giant sidemirrors and juicing the truck forward just as Moos reached out to haul himself onto the back of the truck. The truck would lunge forward shuddering violently, and down would go Moos, a tangle of muffler and vest and yellow rain slicker. Flopping there in the middle of the mountain highway, Moos looked like some madman's kite that had suddenly slammed to the ground.

Meanwhile, Hamadullah's pitiless laughter would roll up and down the mountain.

"What puts you here?" asked Moos, ignoring Hamadullah, attacking his fried-egg sandwich. Moos's shins were bleeding through the torn red spandex pants. Hamadullah snickered. He had toppled poor Moos five times that evening.

"Lost my job," I said.

"Lost . . . you say . . . well, well. Perhaps I can find it."

"Oh, yes. Oh, yes."

"You'd be surprised at what I find. Oh, the goodies, the treasures, the baubles and bangles!

"Oh, yes. Oh, yes.

"You can't tell, you know. Maybe your job went out with the

day's trash. Tossed out. Could be. Mine's in the Dumpster at the university. I'll find it yet."

Moos pointed a cold blue finger at the scum green truck parked beside the road. A glutinous black gruel oozed from the drip pipe at the rear of the truck.

"Can't tell what's in there," he said, smiling wide, showing yellow teeth laced with pieces of egg. "You'll have to see my collection, really. So many valuable things. Once I found a daisy chain of little white angels, their little wings smudged with chewed meat. How they sparkled after I cleaned them up.

"And a cat. Yep, a cat. Kept hearing something in the trash. Such a sad sound, and I dug until I found it—a cat tied up in a blue pillow case.

"You gotta check everything. Could be a job in there or a million dollars or another poor cat or dead human beings. They show up every once in a while."

We walked back to the truck. Hamadullah crawled up into the cab and slept. Moos flicked the last of his third sandwich into the back of the truck.

"Fired?" said Moos as he balanced himself on the back of the truck, sunk his hands and arms into the night's gathering of refuse.

"My friend the CEO never said the word, exactly," I said, mesmerized by Moos as he began pulling out handfuls of garbage, picking through the contents. He slipped a soft, brown apple half into the pocket of his rain slicker.

"Hmmm . . . exactly, how did he put it?" Moos asked, delighted over the discovery of a slimy sack of shiny mock-pearl buttons.

"He implied. I inferred," I said.

"Hmmm," moaned Moos, as he held one of the mock pearl buttons up to the catch the soft yellow moonlight.

"Hmmm . . ."

Each day, just at twilight, county garbage truck No. 2 would lurch forward, pull out of the Piggly Wiggly parking lot and into its own peculiar night world, a biome of the discarded. Above the cackling diesel engine, Woody Moos would be sobbing gently into his muffler. Moos's sobbing was, I soon discovered, actually singing, and this was the song he sang:

> *Row, row, row your boat*
> *Gently down the stream*
> *Merrily, merrily, merrily, merrily,*
> *Life is but a dream.*

Moos could sing even when sobbing. He had a voice that sounded like the tinkling of little bells.

Bells, again.

On those nights when he wasn't being toppled somewhere on the mountain highway by Hamadullah, as he sobbed and sang gently into his scummy green muffler, I learned that over the last year Woody Moos had been nonretained, excessed, laid off, reclassified, given a Mexican raise, and outplaced from eleven jobs.

"Terminated," coughed Moos, spitting a wad of phlegm and bubble gum into the back of the garbage truck. "How I hate that one. I guess because it was the first. The head of the history department said it to me. Just that word. I remember he said it sweetly.

"They all like that one, all the head men, the honchos, the nabobs, taipans, moguls, and magnates. And you can't blame them, really. Think of the rush it must give them to say it, do it. 'Ter-mi-nate.' It's the perfect murder, isn't it? You're as dead as dead gets, and yet, no blood, no body. Poof! The word hits you and suddenly you're a zombie. The only difference between you and the dead is that the dead get more rest.

" 'Terminated.' Poof! and you're among the living dead. You're alive, but your life's gone. Your life is suddenly just so much dead meat.

"I shouldn't fret so," said Moos. "This bad luck won't last. Soon now the day's coming when I'll gleam again, when I'll have that old smell of success. Ah, eau de dough. In preparation for good times, you might say, I've just been deepening my résumé.

"Oh, yes. Oh, yes."

And so he had.

Before he ended up on the back of county garbage truck No. 2, Woody Moos told me, he had worked for a time in footwear maintenance (shoe salesman). Before that, for a month, he had been a member of the catering staff (waiter) at a posh Atlanta hotel. In the spring he had worked as an agrarian assistant (field hand) in west Texas. Hitchhiking back to Birmingham, he landed work as the graveyard deep-sea chef (dishwasher) at the Ocean Spray Cafe just before it was closed down for serving raw oysters infected with cholera. The oysters had been fished out of Mobile Bay and were served with stale crackers and cocktail sauce diluted with watered-down ketchup.

From the kitchen of the Ocean Spray, Moos moved into waste management (trash), becoming a member of the crew of county garbage truck No. 2.

"Some vita, eh?" said Woody Moos, showing his yellow teeth in a wide smile. "Oh, yes. Oh, yes." He had pulled a little silver frame out of a torn garbage bag stuffed with half-eaten microwave dinners. The frame held the photograph of a young woman with auburn hair and tragic brown eyes. She seemed to be looking expectantly off in the distance. Moos wiped her clean. The little frame gleamed.

"Don't they know they can't throw sadness out?" he said. He tossed the frame and photograph indifferently back into the truck. "One more for the landfill," he said. "Just another missing person."

While Moos had been jettisoned, bounced, terminated, shown the door, and given a Mexican raise, he had never been fired, not until the day before Thanksgiving of 1991, anyway, when Woody Moos got caught with a smoked turkey under his yellow rain slicker. The turkey was still warm. Just after sunset, before county garbage truck No. 2 arrived in the parking lot of the Piggly Wiggly to pick us up, I gave Woody Moos a fly-fishing lesson. Under a night sky illuminated by fiery orange moonlight, we walked down to the gorge behind the Piggly Wiggly with sandwiches, coffee, a cold bottle of root beer, and my little rod and reel. We ate and cast over the narrow creek. Wrinkled shadows undulated on the water's surface. Each time he cast, Moos laughed as softly and innocently as a child. For an hour the creek's fast water carried us away.

Carried us away.

While we were casting along the creek, down the gorge from the Piggly Wiggly, as we fished and waited for sunset and the arrival of county garbage truck No. 2, Woody Moos told me about catfish, about how among catfish, the head catfish, the head bull, always has a distinctive smell, one all the other catfish know and respect. When the head catfish is replaced, Moos told me, it takes on a different smell, one that tells all the other catfish that it is no longer the leader, anything special, that it is just another catfish.

"That's the smell I have now," said Moos dreamily. "I'm just another catfish."

Moos grabbed the turkey up on Burlap Road sometime after midnight. The supervisor was waiting in the Piggly Wiggly parking lot when the truck came down the mountain. A woman in a purple bathrobe stood next to him pointing a bony finger toward Woody Moos. A seditious giggle rattled in Hamadullah's throat.

Moos took the turkey from under his yellow rain slicker, wiped it off with his matted green muffler, handed it to the woman in the purple bathrobe, turned, and skipped across the mountain highway, smiling.

There was a black wind rising. Rafts of darkening clouds obscured the moon, and I was thinking of the day a thirty-quart garbage bag full of soiled plastic diapers burst like a cheap balloon instantly transforming Woody Moos into a mosaic of baby turds. How we all howled, especially Hamadullah.

"Don't mean nothing," slurred Moos. "Everyone gets shit on," he said. "Everyone." And as Moos reached for the back of the truck, Hamadullah popped the clutch, sending the truck forward

and toppling Moos onto the cold mountain highway.

The lady in the purple bathrobe threw the turkey into the back of the truck. It was still warm. Little circles of blue smoke rose into the sweet night air. Somewhere across the street, up the mountain, somewhere in the blue-black night, Woody Moos was singing:

> Row, row, row your boat
> Gently down the stream
> Merrily, merrily, merrily, merrily,
> Life is but a dream.

"Wait a minute," said Dr. Mutzpah. "Wait. What about this CEO, your boss, your friend, whatever? Are you saying he never fired you?"

Long, thick shadows filled her office. The light from the table lamp made her kind blue eyes seem liquid, sky deep, sky blue.

"He never said the word," I said. "He was smiling, laughing, patting me enthusiastically on the back. No list of charges, no hand-wringing explanations, no reprimand, no second chances, no mercy. My friend the CEO just kept smiling, and I remember thinking that it was nice one of us was having a good time. He filled my pockets with compliments and ushered me toward the closed door, and all I could do was wonder if I could make the cast from there to the giant round geode that sat on the corner of his desk. I had dug it out of a western mountain while a cold rain fell, wrapped it in work shirts and ties, and carried it back home. I gave it to my friend the CEO. It was one gift of many he received in celebration of his twentieth year with the company. I sawed the top of the stone off just before giving it to him. It was like trepanning. I stared down into that stone cranium, into a wondrous chaos of sparkling blue-gray quartz. Light dripped from the halved geode like blood, a thick stream of blue-gray light, an ancient light, older than man, than memory.

Dr. Mutzpah went on looking for answers, though, all the little incidents that might have triggered my malaise. On one Thursday afternoon, just before I drove out of Denver and into the high mountain country, Dr. Mutzpah asked me what had been the highpoint of my career so far.

"I've never read an issue of *Entertainment Weekly* magazine," I said.

A grin threatened the dignified, professional corners of her mouth. "An attitude like that can get you fired," she said.

"I know," I said. "I know."

I was not prepared for the closed door on that balmy June afternoon. Such a surprise can leave a man frayed, blanched, as his numbed brain fills with dark pools of blood. When I left the building a yellow moon filled the night sky. Tattered shadows drifted among the pines, and there was a cool wind coming off the mountain. Beyond the building's double doors and polished floodlights, I lost what was left of my equilibrium, bounced off a wall of gray and red stones as the sidewalk rose to meet me. I stumbled about like a moonstruck crab until gravity seemed to give way altogether, dumping me into some kind of ridiculous pratfall through time and space that landed me, finally, in the black cozy chair in Dr. Lilly Mutzpah's office in downtown Denver.

There were no warm handshakes or heartfelt good-byes from my friend the CEO or from anyone else, as I recall. Sudden endings are like that. The exception was the lovely senior editor in the office next to mine. On my last day she helped me carry my belongings to the car, and she raised up on her tiptoes and kissed me gently on the cheek.

Of that moment, I can only remember this: how sweet her skin smelled and how the sunlight mixed with her hair.

What a grand good-bye.

In a hotel room somewhere in Kansas, I kept going over in my mind what had happened. Again and again. I tried reducing the entire experience to the purity of mathematics. My friend the CEO, who is an abstract mathematician by training, would have appreciated this effort, I like to think. But nothing balanced, nothing added up to give me a clean, neat, precise answer. That's the trouble with trying to apply mathematics to life. Life refuses to cooperate, to be orderly, predictable, precise, calculable. Too many variables, thank God. Too many possibilities, too many emotions beyond measure. The equation did spit out a wonderful piece of irony, however. On the morning of the day that I lost my job I had made an appointment with my doctor. I was going to haul my melancholy in and have it examined, checked out. Alcoholics at Southern Progress are treated kindly. They leave quietly, with pay, go into treatment, and come back with their breath and life as sweet as peppermint. I looked forward to getting my moods tuned and rotated, my brain rewired, coming back to my job in paradise with my breath and my life as sweet as peppermint. Instead, I cancelled the appointment and wound up in Kansas, the malaria boiling in my blood.

Later, when I finally drove out of Denver and over the peaks of the Front Range and down into the high meadow country of South Park, Colorado, I would meet Kiwi LaReaux, Swami Bill's main squeeze. When I talked to her of paradise, this is what she told me, smiling shyly as she spoke:

"Paradise? There are so many . . . so many."

Which is true, I think. And human beings are forever falling in and out of them, as I did. Indeed, falling in and out of paradise is one of the things human beings do best.

Here is another paradise of mine. When I was a boy, it was my favorite.

My father was a career soldier. The family followed wherever he went, except when he went to war. We were military bedouins, moving from one army base to another. By the time I graduated from high school, I had attended fourteen different schools, mostly army-base schools. I can remember many times when, as students, we had to stand up and talk about our heroes. Of course, we were expected to talk about our fathers, who were really heroes, soldiers with Purple Hearts and Silver Stars and Medals of Honor. They were lucky soldiers. Lucky to be alive. World War II and Korea and later Vietnam were always being fought at our house, down in the basement where my dad had an office, or around the kitchen late at night, the beer and memories flowing, as my father and other soldiers traded stories of fear and luck and survival.

And the kids, when our turn came at school to talk about heroes, or who we admired most, would always talk about their fathers. Except me. To me, soldiers, even soldier heroes, were hardly rare. They were as common as enlisted men. They were everywhere. So when it came my turn to talk, I always talked about one of my father's older brothers, my uncle Ralph, who was a salesman for Nabisco. Every time my uncle Ralph showed up at our place, or when we showed up at his place, or when we all met at my grandmother's house in Shreveport, Louisiana, my uncle Ralph would smile and take me by the hand, walk me down to whatever new huge Chevrolet he was driving. Nabisco gave him a new one every year. He would slowly open the car's huge trunk, and there would be, to my eyes, surely 90 percent of the Oreos and Fig Newtons and Lorna Doones that existed in the free world. Or so it always seemed to me. And my uncle Ralph always let me have as much as I could carry.

Those moments with my uncle Ralph and his huge Chevy, with its immense trunk gorged with cookies and crackers, seemed like paradise to me. So I kept getting up in front of one class or another and not talking about my dad, figuring everyone knew already that he was an honored soldier, but about my amazing uncle Ralph and the little chunk of paradise that he carried around in the trunk of his shiny Chevolet.

Remembering that the little fly rod I had given my friend the CEO on that balmy June morning was still lying on his desk that same afternoon when he fired me joggled my brain, buzzed through my thoughts like lightning as I drove across the Kansas plains, the land rich and dark and flat and endless in every direction. The little rod gave rise to pleasant thoughts of trout, dozens of them rising up off the bottoms of some cold stream toward shimmering pools of deflected sunlight on the stream's surface. Their muscled flanks shuddered in the water. I had not thought of trout or of wild trout water in a long time. Just the image of them sent a chill through me and settled me, calmed me, and I again felt that rhythm of blood and water, bone and wind, muscle and stone.

Things change, always. There are no absolutes, except that things come and go.

Come and go.

That's what I had forgotten behind my friend the CEO's closed door: those rhythms. Life inexorably tangled in the flux of time. I had forgotten that it helps if you expect nothing and anticipate everything.

By the time I crossed the Colorado state line, the fever had broken again, and I thought clearly enough to conclude that I had come down with Albert's disease.

Albert was my great-uncle. I lived with him and my grandfather on their marginal farm in the hardluck Ozark Mountains of northwest Arkansas. Albert's last year was plagued by a swelling mental misery, a cancerous plague of loneliness. And why not? He had lost five wives. They died on him, all five of them. He finally concluded that he was host to some unspeakable virus that killed any woman he loved or even felt attracted to. In the last year of his life, anytime he found himself in the presence of a lady he would cover his mouth and nose with his faded yellow bandana. Not long before he died of a brain tumor, Albert lowered the bandana from his mouth and whispered softly in my ear, "You know, son, a man shouldn't have to lose five of anything."

I remember we were standing knee-deep in the cold waters of

Karen's Pool on Starlight Creek near Elias Wonder's clapboard cabin. Albert flicked his old cane fly rod and his line arched through the light wind as easily as a single strand of spider webbing. After Albert spoke, he placed the yellow bandana back over his mouth and nose.

Thinking about it as I drove into Colorado, I knew I had Albert's disease because I had been losing things, too many things, including my mother.

My mother died of brain cancer, just like Albert.

Albert's mother died of brain cancer.

My grandmother died of brain cancer.

My family has brain tumors the way other families have blue eyes, red hair, double-jointedness.

"There, there," said Dr. Lilly Mutzpah when I told her of the brain tumors eating away the branches of my family tree.

Meanwhile, chemicals in my brain went on souring and burning. Sometimes it felt as though all my neurotransmitters had been zapped, leaving me with a headful of crackling short circuits. Maybe it was fishing in all those electrical storms. Too much time spent on trout rivers.

Or not enough.

Dr. Mutzpah wanted to spend the next several months investigating and mending my upset psyche, even though I assured her that wandering about in my brain was no more stimulating or revealing than an afternoon at Buel Hunkapillar's Gator-Rama near Fish-Eating Creek, Florida, which I remembered featured a water moccasin decked out in a flabby rubber nose and an orange fright wig, turtles on roller skates with poignant Bible passages painted in neon red on their shells, and Tiny, a seventeen-foot alligator. Buel Hunkapillar would stick his head into Tiny's gaping jaws. Whenever Hunkapiller said "chicken," Tiny would salivate, snap its jaws shut, roll over on its back. Buel Hunkapillar liked to tease fate by shouting the word "chicken" while his head was still inside Tiny's trembling jaws.

"How do you cope?" asked Dr. Mutzpah.

"Root beer helps," I said. "The colder the better. It can take the edge off misfortune."

Too, there is something that Woody Moos would later say to me, late one night on the back of county garbage truck No. 2 as he picked through the garbage, something that keeps bobbing up and down in my memory. Moos's words have become something else that can help whenever I need it.

Earlier that night, Moos had found an old sock among the contents of a broken garbage bag, a sock smeared with bacon grease and festooned with bits of eggshell. A knot had been tied in the sock. Moos shook it. I could hear loose change clinking inside. There must have been several dollars in that sock, and yet Moos casually tossed it aside, wiping a smudge of bacon grease on his yellow rain slicker, saying, in almost a whisper, "Certain parts of my soul are not for sale."

Dr. Lilly Mutzpah, by the way, was always scribbling hurriedly in her small green notebook. Sometimes, as the good doctor scribbled away, I would fall into a daydream about wild mountain streams and all the remembered trout of yesteryear, how they had hauled me from here to there and from there to here and everywhere, in and out of time, as the years have gone easily by, even to the far side of experience, to that passing moment where things simply are and there is no need for explanation or reason or interpretation. I never told Dr. Mutzpah about my innocent and harmless daydreams. I did not want to interrupt her scribbling. Too, I never told her about waking up in Biloxi, Mississippi, with Sergeant Muldoon's tattoo freshly embroidered on my left arm, though perhaps I should have.

What did I tell her?

I kept on telling her that the depression bubbling about in my brain and my blood was a drought of the spirit, a relentless palsy of the nerves, a fathomless exhaustion. I told her that my depression seemed to corrupt all the senses, reducing everything to a kind of amorphous bewilderment in which details were lost, in which the world often drifted through endless membranes of thick, clawed shadows, shadows that left it flat and uninteresting. Time did not move, it oozed, moments dripping like globs of melted candle wax down bleak, grimy window panes. Often, I told Dr. Mutzpah, the depression would rise like a sudden black wind, leave me breathless, like I had been kicked in the solar plexus. On the morning I crawled out of the blue sleeping bag in my unfurnished room in Denver, Colorado, grabbed the telephone and the phone book, and eventually found myself staring at Dr. Lilly Mutzpah's address and telephone number, the skin at my fingertips had gone the gray-blue of brooding storm clouds, and my arms and legs were so heavy with fatigue that they felt like dead flesh. It was as though I had suddenly been stricken with cutaneous alogia—that strange state of torment where the nerves go numb, feel nothing, neither pain nor pleasure.

Depression, I told the good doctor, seemed to me more than a shuffle of mood, a persistent, forever-threatening gloom. At its worst, the disease also carries its own special breed of pain, a pain that is at once sweeping and cellular in nature, and in time seems indissoluble, obdurate, unforgiving, and imperishable. It settles like tongues of carbolic acid just below the skin, along the pink interior walls of the skull, along the spine.

Never looking up from her small green notebook, Dr. Mutzpah asked me to please go on, asked for more telling description, details.

And I told her that my depression's pain was animate, urgent, a kind of nonstop mental neuralgia. Tic douloureux of the brain.

"What helps the pain?" asked Dr. Mutzpah. She had stopped scribbling in her small green notebook and was looking at me. Her pale blue eyes twinkled with reflected lamplight.

"Economics," I said.

Unpaid bills. That and sometimes, as I keep saying, I will imagine all the trout that I have tucked deep in the folds of my memory rising in bright rivers, and I imagine casting to them, and letting them take me where they will.

Any place at all.

Depression is a topography not only of pain, but of isolation, a loneliness that is deep and wide, a longing so intense that I felt like a blind and deaf lemming groping about for the sea, any sea.

I joined clubs and societies in which I had little interest, attended meetings to which I had not been invited, bumped purposely into strangers, hung around smoky bars and bad restaurants drinking root beer over crushed ice, called friends long-distance who had trouble remembering me. I listened to conversations while in line at the supermarket, on buses, snatched whispers in dim movie theaters.

What did I hear? The mutter and moan of loneliness, the sad trill of sorrow and desperation. I told Dr. Mutzpah about the man standing in a cold rain along a highway in Kansas, his lips Caribbean blue, his skin chalky white. I stopped, rolled down the car window. The man was mumbling something I could not understand. He just stood there in the cold rain, his eyes colorless save for the cold, gray, autumn light, his lips trembling. And I honked the car horn, once, twice, and still he just stood in the cold rain. There was a terror in his trembling, a bottomless isolation, as though he were the last of his species waiting there on that highway in Kansas in the cold rain for oblivion's consoling touch.

Finally, I rolled the car window up, drove on and did not look back. That is another way to cope, I told Dr. Mutzpah. Taking things as they come. Taking the days one at a time.

Dr. Mutzpah said that every human being is looking for something. The good doctor wondered what I was looking for, searching for. She kept asking.

I told her that I supposed I was looking for the great good place, perhaps a small community of human beings bound together by the common torments and absurdities of life and yet still in love with the earth, still happily bound to it, content with things fundamental—wind and fire, soil and sunlight, moonlight, and fast, cold, rivers.

Dr. Mutzpah wanted to know if I was looking for home.

"Always," I said. "As many as my heart and brain can hold, embrace, some place edged with wildness that can nourish the spirit."

And in such places, for me, there would always be wide, fast, free-flowing rivers, and in that cold, fast water, trout. Where there is such water, where there are such fish, there is still spontaneity and magic, even for a tired, depressed angler whose brain sometimes feels like foam rubber, who has awoken on too many mornings looking like an abscessed gunshot wound, to find himself huddled over a warm can of root beer and a half-eaten can of bean dip, greeting the dawn with toots of digestive theophany.

The sessions with Dr. Mutzpah turned out to be more helpful than harmful. We told each other harmless lies for medicinal reasons.

"There, there," she would say softly, and the words eased through my brain like currents of warm honey.

The good news, as I say, was that my depression turned out to be treatable. There were pharmaceuticals for my dyspeptic chemicals and frayed synapses, psychiatry for my bruised psyche.

Over several months I tried several antidepressants as Dr. Mutzpah searched for just the right medication, the one that would mend the faulty mental wiring in my brain.

Drugs took me up.

Drugs took me down.

Drugs took me round 'n' round.

Some made me sleepy, some made me nervous, some sang me death's sweet, hypnotic lullaby. Some let me rest, others made me squirm, some buzzed in my brain like downed high-voltage wires. Some made me numb. One left me in the blue sleeping bag for days, buried alive. As I say, Dr. Mutzpah found the medication that made my chemicals smile, made my psyche glow, let me dance, in time, out of depression's cromlech and into the fat, warm, comforting arms of homeostasis. Meanwhile, Odell Euclid, who worked at the magazine with me, whose desk was next to mine, offered to cure my case of the meat bucket blues.

"I can get you back on your feet again by midnight," said Odell Euclid. "All you need, friend, is an armload of Marx Brothers films and a bowl of peyote buttons."

My norepinephrines and serotonins and cortisol became as giddy as a young boy's flush chemistry and I packed my rod and reel and the blue sleeping bag and hiked into the high country, walked along fast mountain streams, waded into their cold waters, cast my line over rising trout, my coat pockets full of dreams and heavy-duty vitamins.

THREE

NOW & ZEN

Such a price the gods exact for song, to become what we sing.

—GOETHE

The afternoon I crossed West Colfax Avenue on my way to my first meeting with Dr. Lilly Mutzpah, I had been in Denver less than a week. On that afternoon, my face glistened, was covered with a limpid sheen of sweat. It was snowing, and in the hulking shadows of downtown Denver's dingy buildings, the snow looked first delicate blue, then like globs of mercury as it gathered in the gray streets.

By then my depression had become synclastic, as tight-fitting as surgical gloves. Inside my head, it pressed relentlessly against the moist gray insides of my cranium like a stuck throttle.

I had yet to cross the ragged line of mountains just beyond the city, to journey into the high country. I had not yet walked along the Middle Fork of the South Platte River, heard the trill of its cold, fast waters. I had not yet looked into that wide, deep pool and seen the big brown trout with the achromatic eyes, eyes that were opaque, blind. I had not yet seen the old trout rise in the river's current, all grace and wild instinct flashing in the chilly late autumn sunlight.

Instead, I was standing in downtown Denver, the sky a whorl

of delicate blue snowflakes. I was coatless, and malaria fevers boiled in my brain and in my blood. There was the feral, indifferent smell of mountains in that snowstorm, in the icy wind that blew hard out of the north and west, a wind that groaned heavily down among the city's tall buildings, scraping the surface of its dull gray streets.

While waiting for the right alchemus of medicines to take hold, I got better by talking each week to Dr. Mutzpah and to her other Thursday-afternoon patients as we waited our turn in the calming off-white alcove that served as Dr. Mutzpah's waiting room. My Thursdays were filled with talking and listening. Each Thursday, before I went to Dr. Mutzpah's office, I stood outside, on the corner of Stout and Seventeenth streets, listening to Dr. Truth's electric voice.

Dr. Truth with his booming, sonorous voice. Dr. Truth with his unshaven white and gray stubble, his untrimmed mustache, his tangle of platinum-colored hair tucked haphazardly under a crumbled and faded brown fedora.

Dr. Truth in his mismatched shoes and Stygian black trenchcoat, his narrow eyes often hidden behind designer sunglasses with sky blue lenses.

Dr. Truth standing on the brown folding chair at the corner of Stout and Seventeenth streets in downtown Denver, there in the sheets of rain, under sunny skies, in sudden showers of ice and snow, always flailing his arms, pounding his small fists, his piebald skin glowing in patches of pallid blue and bruised yellow.

Dr. Truth yowled and shook his small fists at every passerby, his thin lips tight and his blackening teeth showing, his brown chair shifting dramatically as he stomped his feet urgently. I listened to Truth for months and his message never changed.

"People of Denver, come close. No, no. Closer still. Get right up here, right up next to me. Truth's the name. Come on, take a look. Inhale and get a smell.

"Truth's an ugly thing, isn't it? And smelly.

"Yes, I'm fallen, a broken human being. A walking, breathing, failed product of the good ol' U.S. of A.

"I'm the Eagle's shit, Uncle Sam's bad breath, Miss Liberty's forgotten.

"That and more. Come close now. Closer.

"I'm your worst nightmare, your greatest fears.

"Hear me now, hear me. Oh, come on, get closer. CLOSER!!

"Let me tell you my story, your story, our story.

"I had a job. Had a house, big and roomy. Shade trees and a grassy yard that I mowed and kept tidy. Had a beautiful wife to sleep with, laugh with, make love to. Had two children, a boy for me, a girl for her. I carried their sweet little photographs. Had two cars, a wallet full of credit cards. Had the respect of my neighbors and fellow workers. Always had a pocketful of frog green dollars.

"Friends, I had it all. Just like you have it. Had it all and lost it all. Didn't lose it to crime or the government or bad nutrition. Didn't lose it to booze or drugs. The booze came later.

"Things just went sour. Life crumbled. The job went first. Mine and fifty-nine thousand others, all in a single day. Imagine that.

"So, no job, then pretty soon no more of that magical frog green money. No more frog green money and pretty soon no more roomy house and grassy yard. My beautiful wife lost interest in making love to me, then simply lost interest, then took off. I can't find her anywhere. If any of you see her, let me know. She's Truth's wife. She has Truth's children and their sweet little photographs.

"All gone in—what?—a week, a month? I forget. Hocus-pocus. You have it all, then you don't.

"You're an ordinary guy, Mr. Average U.S.A. of St. Louis, M-O, then you're Dr. Truth, and all Truth's got is this chair and these clothes and a cardboard condo in a dark alley where the cold wind isn't so bad, and mission stew and all the old, green government cheese you can stuff in your coat pockets.

"One moment you got friends and station, the next no one

knows you, and even your style is gone, withered up.

"One moment you're visible, the next there's less to you than a ghost.

"You want to see the last of Dr. Truth, you want to get me off this chair, off this corner, out of this city, off your mind and conscience?

"Don't give me your spare change, don't give me food or clothes or a new cardboard box. Spare me your pity or sympathy. Don't whisper among yourselves the great, comforting lie that I somehow brought all this misery and sorrow on myself.

"Hell, forget all that. Just give me a job. Let me work again. Just that. Work. And then Truth shall set us both free."

I mentioned Dr. Truth to Dr. Lilly Mutzpah only once. Dr. Mutzpah thought Dr. Truth was an alcoholic suffering from Korsakoff's Syndrome, severe dementia. It was true, I suppose. Dr. Truth *was* a sloppy drunk. And why not? Life can do anything, even drive Truth to drink. If Dr. Truth had been an employee of Southern Progress Corporation he could have gone away, gotten some rest, some peace and quiet, dried out, and come back to work with his breath and his disposition as sweet and tingly as breath mints.

I listened to Dr. Truth every Thursday afternoon, standing among a tiny crowd of people that gathered around him, shaking their collective heads then moving on. Even so, no matter the weather or time of year, there were people there, I like to think, quiet and listening, as though hoping for some private message that would lessen their own misery, ease their sorrow, ease their own pain.

I didn't have a job for Dr. Truth, so each Thursday I left a couple of wrinkled frog green dollars in the Nike shoebox under Dr. Truth's brown metal chair.

Dr. Truth looked like a man of considerable talent to me, and I asked my editor at the magazine about putting Truth on the payroll. My editor grimaced and shook his head, told me his own version of the truth: "People get what they deserve."

There was just too much truth stuck to Dr. Truth. People stopped in the street to listen, took one look, snickered, and

moved on quickly. They found Truth ugly and useless, repulsive, a want ad for perversion, venality, atheism, alcoholism, laziness, poverty, fatalism, insanity, hunger, homelessness, and unemployment.

Getting to Dr. Mutzpah's office, though, meant getting past Dr. Truth. After a couple of weeks, Dr. Truth recognized me as one of his flock, stepped down off his brown metal chair, patted me on the shoulder as I dropped a crinkled frog green dollar bill into his shoebox, said to me, "It's okay, friend, half-truths are gladly accepted. Even Dr. Truth's got to keep his belly full and his head warm."

Past Dr. Truth, through the revolving doors, up seven floors was the man with no name. He, too, was a patient of the kind Dr. Lilly Mutzpah. He was always there, slouched down in one of the small, marble white couches in Dr. Mutzpah's calming white waiting room.

The man with no name had big bottle green eyes and narcesant hair. Every Thursday afternoon he greeted me and told me brightly that since he had forgotten, more or less, who he was, he had lived a life of complete happiness. Then he would slouch down further into the soft couch and recite episodes of old television shows. He especially liked "The Flintstones" and "Gilligan's Island."

One Thursday afternoon the man with no name quit reciting the dialogue from "Father Knows Best." "I can't sleep anymore," he said, his face suddenly just inches from mine, his bottle green eyes bulging.

"Why not?" I said.

He cast a watchful glare at Dr. Mutzpah's door.

"I keep hearing a choir of crickets beneath the floorboards. You know what they're singing?"

"No," I said.

"Neither do I," said the man with no name. "Neither do I."

The man with no name was determined that no matter how hard Dr. Mutzpah tried, he would go right on not knowing who he was and being deliriously happy.

"Ignorance is bliss," said the man with no name every Thursday afternoon.

Miss Piggot scoffed every time she heard this.

Miss Piggot had a mole the color of wet cocoa at the corner of her small, pinched mouth. Roiling mists, as black as thunderheads, drifted in her brown eyes.

"I love you," she said, moving next to me on the couch. Her smile revealed a mouth full of crooked teeth.

Miss Piggot leaned closer, brushing her stringy brown hair against my shoulder. She wore a glaring orange headband on which she had stitched boldly DEUS ABSCONDITUS.

Miss Piggot's head was getting better, was doing just fine.

"Vitamins," she told me discreetly. "Lots of them, all the time. They've made my life's goals so much clearer."

Velveeta Cheese told me to beware of Miss Piggot.

"The bitch is deadly," he or she said in a high, reedy voice.

I say he or she because with Velveeta Cheese I was never quite sure and it never seemed to matter.

Velveeta Cheese worked as a stand-up comic, part-time bricklayer, and fashion designer, or so she told me the day we sat across from each other in Dr. Mutzpah's waiting room while outside it snowed a wild, electric blue snow.

"Mutzpah wants to zap me," said Velveeta Cheese breezily. I'm pretty sure it was Ms. Cheese that day, since she was decked out in a golden mufti festooned with flashing rhinestones, purple hose, and yellow tennis shoes. She had misted and twisted her thinning hair into an adorable bohemian bob.

"Zap you?"

"Yeah, you know, give me the juice, fry my gray matter, buzz me with a few jillion watts of electricity."

"But why . . . ?" I had wanted to say so much more. I had wanted to say, "It's okay, Velveeta. Things work out. There, there." But nothing came out except a startled "But why?"

"Because being Velveeta Cheese ain't easy. I have this compulsion to spread myself around," said Ms. Cheese, patiently smoothing a single greasy strand of her bootblack hair over her bald pate.

Velveeta Cheese had ECT, electroconvulsive therapy. The week she came back she had become a he and was wearing a handsome, dark blue pinstripe suit. This is what Mr. Cheese said to me across Dr. Mutzpah's waiting room:

"It's okay. Things have a way of working out. My brain feels like a vat of warm, melted honey."

That and no more. From that day until the Thursday afternoon I saw her last, Velveeta Cheese never stopped smiling.

What had brought me west, though, plopped me down in Denver, was something less romantic than the vast sprawl of the Rocky Mountains, the high mountain country west of the city, some of which has a wild edge to it. I had come not to let the mountain country whisper to me, tempt me; I had come for work, a paycheck, handfuls of Dr. Truth's frog green dollars.

Being a writer in Birmingham, Alabama, had always been something of a whimsical proposition, an oxymoron of vaudevillian proportions, as vexing and ruinous as being a wool salesman on an atoll in the South Pacific.

I walked out of my friend the CEO's office on that warm, beautiful June afternoon and hit the road again, moved on, a bedouin of the interstate system, once again an explorer searching for the great good place. I would know it when I found it or when it found me, and I would embrace it like a long lost ancestor, tell myself harmless, comforting and beautiful lies about it, including the most comforting lie of all—that it was and always had been my one and only true home, my piece of the good earth, the place where I have always inevitably belonged, a place marked by family and friends, peace and solace, stained with an unyielding wildness.

Mi Oh, the beautiful young hostess at the Now & Zen restaurant in Denver, would later tell me how Japan had solved the problem of human loneliness, just as it had solved the problem of reliable automobiles and high-quality cheap technology. In Japan, Mi Oh told me, old and lonely human beings who had the money could rent families of their very own. For just $350 a month, the lonely could rent beautiful and handsome and successful sons and daughters, complete with lovely and sweet grandchildren. And their new families visit them regularly, hug them and kiss them and shake their hands, tell them about their exciting and full lives, tell them all about what wonderful things their rented grandchildren were doing. Mi Oh told me that the best thing about the rented families was that after whoever had rented them was full of pride and happiness and no longer lonely, the family did what real families almost never did. There were more hugs and kisses and great big smiles, and then they left, said good-bye. Flush with pride and wonder at the beauty and warmth of his rented family he would wave to them, and the family would wave back happily and tell him to cheer up, that his lonely days were over, that they would make sure he was lonely no more.

Lonely no more.

You can rent just about anything in Denver except a beautiful and handsome and successful family that will come over and help you chase away the blues, end your loneliness. Denver is just another large American city, and cities take their toll, as do wars and poverty, technology, insanity, heaven and hell, and eternity.

Eternity's toll, Swami Bill would tell me later, is that it just goes on and on.

Denver was a pulsating dollar sign, one I drove thirty hours straight to snuggle with, seduce, introduce to my obligations.

The job and my obligations shook hands, embraced, sat down and feasted together, and struck a deal. In the end, the only thing that separated me from Dr. Truth and his yellow teeth and his breath that smelled like a bucket of fish heads, Dr. Truth yowling nonstop from atop his metal chair at the corner of Stout and Sev-

enteenth streets, was not style, heritage, background, talent, handsomeness, manners, breeding, education, experience, beauty, grace, friends, or sophistication. All that separated us was the most fragile membrane of all—dumb luck and two hundred frog green dollars a week.

Standing there on West Colfax in a snow that looked like a storm of blue confetti, there in front of the Denver Mint, a building with a Brobdingnagian presence, a dreary white facade and a belly full of shiny new money, standing there with a cold wind stinging my face, clawing at my gloveless hands, I remembered the first words I had heard Dr. Truth say, "Friends, it isn't so much that the American dream is gone, exhausted, dead. It's that even the dream of the dream is rotten and hollow."

A crust of fragile blue snowflakes gathered on Dr. Truth's hat and nose, on his cheeks and bright violet lips.

Dr. Truth yelled and screamed. Pale blue snowflakes melted on his wagging tongue as he screeched at those who waddled through the storm that he had been just like them, that he, too, had once believed in endless head-over-heels, never-ending, more-ever-more riches and prosperity. Now, all he had was fifty-eight cents, a cardboard condo and a warm, pretty, and fading hallucination of getting another job, the chance to earn a living, hang on, survive.

Among Dr. Truth's messages was this: sooner or later life comes down to maintenance. That's one of the things I was thinking about on that Denver Street in the snow—maintenance: How to maintain the little home in the foothills of the Appalachian Mountains that sheltered my family, my young sons and too many books and a basement overstuffed with dreams and ghosts, fly rods and boxes of fossils and ancient bones, and stones of every color, stones shaped by wind and cold and the endless press of moving water, mountain rivers, and streams. The stones come from every stream and river and creek I have fished. Each one of them tells a story, embraces a world, a universe wrinkled not only with the memory of time, but with every moment spent or unfolding or yet to come, every past, every future, every vital present, even the one that found me standing on a street in downtown Denver in clouds of blue snow.

While I was looking up into the blowing blue snow, I thought about my great-uncle Albert and Elias Wonder, the old Sioux lunatic. Albert and my grandfather, as I say, had a farm in the Ozark Mountains of northwest Arkansas. Wonder lived in a crumbling clapboard shanty down the creek from the old farmhouse at the edge of Karen's Pool. According to a report filed by the county agent, my grandfather and great-uncle Albert and Elias Wonder were men of no measurable value who lived on worthless land and did no work that showed a healthy profit. Among the worthless things they had were geese flooding autumn skies, wild quail in the tangled hedges at the edges of the fields, deer in the thick mountain woods, woodcock down in the damp sloughs along the creek, trout hanging at the edges of the current, in the fast waters of Starlight Creek, a good tin roof that kept out the wind and most of the rain, five worn fly rods and fraudulent flies fashioned out of belly fur, chicken hackles, bird feathers, colored threads, flies that sometimes worked. Whether they worked or not never really mattered, because we almost never kept the trout, anyway. They each had a good hat. There was a warm blanket on every bed. Cold springwater ran out of a section of pipe that had been driven down through a gallery of dark stones, down through layers of porous, percolating limestone behind the barn. The water was clear, clean, and cold, and ran down the face of the stones and into a tiny, nameless, narrow stream of water that emptied into Starlight Creek. Endless ranges and slants of light and wind and shadow came off the mountains. And that country to them and to me was all we knew of god—bountiful, merciless, relentless, inexplicable, and abiding.

I lived with the old men for a while. We worked, we fished, we dreamed, and every moment, it seemed to me then, burned with possibility. Each day, my work done, I would go down to the creek, wade into its cold, fast water and suddenly be embraced, or so it seems to me now, by the participatory universe, becoming a motion among motions, fly rod in hand, casting to

rising trout, yearning for connection, that moment when there is
no difference between the observer and the observed. While I
was only a boy, I seemed to know even then, in some deep and
silent way, that the wild water heavy with trout could haul me
here and there, anywhere and everywhere, even to the edges of
the universe.

Those days on the water, fly rod in hand, had a rhythm. I could
sense it in my flesh, in my blood, in the folds of my brain, a pulse
of blood and breathing, the dim glow of ancient memory. Elias
Wonder, the old Sioux lunatic, put it into words that still flow
through my memory, the words that he told the county agent
who came around to tell the old men that they were poor failures
because they were not ambitious enough, were too unmotivated
and lazy to cooperate with modern technology, would not culti-
vate prosperity by damming the creek, slashing and burning their
thick stands of hardwood, turning their hovel into a pine planta-
tion, a place of pride that could provide the state of Arkansas, the
South, the nation, with what it really needed, more telephone
poles.

These are the words the smiling and barefoot Elias Wonder
said to the county agent: "Things come and go."

I noticed while I was looking up at the falling blue snow that I
was leaning against yet another telephone pole the old men had
proudly not planted, grown, cut down, and processed to help
maintain the world's prosperity.

In another five minutes I found myself seven floors above the
city, sitting bathed in the neutral, peaceful, sedating light of Dr.
Lilly Mutzpah's office, staring out the big picture window toward
the peaks of the Front Range, which were covered in a shawl of
fresh, soft, blue-white snow. Where the highest summits pierced
the snowy sky, there were tendrils of grizzled, eddying clouds
and around each a thin aureole of coral light shimmered like
shadows over water.

At that moment, a word broke loose in my brain. *Shuzin,* a Japanese word I had learned years ago on the island of Okinawa before my friend Norwood pulled the pin on a World War II Japanese hand grenade and became, in an instant, cosmic.

The hand grenade was in excellent condition, as good as new, a little metal box of death still waiting to be opened. We found it in a lovely little stream beneath a canopy of lush green jungle. Since Norwood was the oldest boy among us, the honor of pulling the pin, opening the grenade's little metal box of death, went to him. The rest of us were sad and disappointed. We wanted to pull the pin. After all, we were the sons of combat soldiers. Our fathers were busy pulling the pins off hand grenades in Vietnam. Good sons, we wanted to be just like them.

While we lived on Okinawa, my mother employed a beautiful young Okinawan college student as a maid. Her name was Suzy. Suzy had long, silky, black hair, which she wore loose, ebony eyes, and soft, xanthic skin and a tiny voice.

I loved her desperately, or as desperately as a boy could. It was Suzy who taught me about *shuzin,* the warm and generous idea that home is not any one place, but many, that the human soul is inexorably bound to this little blue planet, to all of it, as a whole. While I looked numbly into her moist, black eyes, Suzy told me that a human being searching for God should not lift his head and eyes to the skies. Rather, he should get down on his knees and consider the earth, which is, said Suzy, just another word for heaven, and that the doors of heaven are always open wide.

Shuzin. My memory is a river of such moments, a river that is forever flooding, then retreating, beaching all kinds of interesting debris in the mind. Things like *shuzin,* which according to Suzy has always been mingled in the blood and bone and tissue of human beings, even when we were not yet human beings, even when we were thoughtless little blobs of life, tiny bacteria squirming down in the blue-green scum bullying the rest of microbial society.

Shuzin. I kept whispering it, as though it were some newly discovered language. And I watched the sunlight in the distance,

how it mixed with the snow, glinted off the high peaks, threw tempting shadows down along the ragged slopes of the high country. As I stared out Dr. Mutzpah's window, while the blue snow fell and the eerie light beyond the mountains glowed, the future, like the present, seemed wide open.

Autumn had just begun to settle in the mountains and the high country when I arrived in Denver.

I rented a small, unfurnished room in a three-story, faded red-brick building just off Colorado Boulevard.

"How much?" I asked the young Asian woman who had sidled up to me, tapped me on the shoulder, smiled generously.

She had a big blue-steel handgun in one hand and a wooden flute in the other.

"For you, ten dol-lah a day, plus a hunred-dol-lah deposit.

"You know, case you slip-a-roo in the night."

Putting the wooden flute under her arm, she held up the wad of twenties I handed her to the midday Denver sunlight, which, thanks to an almost permanent cloak of pollution, is the color of cancerous liver.

"You got yourself a room, my gaijin-baby," she said, stuffing the twenties into the pocket of her jeans. "I'm Mi Oh."

"Myoh?"

"No, Mi and Oh. Mi first name, Oh last. Mi Oh."

"Oh my, oh me oh my oh."

"No, no, gaijin-baby. Mi and Oh. Mi Oh."

She slipped the shiny blue-steel gun into the pocket where she had deposited the twenties.

"Let me be first wel-come you, my gaijin-baby, to paradise and to the Now & Zen, there on corner. It belongs to my father, like this fine guest house. The Now & Zen has best Asian food in Den-ber."

"Oh my."

"No, my gaijin-baby, Mi Oh."

Mi Oh took off her lemon yellow sunglasses with the electric gold lenses and winked. She wore a pink Grateful Dead T-shirt, which was tucked neatly into her designer blue jeans. Mi Oh slipped the sunglasses back over her beautiful melanous eyes, and the Denver sunlight glared off the lenses in ugly little brown streaks.

I noticed that Mi Oh was chewing on a great wad of purple bubble gum. As Mi Oh walked away, she blew and popped big violet halos of gum, patted the pocket stuffed with the blue-steel handgun, and crumpled twenty-dollar bills, and seductively shook her tiny little hips.

I emptied the contents of the Toyota and my throbbing head into my little room. After thirty hours on the road, most of it, it seemed to me, spent driving across the monotonous flats of Kansas, my brain felt like three pounds of turtle green Jell-O sloshing about in a one-pound bowl.

That night I walked over to the Now & Zen, scooted into a red leatherette booth, opened the plastic-coated menu, abandoned minimalism, and had numbers 67, 49, and 85, heavy on the Mongolian beef and moo shu, and all of it western style, which turned out to be on a plate decorated with dragons in cowboy hats twisting menacingly about little tangles of skiers racing happily down snow-covered mountain slopes.

Below the twisting dragons and cheerful skiers were fish, some mythic species perhaps, with curling, black, whiplike whiskers, blue scales, vacant yellow eyes, and thick tomato red lips drawn back to reveal double rows of fiercely barbed teeth. There were lovely little red letters on the teeth. This is what was written into the fish's snarling grin: THANK YOU AND HAVE A NICE DAY.

The Now & Zen was as dimly lit as a geomancer's parlor. Over each red leatherette booth and open table hung a single soft forty-watt bulb tucked delicately inside a red paper lantern, on which were painted peaceful scenes of immaculate rock gardens, silver rivers bathed in golden moonlight, warm golden pagodas, bright blue and orange Shinto temples, black serpents rising out of roiling quince seas. Between the booths and tables, for pri-

vacy, were tall, honey-colored wooden screens. Carved on the screens were leaping tigers and graceful cranes and great spreading maple trees. Rainbow-colored silk fans, Zen sumi-e paintings, and M. C. Escher prints decorated the restaurant's pale green walls. Dozens and dozens of tiny bells were hung from the ceiling. Every time customers entered or left, the bells would toll gently.

Bells, again.

Mi Oh told me that it was not air or wind that moved the bells, made them sing so mournfully, but rather the spirits of the dead letting the living know that death is not so bad. I would later tell Mi Oh that my mother had heard bells as the tumors in her brain went about killing her. I would tell her, too, what my mother had told me about the bells she heard—that they tolled and tolled, not just for her, but for everyone. When I told her this, Mi Oh smiled. The door to the restaurant opened, and the bells hanging from the ceiling chimed delicately. Mi Oh told me that my mother's spirit was a part of that wind, that wind that moved about the bells, making them sing gently, sweetly.

That first night at the Now & Zen, I could not stop eating. I kept ordering the sweet-and-sour pork with the chef's special sagebrush sauce. The chef turned out to be Mi Oh's brother, Johnny Oh. Late one night, as we sat in the red leatherette booth, Mi Oh whispered the contents of Johnny Oh's special sagebrush sauce into my ear: Tabasco sauce, garlic, hoisin, chopped young chili peppers, and heaps of good old MSG—monosodium glutamate, glutamic acid, one of the good earth's many natural amino acids, found naturally in seaweed, cereal gluten, even beets. In the 1920s a process was discovered that reduced MSG into a powder.

I asked Mi Oh who had discovered how to fashion MSG into such a titillating taste. "The Japanese, my gaijin-baby," she whispered.

"Figures."

"Who else, my gaijin-baby," she cooed. "We make everything."

Mi Oh winked seductively at me from behind the coral pink

and lime green cash register, and I felt something stir inside me, some yearning not even Johnny Oh's special sagebrush sauce could assuage. Polishing off the last plate of sweet-and-sour pork, the exotic fish on my plate seemed caught in mid-jump, its tomato red eyes fixed on a pool of rice and dark dollops of gummy monosodium glutamate.

Mi Oh's father and mother, she told me, were from Kyoto. There was a color photograph behind the cash register of the Kiyomizu Temple, the Temple of Pure Water, one of Kyoto's most famous temples.

I kept going back to the Now & Zen, drawn there not so much by the food, but by Mi Oh and the lure of the Temple of Pure Water.

Over tiny cups of warm green tea, Mi Oh and I talked. I asked her about the restaurant's name.

"Zen, my gaijin-baby," she said, "is the way." Tiny swirls of smoke rose in tight spirals from the little cups of green tea. Mi Oh wore no makeup. Under the soft light of the red lanterns, her skin looked dreamily flawless and smooth. Tiny golden flecks of soft red lantern light gathered in her black eyes.

"The way . . . ? Ahhh, and what is the way?"

Mi Oh giggled. "Sen is the way, the American way."

"The way is Zen and Zen is the way?"

Mi Oh's giggles matured into a full-blown laugh, as she tossed her head side to side knowingly. Her beautiful long black hair swayed like shadows across heavy seas.

"No, no, no, my gaijin-baby. *Sen* is the way. S-E-N."

"Sen?"

"Dol-lahs," said Mi Oh. "Money." "And the more sen you get, the more Zen you can buy, any Way, as many Paths you like. You see."

"I see."

I had the shrimp fried rice and plenty of yakitori, worked my way through it all, down to the fish rising across the red and blue plate. I let my imagination turn it into a leaping trout, any trout. It had been so long since I had been in the high country, waded the

cold, fast waters of a mountain river, fly rod in hand, felt a river's cold inexhaustible pull, watched inky shadows dart through the water, wrinkling at the current's edge, cast my line, dropping a fly on the water like an offering, hoping for some fish to swallow it and haul me away.

Haul me away.

I do not know how long Mi Oh had been standing next to the booth. She was dressed in her red silk hostess dress which was slit to the thigh. A dragon fashioned from silver and gold thread twisted amorously across her breasts. This is all I could think of to say:

"Oh, my. Oh, my. Oh, me, oh-my-o."

She giggled, left my bill and two fortune cookies. I cracked the two cookies open, let the tiny little pieces of paper folded inside them fall to my plate. This is what the first one said:

"The farther you go, the less you know."

The second message, written by hand, had this to say, no kidding:

"I like you fine. Tao you you feel about me, my gaijin baby?"

Mi Oh giggled from behind the cash register. Soft red light bathed the big color photograph of the Temple of Pure Water. The door closed and the tinkling of the tiny silver bells filled the restaurant.

Trying to simplify my life and my economy, in a week's time I culled my possessions so that I could, with room to spare, stuff everything in one duffle bag and the worn gray-and-yellow backpack. Sitting on the floor of my unfurnished room wrapped in the blue sleeping bag, I looked around me, taking stock of my efforts at frugality and austerity.

Other than the addition of a single milk white reading lamp, my unfurnished room stayed that way. The milk white lamp stood like a sentry beside one of the three wooden vegetable crates I picked out of the big Dumpsters behind the King Super super-

market down the street. Balanced on the crate beside the lamp was my beat-up old Underwood typewriter.

The Underwood and I have been through a lot together. Its keys and gears, elements, molecules, atoms, and chemistry are, as far as I know, in good shape and have never gone sour or haywire. Unlike so many other things, including the chemicals in my head and in the heads of so many other human beings, the Underwood has never let me down. It keeps going on and on.

The two other empty vegetable crates in my room in Denver served as both bookcases and bureau. There is nothing ignoble or disrespectful about tucking Flaubert and Annie Dillard, Vonnegut and Joseph Heller, Twain and Thoreau in with fresh socks and clean underwear, piling John Nichols, Barry Lopez, and Gretel Ehrlich in with laundered shirts, folded pants, and colorful ties.

The sleeping arrangements were easiest of all: in the middle of the room's stained, pus green carpet, I unrolled my old blue sleeping bag. Its soft, thick pockets of down seem permanently saturated with the smells of every wood and river and mountain I have known. There are traces of the redolent marsh gas, dark bayous, and the trembling islands of Okefenokee swamp; folds of the Pacific's cold, rich breath; a hint of chalky sea-salt stain from lying coiled beside the red-and-yellow sea kayak on an island in Baja's Magdalena Bay, fighting sleep, listening to the night, the sound of gray whales rising, spouting in the bay's dark, cool waters; and the pungent spoor of fever and sweat rubbed deep into the bag on the Bay Islands of Honduras where iguanas rattled about in the branches of the trees and tarantulas the size of mice curled up harmlessly in the warm, dark bottom of the blue sleeping bag, tickling the bottom of my feet. Faded watermarks darken the bag, in each one the essence of rivers and streams, wild water. Hazel Creek, Snowbird Creek, the wide blue waters of the saltwater flats off the Florida Keys, Starlight Creek, the White River, the Rio Grande, Deep Creek, the gray-green rivers of the Blue Ridge Mountains, the deep, wide streams of Utah's high

country, the pale green waters of the San Juan River in the Four Corners region of northern New Mexico. Years of sleeping among the cool shadows of stones have left the bottom of the blue bag marked with its own colored chronicle of time, wildness left in traces of dirt and rock, time's footsteps outlined in smudges of earth.

Each night I unrolled the blue sleeping bag near the room's single window that reached from floor to ceiling. From the window, I could look beyond the narrow alley, to the scrap yard that sprawled over the next block, a netherworld of abandoned cars, their gutted metal corpses heaped in bizarre poses of industrial and technological decay. Among the dead were eviscerated VWs, obsolescent Fords and Chevrolets, decanted Buicks and Cadillacs, all covered with a lovely patina of rust the color of dried blood. Mornings crept up over these twisted hulks of metal and plastic, carcasses of soured, wrecked, oxidizing dreams and unfulfilled promises. Whenever it rained or snowed, the wind coming off the scrap yard was soaked in the sad smell of ruin.

Beyond the scrap yard was the highway, and beyond the highway, down a ribbon of black road, was a scattering of dilapidated houses, and beyond them a sudden, urgent spread of open ground, open skies, a bloat of light and shadow that broadened all the way to the foothills of the Front Range. From my room's window their ragged, snow-covered peaks seemed fixed hard against the abbreviated horizon. On the clearest days the distant mountain summits looked like the gargantuan shards of some undisturbed dinosaurian boneyard.

Whatever the weather, I liked keeping the room's window open wide, so that the days and nights could come and go, press against the room's walls, fill it with each day's touch, complexion, and mood.

As night's early shadows pooled in the corners of my room, as moon glow dripped down the beige walls, I would crawl deeper into the blue sleeping bag, deeper into all its stains of memory and dream.

After I started seeing Dr. Lilly Mutzpah, after the boil of depression in my brain calmed and the bout of malaria in my blood cooled, after I started spending my weekends, all my free time, in the high country of South Park, down in the valley of the Middle Fork of the South Platte River, there was a dream that often came visiting me in my blue sleeping bag, stayed with me through many a late autumn night and stays with me still. It always begins with an awkward choreography of myoclonic spasms that dissolve into a vast mountain valley. In the belly of the valley is a wide river, a great shimmering, meandering ribbon of bright, blue-green water. There is a cool wind blowing down the mountains, bending the thick clumps of honey-colored grass along the river. Overhead, the sky is a spreading broth of blues and reds. The edges of the clouds flash soft purple, burnt orange. In one of the many bends in the silver blue river is a deep pool of water. There is a shoal of blue-black stones above the pool. Below, where the river narrows, there is a sluice of faster water, and sunlight comes off the surface of the river in hard, edged angles, like light coming off broken glass. Shadows of fish undulate in the current at the head of the deep pool. Of a sudden, a fish rolls at the surface. In the dream I see it clearly. It is the blind brown trout. I see only one eye, the center anemic, drained of color, etiolated, waxen, not yet entirely opaque, but adiaphanous. Around its tenebrous nucleus glow countless shadows and penumbras, a seemingly infinite array of flashing auras, rings, halos, coronas, mock suns, deeply colored streams of light: flares, rays, ribbons, facula.

What a show. What a dream: to be pulled into a blind trout's eye and find there the undiluted press of life, a flood of memory and experience, the lost and the found, swimming there in endless pools of plenumic light, as much felt and imagined as seen, light absorbed rather than reflected, a light that stirred in a sightless trout's eye and seemed to radiate with the history of time.

This dream came often and helped the days pass easily until I

would again drive out of the city and into the high country, over the rocky vertebrae of Kenosha Pass and down into the wide valley where the waters of the Middle Fork of the South Platte River glowed silver blue.

When I drove over Kenosha Pass for the first time, I pulled the car to the side of the highway, climbed along a nearby spine of weathered red stone that looked out over the valley. The sky and the jagged line of mountains glowed in what seemed a bottomless, infinite light, a light that shimmered through shades of red and blue that I had no memory of, a light that seemed hard and honest enough, bright enough to have been vestiges of aureate light, that light in which the universe was born.

West of Kenosha Pass, the land looked like a measureless earthen bowl, one filled with wind and relentless casts of sunlight and shadow, a chaos of rock and stone and tall, swaying grasses, huddled stands of gnarled trees. Embracing it all were the mountains, the eastern flank of the Rockies, the crenellated peaks of the Continental Divide tearing at vast autumn blue skies, and through its heart the river moved, creating and destroying, shaping what it touched while it probed for its own kind, that place where it would finally join with the sea.

In that river, in a deep, wide pool of bright water, moving water, was the brown trout that rose sightless toward the river's surface, whose belly was the soft yellow of a rising winter moon.

Despite my room's antiseptic look and often tubercular feel, it was functional, even cozy.

Most mornings, I crawled out of my blue sleeping bag with crusted eyes and a mouth that felt vaguely metallic. Beyond my window, in the scrap yard, lovely tinctures of morning light coiled out of the gutted skeletons of rusting cars, dripped down fractured, grimy windshields, probing among the heaps of wrecked metal. There is, for me, something haunting about morning light, as though with its coming is some intimation of the first light, its own Big Bang, a daily bow to chaos, time's swelling entropy.

Such a light deserves a greeting. I greeted it wrapped in the blue sleeping bag, toasted it with ice-cold root beer and bean dip, and suddenly the feel of the light would change, the texture would crumble, the morning's sweet silence would give way to the sounds of Denver shaking off the night, emerging from its quilt of shadows, quaking back to life through rising crescendos of sound and motion, everything sizzling, shuffling, scrambling, rotating, gyrating, spinning, whirling, stirring—all of it corroborating the Second Law of Thermodynamics as certainly as a drunk suddenly faced with ten flights of stairs.

After the metallic cough of swelling traffic, the first sounds to drift through my open window and into my room each morning came from the twin blue garbage dumpsters in the parking lot two floors below and the rodential scratchings of the man in the titian red cape as he scavenged through the dumpster's load of chaff and culm. After that my neighbor's phlegmatic pulmonary hack vibrated our common wall.

My neighbor's cough would eventually settle like a death rattle in his throat, a noise that never failed to kick me out of night's dreams; haul me up through vaults of light and shadow, whirling clouds the color of mashed mangos, forests as dark as black velvet; pluck me off some stretch of fast, wild river full of menacing trout; pull me, reluctantly, from Kiwi LaReaux's perfect green eyes, or out of Mi Oh's soft, small arms, her tiny hands always full of freshly baked fortune cookies stuffed with hints of inevitability, shades of destiny.

Awake, I would check my watch, see what direction time and I seemed to be moving in, get dressed, pace about my monastic room like a paramecium sloshing about in a drop of water, walk down the hall to the second floor's common bathroom, look in the mirror only to discover that I had the look of a freshly etiolated cat—a road kill, something you often see sad-eyed children praying over, singing threnodies to, as they scoop it into a shoebox and plant it under Mom's begonias.

Every morning, as I left the bathroom, the man in 2C would be waiting patiently to get in, standing there in his underwear and black slippers. The man in 2C had a puckered red scar that meandered from his left shoulder to his hairless belly. Standing there each morning, outside the bathroom door, the man in 2C cast a mealy white shadow across the cold brown hallway floor, an oval shadow, like the shadow of a tombstone.

Each morning I would nervously sidestep the man with the mealy white shadow, hurry down the stairs, out the door, and into the pathogenic Denver atmosphere, nearly always visibly brown and thick. The man in the titian red cape leapt up out of the bold blue garbage dumpsters each time the building's door swung open. Under the cape he had on pale yellow pajamas that had hundreds of little green Guernsey cows printed all over them.

The man in the titian red cape and yellow-flannel cow pajamas wished me godspeed, a good day. One morning he leapt out of the trash full of caution and urgent warning, telling me over and over again to beware, a dollop of brown limp lettuce on his cheek, a smudge of some kind of meat glistening from his ivory white lips.

"Not a safe place out there," he said, pointing a bony finger past the building, beyond the scrap yard, out toward Colorado Boulevard.

"Ya gotta be careful, man. Real careful. Garbage giveth and the street taketh away, ya'know, man. He-he-he."

He leapt from one dumpster to the other, his cape stuck greasily to his back, and I leapt into the Toyota, into traffic, on to Colorado Boulevard and through Denver's tabetic heart. The offices of the magazine where I had found work were at the edge of the city, in a building that had the runny brown pallor of an oozing infection. At that time of the morning, all of Denver, like the man in the soiled titian red cape jumping among the garbage Dumpsters, shimmered like something drifting at the edge of a bad dream.

My work at the magazine involved hardly any work at all. It was my job—it was the job of every staff writer there—to fill space. I had to fill about a hundred inches a month. Truly the work was more a matter of efficient technology and engineering than of imagination and writing. Minzo Root, the editor of the magazine, told me that what was in the magazine did not matter much anyway because the magazine game had become one of presentation and image rather than of substance, which probably explains why the magazine employed more managers, administrators, advertising salespeople, computer experts, and gadgeteers than reporters and writers. The publisher of the magazine paid thousands and thousands of dollars to find out what the magazine's readers really wanted. Focus groups of eight to ten people were brought in, given lunch, paid $25 each. In return, they told management what they expected from the magazines they read.

They wanted less and less detail, more and more revealing color photographs, especially of celebrities, disasters, murders, and so on and so on. Too, they wanted the winning numbers of the state lottery printed on the first page of the magazine each month in gigantic, easy-to-read red print.

They wanted fewer words.

Since it was clear the readers did not care about news or human interest or about much of anything, said the editor and publisher, why should we?

So we gave the readers what they wanted, lots of revealing, detailed color photography and fewer words, broken up by pages and pages of dazzling, tempting ads.

"You're trying too goddamned hard," Minzo Root was always telling me. What he meant was that I was writing far too many words, pages and pages that would never be used because they were of no interest.

The first morning that Minzo Root told me that I was trying too goddamned hard, he had just come into the office and still had on a bright red-and-white ski mask pulled down tight over his face. There was a dainty blue tassle on top of the ski mask that would orbit Root's moon-shaped head each time he spoke.

Minzo Root went on to explain to me that the average reader of the magazine had the interests and the attention span of a twelve-year-old.

"You wanna know the most important stuff we print?" said Minzo Root, the small blue tassle on the top of his ski mask spinning round and round his head.

"Horoscopes, crossword puzzles, travel calendars, celebrity gossip, cartoons, and any kind of human atrocity. Flush everything else out of your head, boy."

Minzo Root had some more advice for me. He had heard rumors that I wrote books. "Listen, boy, I'm afraid books don't mean shit here," said Minzo Root. "Hell, they don't mean shit anywhere that I know of."

Odell Euclid was smiling as Minzo Root spoke. Odell Euclid sat at the desk across from mine, next to the woman feature writer who had not left the office in five years. She did all her stories by telephone.

"Life's a lot less messy by phone," she would later tell me.

Odell Euclid was the magazine's utility man, though he had a passion for writing poignant, deeply moving tributes to the dead, which never ran. He also wrote candid and lurid stories of murder that always ran accompanied by plenty of revealing, detailed color photographs.

You could always tell when inspiration was whispering to Odell Euclid—the entire office vibrated with the wild paradiddle of his two-fingered typing.

Whenever inspiration went cold, Euclid would send me electronic messages that flashed across my computer monitor in Martian green.

After Minzo Root told me about the tastes and interests of the magazine's readers, this is the message that Odell Euclid flashed across my screen: "Whatever you write around here, throw in plastic explosives. Swing a baseball bat, leave a smear of blood, a piece of ripped flesh, a spatter of fresh brains. Such warm touches will perk up any piece, even recipes, gardening tips, and restaurant reviews."

As it turned out, I did not have to throw in anything. Life took care of the details. It always does. My days were filled with mildly interesting white-collar crimes, child abuse, gangs, battered wives, AIDS, battered husbands, drugs, catastrophes natural and unnatural, racial hatreds, environmental ruin, political corruption, the shrinking expectations of middle class America, the unnerving giggles of the insane, the despair of the homeless and the hopeless. And of course, none of it ever ran: too many words.

"Some world, isn't it?" Odell Euclid would say every evening as we walked out of the office and into the deepening Denver night. The city nights, by the way, had a peculiar sound, like the grinding of immense mechanical teeth.

So the days went. I spent the mornings filling my copy with stinging description, pathos and bathos, humanity's common misery, and small joys, and the afternoons taking it all out. In the mornings, I marched powerful verbs and nouns across my computer screen and in the afternoons I crossed them all out, leaving life to slog about in the passive voice.

And Odell Euclid was always zapping me with fresh electronic messages. The words shimmered across my screen dressed in Martian green. One afternoon, Euclid's message was that "any automaton could do-do-dooly-do what we did-diddly-did and still have time to paste up, sweep up, and lock up."

"Everything but the horoscopes," I yelled, and looked up to see Odell Euclid giving me a bemused, conspiratorial smile.

Late the night before, over the endless buzz of the police scanner, the monotonous crackle of suicides, stabbings, hangings, robberies, shootings, axings, after too much cold pizza and too many pots of bad coffee, in a moment of angst and exhaustion, we decided to rewrite the monthly horoscopes, to give fate and fortune a helping hand.

This, for instance, is what fate and fortune had in store for Capricorns. "The death of a loved one is at hand, but fear not. A dead mouse feels no cold. It looks like a month of financial trouble and woes, as well. But you will find comfort in the under-

standing that, come Judgment Day, a pound of gold and a pock-etful of lint are of equal value."

Odell Euclid was a little man with tiny bright eyes. His skin was so white that he often looked as though he had been carved from a bar of cheap soap. On top of his acromegalic head he wore a red baseball cap that was too small for his great head and gave him, at once, a ridiculous and endearing childlike appearance.

Odell Euclid was kind hearted, decent, honest, hardworking, quiet, shy, free of pretense, and therefore a completely extraordinary human being.

Euclid and I became good friends, as close as war buddies, especially after we fiddled with the horoscopes, recklessly fiddling with the fortune and fate of Denver's minions with a jocular flick of our computer keys.

As I said, Odell Euclid's moving tributes to the dead were legendary, or at least secretly so.

Minzo Root would read Euclid's tributes to the dead and quickly tell Euclid that he would never amount to diddly because he was as odd as the blue-footed booby and about as likable as spoiled eggs.

When Minzo Root turned his back, Euclid flapped his arms like the great wings of blue-footed booby, smiling wildly.

Odell Euclid.

God bless him.

Odell Euclid, by the way, was a Benthamite, a follower of the moral philosophy of Jeremy Bentham, who stepped out of the chaos of time between 1748 and 1832. Jeremy Bentham was the father of utilitarianism, an innocent theology based on one simple creed, a belief as harmless as a baby's coo—the belief that there is in life only pleasure and pain, and that human beings are creatures who embrace pleasure and flee from pain.

Jeremy Bentham also believed that human beings, once dead, could still lead useful and fulfilling lives as sculpture and lawn statuary. Bentham made it clear that after his own death he wanted his body to keep on working, to be as useful as ever by being used as sculpture. What is left of Jeremy Bentham, a brittle little skeleton, was at one time kept in a closet at University College in London and was wheeled out from time to time, complete with Bentham's old walking cane.

Whenever Euclid found himself writing about the violent death of a human being, he would shake his great head and mutter to himself sadly, "Roll out Jeremy." This was Euclid's way of saying how fragile and short, how comic and tragic, how pitiful, embarrassing, and ridiculous life is.

Roll out Jeremy.

Euclid and I would often spend our afternoons walking around downtown Denver buying illegal burritos and tacos from friendly, generous Hispanic Americans down on their luck.

These criminal street vendors carried small, brightly colored Coleman coolers. The coolers were stuffed with delicious warm tacos and burritos. The street food was filling and nourishing, good and cheap, whereas most of Denver's restaurant fare is boiled or comes in a paper bag. Too, Denver food is always lukewarm, even the soup.

Like so many big American cities these days, Denver is a city with a self-congratulatory flair, one that matches its penchant for fashion rather than style. Along with so many other large cities, it stumbles along toward the millennium like some dazed, mechanical troglodyte, while its citizens take bets on whether or not it will make it, whether it will survive or collapse under the weight of its own urban dissipation, whether it will join a host of other large cities in some futuristic urban apocalypse or somehow avert that fate and rise out of looming catastrophe as the symbol of the rising west.

Just beneath its patina of grace, hip vitality and sophistication,

its hyperbole and image of nonstop prosperity, Denver is a thick gruel of dismay and despair, a gummy stew of the bleak and the phony, the hopeless and the broken down.

Denver has a slightly vaudevillian cast, especially after twilight as the city's lights go on and when, from a distance, Denver does not seem rise out of the land, but to rise in spite of it, to rest on its broken back. Denver, consequently, is not a city that engenders loyalty. Even though I wandered about Denver for months, there is really not much to tell. The people there are bright and shiny, as bright and shiny as the pennies made at the Denver Mint. The Denver Mint, by the way, makes twenty-one million bright and shiny new pennies a day.

Imagine that.

Denver prides itself on being the gateway to the Rocky Mountains. There may be more outdoor stores in Denver than in any other city on the planet. To the west of the city, up in the high country of the Rocky Mountains, are dozens of bright and shiny ski resorts. On some winter nights when the wind is right, when it is coming off the western slopes of the mountains, you can hear, even above the noise of traffic and sirens, the sound of merriment and gaiety rising from the ski slopes, the sound of all that slaloming and shussing.

Denver is the result of a happy accident, the happy accident of gold being discovered near the juncture of the South Platte River and Cherry Creek. The gold did not last.

It never does.

Perhaps that is why, Odell Euclid told me, the city greets each new resident with the same two words.

Good luck.

Besides its swelling population of Frozen Urban Refugees, as Denver's two million residents like to call themselves, Denver has a whopping population of transient human beings. They come to the city like lemmings. There are knots of them on almost every street corner—the incurable, irredeemable, irreparable, the displaced and misplaced, misfits and the permanently impoverished, the terminally luckless, the ruined and forlorn, the dejected

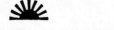
and despondent, America's taedium vitae overwhelmed by loss, gloom, misery, and sorrow. Somewhere in all those crowds was Dr. Truth. Odell Euclid was there too. So was I.

Mixed in with the city's crowd of tired and hopeless were frauds and swindlers, con men and hustlers, hookers and drug dealers, petty criminals and nervous murderers, all wanting to help the human lemmings empty their pockets before they leapt into Denver's cold, dark, roiling urban sea.

Odell Euclid and I were supposed to keep an eye on this human drama in case there were any titillating mass murders or pitiful suicides. We walked the city's streets, and no matter where in the city we drifted, I cannot remember ever meeting anyone who was actually born in Denver. They were all coming or going, coming for a job, looking for a place to live or a hot meal, a corner to work, or just passing through because they had heard that things were better in Nevada, that there was hope in Seattle, work in Texas, genuine concern in Atlanta, refuge and endless sunny days in Florida.

"Things are never better, no matter where you pull up," said Bronton Phelps, who had drifted into Denver from North Dakota, where his family ranch had failed not once but four times.

Bronton Phelps was wrapped in a cloak of vented steam hissing and rising from a grate in an alley off Nineteenth Street. His eyes glowed dimly, like failing zircon lamps, and his lips were cracked, the color of bruised plums. His teeth clacked together when he was not talking, so that he made a noise, standing there in that fog of rising steam, like a gravely wounded woodpecker.

Phelps told us he was wearing every piece of clothing he owned, the same clothes he had been wearing ever since he had been forced off his family's failed ranch. He listed his belongings: two sweaters, long underwear, overalls, three pairs of wool socks, wool gloves, and cowboy boots, all of it hidden beneath a

huge hunter's camouflage coat and camouflage hat. Bronton Phelps laughed about the coat and cap and told us that when his luck finally ran out, he could just walk away and become invisible, disappear.

Odell Euclid reminded me that Bronton Phelps, in the eyes of Denver, Colorado, America, and planet Earth, was already invisible. Odell Euclid also reminded me that North Dakota was a place of such emptiness and isolation that one of every fifteen males in the state is an elk.

"Things never are," said Phelps vacantly, a puff of his thin gray breath rising with the hissing steam.

"Never are what?" I said, moving deeper into the alley.

"Any better," said Phelps. "Things are never any better no matter where a man goes these days."

For Bronton Phelps, Denver turned out to be just another disappointment, more bad times. He told us he had hitched a ride into the city in the spring, had had six jobs, none of which had lasted more than a week.

"I got sixty-three dollars and change," said Phelps, reaching through his layers of clothes to his pocket, jingling the loose coins with weak reassurance. "It's enough to get me South, maybe, and outta this cold and the coming snows.

"Knew a guy named Morton. Rolled through here coupla weeks ago. We washed pots together for a day. Morton got his pay and took off, headed for Orlando, you know, where Disney World is at. Think maybe I'll head that way myself. Morton talked and talked about the place while we scrubbed pots, talked on and on about how there is plenty of work and cheap, clean places to live, how times there was real good, 'cause, you know, Mickey Mouse is runnin' the place.

"Jesus Christ," said Phelps, shaking his head, shoving his hands deeper into his huge coat. "It's come to that, it's come to bettin' your life, bettin' it all, on a friggin' mouse.

"Go figure," said Bronton Phelps.

Go figure.

Phelps planned on walking out of downtown Denver the next morning, getting to the side of the interstate heading south by sunrise.

"Maybe the mouse can spare some cheese?" said Phelps. "Who knows. Who knows anything anymore," said Bronton Phelps as he stood in the warming fog rising off the grate, leaned stiffly against the brick wall as though his flesh was being slowly, wonderfully mummified in the rising spout of steam.

Odell Euclid wrote a story about Bronton Phelps. It was called "Looking for the Cheese."

Minzo Root refused to run it. The homeless, after all, were not news, either in life or in death, or anywhere in between, even on a highway headed south toward the warm, caring embrace of Mickey Mouse.

Dr. Truth was never news, either. We found that out while gathering facts about a murder outside a bar near the old warehouse district. The murder had just happened. We heard all about it on the police scanner. Paramedics were already there collecting the dead human being, shoving him into a black plastic body bag.

The paramedics were complaining because they had rolled a double, which meant that there were suddenly two heavy, dead human beings to haul off instead of one.

Odell Euclid was the cause of the paramedics' anger. He had tripped over a pair of shoeless feet behind the bar. The feet were sticking out from under a pile of holly green garbage bags. The shoeless feet were a lovely shade of delicate blue.

It was almost dusk when Euclid tripped over the shoeless, delicate blue feet. The feet glowed in the twilight like polished soapstone. The paramedics dug down among the pile of holly green garbage bags, revealing who those delicate blue feet belonged to.

They belonged to Dr. Truth.

Truth was dead, a great slab of frozen meat. His coat was gone. So were his shoes, his dingy, emerald green slippers. Odell Euclid noticed that Dr. Truth had stuffed his clothes with layers of newspapers and crumpled-up brown paper bags. There were long shreds of newspaper and paper bags tucked around his neck and ankles, as well. Lying there, dead and frozen and shoeless among all those holly green garbage bags, Truth looked like a cheap scarecrow, shrunken and pathetic, laughable. Dr. Truth's eyes were open. There were no longer bright prisms of colored light. They were only one color, crystal blue, and they were staring blankly up at the darkening Denver sky. Little tears of blue light had dropped from each dead eye and had frozen on Truth's sunken, blue cheeks. The paramedics thought Dr. Truth had been under the holly green garbage bags for some time. He smelled of runny ulcers and pure despair, of Italian salad dressing and tomato paste, of vomit and rotting apples.

Staring down at Dr. Truth, Odell Euclid said only this:

"Roll out Jeremy."

I had seen and heard Dr. Truth the day before, heard him yowl as always from atop his brown metal folding chair at the corner of Seventeenth Street & Stout. His eyes were still burning with color then, and no one had yet stolen his frayed coat and his dirty emerald green slippers.

I was on my way to my Thursday afternoon appointment with Dr. Mutzpah. I stopped and listened to Dr. Truth, as I always did. He was screaming that talent and love, commitment, looks, position and power, sex, real estate, loyalty, bonds, the Comedy Channel, and health don't mean squat. Truth had had all that and more, he said. It all goes, he screamed. It all goes. It all fades and crumbles. And Truth really didn't want any of it back.

"Friends," howled Dr. Truth, "I'll tell you what Truth wants. It's just a little thing, really.

"While I'm here, friends," said Truth, "while I'm on this side of the dirt, I only want what every human being wants—to be useful.

"That's my desire. To be useful, again. That's the truth."

And a policeman showed up and hauled Dr. Truth off his chair, told him to move along, and to just keep on going, to get out of town. Truth was always being shown the door. But he had always come back, always shown up the next day, back atop his brown chair, filthy and ragged, his yellow teeth showing in a wide smile, as nervous knots of whispering people drifted by averting their eyes because they had already learned that this Truth had nothing to offer them but more of what they already had plenty of—desperation and heartache, loneliness and fear, sorrow and regret.

The police detectives who were investigating the murder at the bar eventually came outside, saw Dr. Truth stretched out among the holly green garbage bags. They went through his pockets and discovered that Dr. Truth's real name was Neddy Finn. Underneath all those layers of rags and newspapers and shredded paper bags the detectives discovered something else: thousands and thousands of frog green hundred-dollar bills pinned to Neddy Finn's orange and yellow underwear.

Go figure.

Just after the detectives had finished going through Truth's pockets, as the paramedics were sliding Truth's frozen body into another black plastic body bag, I felt a hand on my shoulder and turned to find myself looking into a sagging, jaundiced, toothless grin.

The grin was stuck on a tiny face sunk into a cascade of sagging brown wrinkles, and on top of the wrinkled face and head were tiny tufts of silver hair.

The grin became a voice, a wheezing, phthisic sound.

"I got hair." The words were said slowly, precisely, as though they were encased in perfect atonement.

"Hair?" I said, backpedaling toward Odell Euclid, who was still trying to take revealing, detailed color photographs of Truth's stiff corpse.

"I got plenty," said the grin.

The grin and all those sagging wrinkles and those sunken little pig eyes and tiny tufts of silver hair and wheezing lungs had a name.

Lucy. Miss Lucy.

"Whose hair?" I asked, expecting that Miss Lucy would retrieve fistfuls of shrunken heads from her bulging, bright, blue-and-white Pepsi tote sack.

"Whose do you wish, eh, young man?" said Miss Lucy. "Whose do you wish?" Miss Lucy giggled and gurgled, keeping one of her tiny pig eyes on the nearby detectives and paramedics.

Miss Lucy, it turned out, hawked literary locks. There were enough tangles and wads of hair in her bright blue-and-white Pepsi tote sack to stuff a mattress.

Curly hair, straight hair, wavy, dainty bobs, single strands and curls, whole cowlicks. Hair of every color and texture. Coarse and fine, shiny and dull. Tousled and matted, shaggy and thin, bangs and ringlets. Bleached hair, argentine hair, hair that still reeked of peroxide and Javelle water. Fair hair and hair the color of lint. Hair that was Quaker gray and hair the color of lead carbonate. Chrome black hair and hair that was Havana brown and wild siena, butter yellow and cerulescent.

There was hair in small envelopes and hair in Ziplock plastic freezer bags. Hair in tiny boxes and wrapped in pieces of cellophane.

Miss Lucy dug through her load of literary treasure, settled finally on a Ziplock bag, pulled it out, opened it, and produced a pinch of thick oyster gray hair, tightly curled.

"Mailer," said Miss Lucy. "Or maybe you're the Updike type. I've got him somewhere—dark phase, graying, and silver."

Miss Lucy said she had them all, the living and the dead. Thurber and Cheever, DeLillo and Sanchez, Amy Tan (long strands of raven black hair held together by a yellow paperclip), Steinbeck, and shavings from Hemingway's beard (silver gray phase).

"Only a dollar each," said Miss Lucy.

Behind us, the paramedics had tagged, shoved, and bagged the remains of Truth and hoisted the black body bag into the back of the ambulance.

"Don't see the one you want, huh, mister?" said Miss Lucy.

"I can get it, the hair right off the head of any writer you can name.

"Yeah, sure. And it's all legal, too. This is kind of a sacred thing with me, really. I mean, I take care of their hair the way a bookstore takes care of their books, you see.

"You see."

I looked at Euclid. Euclid looked at me. Euclid bought a locket of Twain. I took a snippet of Heller. We said good-bye to Miss Lucy, climbed into the back of the ambulance, and sat on either side of Truth's bagged body.

Odell Euclid wrote a story about the death of Truth, about the life and times of Neddy Finn. Euclid had trouble deciding on a title for his story. It was either going to be "A Dead Truth Feels No Pain" or simply "The Francium Blues."

I liked "The Francium Blues." Francium is the most unstable natural element yet discovered. It is formed by the decay of actinium, a radioactive element. Francium is itself radioactive and has a half-life similar to that of most truths, about twenty-one minutes. And like truth, francium has never been seen or measured or weighed. Too, at any given moment there is about as much francium on the planet as there is truth: less than half an ounce.

Imagine.

Odell Euclid signed his story about Dr. Truth, about the life and times of Neddy Finn, this way: "A Dead Truth Feels No Pain, or, The Francium Blues," by The Blue-Footed Booby.

Minzo Root made sure it never ran.

Two days later, on a Friday afternoon, Odell Euclid was called into Minzo Root's office. The door was closed. A bad sign, like the unexpected white blur on routine X rays.

It was a late autumn afternoon. Darkness seemed to seep from the ground, take hold of the city from the inside out.

Odell Euclid was not fired or terminated or given a Mexican raise. He was not bounced, given the shaft, or the boot.

Odell Euclid was let go.

After leaving Minzo Root's office, Euclid sat for a long time at his desk just staring out the windows. Then there was this last Martian green flashing across my screen.

"Roll out Jeremy."

Dr. Truth's corner did not stay vacant for long. It was a popular corner, evidently one where a man might change his luck, his fortune, his fate, find work, get a hot meal and a warm bed at the mission, get a hot shower and a way out of town. Three days after Truth's death, a lady climbed up on his brown metal chair and auctioned off her sorrows: a lost husband, a missing child. Someone else announced that they were dying of lung cancer and had no health insurance. The man begged and pleaded for money to buy the pills that would ease his pain.

Ease his pain.

Another man leapt up on the chair and confessed that he wanted to die but that he did not believe in suicide. Yet another wanted love, and another refuge, and another asked only if there was someone who could spare a jacket, something to warm her against the cold. Another hopped up on the chair and wanted to know if anyone knew what had become of hope. On the day Velveeta Cheese shared with me what he was sure was the funniest joke on the planet, there was a small, thin woman up on the brown, metal chair. She wanted to give her little daughter to anyone who had a good home, could give her more than bad luck and hunger and the misery of the streets.

The few people on hand averted their eyes and walked quietly away. I walked out of the cold and into the cozy, warm elevator that carried me up the seven floors to the offices of Dr. Lilly Mutzpah. Velveeta Cheese was in the waiting room thumbing through a yellowed copy of *Ulysses*. Cheese looked like a haberdasher's dream. He was dressed in a puce dickey, red bolero sweater, yellow ski pants, Wellington boots, sparkling Chaqueta jacket, black boa, and a heavy blue Inverness coat. Covering his shiny bald spot was a blue porkpie hat.

At his feet were a hot plate, a pot half-filled with already boiling water, and several packages of spaghetti.

Velveeta Cheese caught me gawking.

"Visual aids," he said, reaching down to stir in another handful of snapped spaghetti strands.

"Audiences go nuts for visual aids," said Velveeta Cheese.

"Really. If I walked out on stage, soaked a dead cat in gasoline, lit it, and swung it enticingly over my head while reading the Denver yellow pages, I'd get laughs galore."

Velveeta Cheese rhythmically stirred the spaghetti noodles down into the still-boiling water. "Drum roll, please," said Velveeta Cheese.

"Okay . . . Picture this. The lights go down and there's only a single white spotlight. I come on stage slowly. It's got to be slow, you see, 'cause I'm pushing a little table with wheels. It's got all this stuff on it. The water's already been boiled and is still boiling. I'll boil it backstage while Tommy, the club's MC, whips up the audience, gets them pumped. He's got this dog that has real bad gas or something. Thing burps and farts and belches all the time. But Tommy's trained it, ya' see, to belch and fart so it sounds like the damn dog is singing 'You Ain't Nothin' But a Hound Dog.'

"Knocks 'em dead every night.

"Then, suddenly, I'm there in that single white spotlight with my rolling table, with the boiled water and my package of spaghetti."

Velveeta Cheese got up from his chair, knelt close to the pot of bubbling water, and spooned up a big glob of noodles.

"See, the audience won't know about the boiling water and the spaghetti at first. The whole bit will take 'em by surprise.

"So first I'll hold up a big handful of stiff spaghetti and give 'em a sexy smirk. That's to let 'em know that something good is coming, something drop-dead funny.

"Then, smooth and quick like, with just a tiny pause, I fork up a bunch of the boiled goo from the bottom of the pot. So now in one hand I have a bunch of stiff spaghetti, and in the other a shimmering spoonful of smoking, limp spaghetti, and I say oh-so-slowly, oh-so-seductively, as I shove the hand with the stiff spaghetti forward, 'This is your dick!' and then, as I hold up the limp, dripping, blanched noodles, I pout, 'And this is your dick on drugs!'"

Velveeta Cheese laughed and laughed as he scraped the clump

of boiled noodles back into the pot, and put the unused spaghetti back into his bag.

"Great stuff, huh?" said Velveeta Cheese, his shoulders shaking, as he went on laughing and laughing, making a sound like a band of talentless children, all playing the piccolo.

Dr. Mutzpah appeared at the door, her arm wrapped tenderly around Miss Piggot's quivering shoulders. Velveeta Cheese gave me a wink, scooped the rest of his visual aids into his bag, and bolted for the good doctor's open door.

On her way out, Miss Piggot stopped by the couch where I was sitting. She smiled as Velveeta Cheese rushed past her. Miss Piggot told me that while looking out her kitchen window she had discovered that she could see forever.

"What does it look like?" I asked in a hushed voice.

Miss Piggot began sobbing, shaking her head back and forth, saying, "That's just it. I don't know. It was all a blur, a goddam blur in every direction."

After Truth's death Odell Euclid told me about a murder he had covered where the murderer got into the victim's house by posing as a delivery man from a local florist.

"Who can say no to flowers?" said Odell Euclid. "As you can imagine, the young woman opened the door, saw the beautiful flowers, and was rosy with expectation. She wasn't disappointed.

"Roll out Jeremy."

Euclid believed in many things. One of the things he believed in was that every human being, like the young woman who had opened her door once she saw it was a delivery of beautiful, unexpected flowers, was waiting for a messenger and his message—a word, a look, a sentence, the beauty of unexpected flowers, something, anything—that would illuminate their lives, save them or end them. As it turned out, Dr. Mutzpah was my messenger and this was her message.

"Why don't you get out of town," Dr. Mutzpah told me on the

day that Miss Piggot let me know that she could see forever and that it was a blur in all directions.

When Dr. Mutzpah delivered her message, I was looking out her big office windows at the mountains in the distance. Immense streams of soft amber sunlight flowed down their peaks and ridges. I went from staring at the mountains to staring at the beautiful oversized salmon fly that Dr. Mutzpah had framed and hung on her wall. The good doctor told me that she had put it in her office to remind her of Alaska. When the spawning runs are on, many Alaska rivers are so thick with salmon and steelhead that the rivers seem to boil with fish. Most of the salmon and steelhead trout in those rivers are trying to do what a lot of human beings would like to do: get home so they can die where they were born, end where they began.

By the way, I took the good doctor's advice.

I got out of town.

That Friday, I learned the true secret of Denver's appeal and its success. It is easy to get out of. Escape is child's play. I drove up and over Kenosha Pass, headed for the great valley of South Park and the little town of Fairplay. I liked the name. Odell Euclid told me about Fairplay, said I should stop there.

"More than two million Americans play the accordion," said Odell Euclid. "And as far as I know, none of them live in Fairplay."

That was all the recommendation I needed.

MANNA FROM HEAVEN

Everything is the way it is because it got that way.

—D'ARCY THOMPSON

~~~~~~~~~~~~~~~~~~~~~~

I mentioned that the first time I drove out of Denver, headed west toward the blood red ridges of the Front Range, I stopped at the crest of Kenosha Pass, parked the Toyota, climbed along the edge of ragged, ochre-colored stones that looked out over an immense valley under a dome of blue skies. The valley and the surface of the Middle Fork of the South Platte River, which meandered in gleaming lazy bends through the valley, seemed drenched in shimmering waves of lustral light.

It was a quality of light, a degree of illumination, that only lasted a moment then dissolved, the light receding beneath dark shadows, the darkening surface of the river, joining all the other moments that had ever pressed against the mountains, mingled with the moving river. There are, I like to think, fossils of light, just as there are fossils of the long dead, the teeth of the departed, the sand-filled skulls of the extinct, imprints in stone of lost seas. Microwaves are the fossils of light left over from the creation of the universe, the instant of the Big Bang.

Think of that.

Traces of creation left as fossils of light, a light not seen but heard, wrinkles of energy still sizzling and crackling with the news of beginnings. And in the beginning, everything was night, sweet night, Mother night, where the first light wrinkled like a wind in the darkness, blistering the night's perfect black membrane.

Like the light I saw shimmering across the damp meadows of South Park from Kenosha Pass, perhaps: a light beyond the corruption of form and substance, a crush of pure colors and perfect shadows. Wherever wildness hangs on, lingers, some speck or ray or shaft or gleam of this ancient fossil light, this creative light, is near, marking the continuum of earth and time.

I have stumbled on such ranges of light before along mountain streams, in cool, shadow-filled forests, in the glint of a trout's dark eye as it rises, or flashing off the backs of stones. It was the same light that was in Dr. Truth's dead eyes, and in my mother's eyes when they turned from pale green to bright blue as the cancer in her brain grew and grew.

According to Odell Euclid, Fairplay was somewhere down in the valley, somewhere down in that immense earthen bowl of color and sunlight and rippling shadows, down below the flanks of the mountains, on the eastern slope of the Great Divide.

Fairplay is something of a fossil, too. Long ago, a group of human beings gathered there and decided it was the great good place. They decided it was the great good place because gold had been discovered nearby. Once the gold played out, most of the people left, hit the road, believing that the great good place was elsewhere, maybe over the next high mountain pass, maybe in the next valley, in the next great earthen bowl filled with sunlight and soft wind, with high mountains all around and a bright river meandering through it. Maybe the great good place was in Utah or Wyoming or northern New Mexico or Montana.

The trouble with finding the great good place is that there is always something on hand to ruin it. Either it's too many people or too many cows. Too many fences or not enough chili peppers. Too many anglers and not enough fish, or too many broken-down writers and not enough wild woods and streams. Too much indifference or not enough. Too much poverty. Too much style and not enough life.

It seems there are too many destinations and not enough places.

It's always something.

These days that something is usually time and money. That's what it takes to get to country that is still interesting. That's what most of us don't have. I had just enough of both to get me as far west as Fairplay, Colorado. America, in general, is headed west. Bad news for Montana and Idaho, Utah and New Mexico. The drift west seems unstoppable. Every day the bulk of America's population creeps fifty-eight feet west. As I say, I followed the national trend as far as Fairplay, then stepped out of the rush. Something caught my eye, got my attention. The mountains all around, the great valley with a bright river winding through it. All that and a little stooped man with bushy orange eyebrows bobbing over a pair of bright eyes, one brown, one blue. The stooped man was driving a butter yellow Volkswagen beetle and honking madly, waving urgently for me to pull over. As he stepped out of the butter yellow Volkswagen beetle, I noticed for the first time that the stooped man had a parrot on his rounded shoulder.

As it turned out, the parrot was stuffed.

I asked the stooped little man with the stuffed parrot on his shoulder what his name was.

His name was Swami Bill.

I traveled west from Denver on Hampden Avenue, which becomes Colorado Highway 285 as soon as it sheds its urban burden. I drove to Fairplay over Kenosha Pass every weekend for more than three months, leaving my desk at the magazine early each Friday and pulling into Fairplay just as the thin, pale, autumn-afternoon sunlight began to dissolve, recede over the broken-knuckled ridge line of the mountains pressed against the western sky.

I liked the town. It seemed as good a place as any to empty my head, see what the depression had gobbled up, wounded, and destroyed, and what had stuck with me, hung on and survived.

Odell Euclid had told me, by the way, that there was not a single accordion player in Fairplay. He was right.

Swami Bill was the first person I met in Fairplay.

After he stepped out of his butter yellow VW, he tapped on my car window.

Our cars were side by side at the town's little-used traffic light swaying indifferently above the intersection that leads into downtown Fairplay.

I probably wouldn't have rolled down my car window if it had not been for the bright blue-green parrot attached to Swami Bill's rounded left shoulder.

Swami Bill had on an apple green monk's robe tied about his waist with a piece of frayed black electrical cord.

His lovely pastel beret seemed not so much to sit on his tiny head as attack it. Tufts of burnt orange hair stuck out everywhere, as if trying desperately to escape.

Swami Bill's tiny ivory white feet were sunk deep into the foam of a pair of pink flip-flops.

The parrot on his shoulder had glass eyes the color of ripe cherries and was dressed in a tiny bold blue cummerbund.

Later I would learn that there were wires in the parrot's stiff yellow feet that were woven into the shoulder of the apple green monk's robe, wires that kept the parrot on Swami Bill's shoulder, though it always listed slightly to the right as though it was whispering something into Swami Bill's ear.

Wires ran down the floppy sleeve of the monk's robe to Swami

Bill's left hand. Every time Bill pinched the wires together, the parrot's dusty blue-green wings would flap lifelessly.

I began rolling down the car window even before Swami Bill tapped on it. The parrot on his shoulder was already flapping its wings and appeared to be squawking something into Bill's ear.

Caught in a chilly mountain wind, frayed, dull, blue-and-green feathers spiraled above Bill's pastel beret.

Swami Bill was smiling wildly, his head tilted toward the listing parrot's sparkling red glass eyes.

Swami Bill leaned closer, revealing bits of healthy whole grain cereal wedged between enormous gleaming white teeth. He had stopped smiling. He told me, with a flash of his wallet, that he was an agent working with a special task force assigned to the Park County Chamber of Commerce and informed me that I had been waved over for suspicion of driving without an aura.

"It's a serious offense," he said earnestly. "Indeed, in Boulder, it's a felony of tragic proportions."

The parrot flapped its wings again, slipped a little farther down Bill's shoulder.

"Not to mention that's it's just plain sad and pitiful," said Swami Bill.

"Kiwi picked up your scorched vibes before you even pulled into town. She's been having crying jags ever since."

Kiwi was Kiwi LaReaux, Swami Bill's main squeeze. Dressed in a sarong decorated with brightly colored tropical-bird feathers, Kiwi LaReaux was sitting in the butter yellow VW gently sobbing into a red-and-blue bandana.

Swami Bill and Kiwi LaReaux, I would learn, spent most of their weekends working the mountain highways west of Denver, searching out tourists and drifters, the lost and the lonely, the perplexed, the giddy, the forlorn, the bewildered and the karma-less, to repair their souls and their psyches and to sell them Swami Bill's boxed set of Zen self-help tapes. Each tape was forty minutes of whale songs and tropical rain showers and audible subliminal messages.

Swami Bill and Kiwi LaReaux lived outside Boulder, where

they owned and operated the Holistic Motor Court, Ashram & Coin Laundry.

Standing there along the highway into Fairplay, Swami Bill reached underneath his apple green monk's robe and produced an innocent-looking spray bottle, squeezed the trigger, and filled my car with a delicate, perfumed mist.

There was a colorful handwritten label on the bottle which read SWAMI BILL'S KARMA IN A CAN. USE REGULARLY FOR INSTANT CONTENTMENT.

I did something I had not done in a long time. I laughed and laughed.

So did Swami Bill. So did Kiwi LaReaux, who had gotten out of the VW, stopped sobbing into her red-and-blue bandana, and was standing next to Bill, carefully poking faded blue-and-green feathers back into the stuffed parrot's wings.

Kiwi LaReaux had perfect green eyes and warm red hair. Beneath the sarong of tropical bird feathers, I imagined her skin was a wonderful chaos of freckles.

Kiwi LaReaux smiled and I fell in love, yearned for her desperately, tragically.

Before Swami Bill and Kiwi LaReaux walked back to the butter yellow VW, Kiwi pressed a small leather pouch into my hand.

I emptied the contents of the pouch into my hand.

Stones.

Icy blue-green hexagonal prisms of aquamarine. Bits of bright mica and smoky quartz. Shards of raw garnet and smooth amethyst. Haunting flecks of turquoise and eroded pieces of yellow beryl, smooth as the throats of wild flowers. A delicate detail of rose quartz the color of an autumn mountain sunrise and a blood red crystal of moody tourmaline.

Kiwi LaReaux pointed back toward the mountains crowding the sky, their ridges and summits looking like great drifting bright islands of crushed glass. Flecks of the soft afternoon sunlight, intense and clear, flashed at the edges of her deep green eyes.

Looking down at the stones glowing in the palm of my hand, this is what Kiwi LaReaux said:

"Manna from Heaven."

The yellow VW pulled back onto the valley highway, headed east, back toward Boulder, back toward the Holistic Motor Court, Ashram & Coin Laundry. Home sweet home for Swami Bill and Kiwi LaReaux.

Swami Bill's parrot appeared to be screaming out the VW's window as they drove away, screaming in Bill's voice, screaming a phrase I would hear the parrot shout and yodel, whisper and chortle, yawp and sing over and over for months to come.

This is what Swami Bill's stuffed parrot was screaming in Bill's cracked, glottal voice:

"OLLIE-OLLIE-OXEN-FREE!

"OLLIE-OLLIE-OXEN-FREE!"

I drove through Fairplay, then up Highway 9 to the crest of Hoosier Pass, where I pulled off the road and parked. I climbed along the stones along the pass until I came to a wide, sun-drenched bench of a rose-colored stone tilted west. I lay down on that warm slab of rock for a long time, my back pressed flat against the stone. If I had read my maps right, this bench of ragged, rose-colored stone tilted west off the crest of Hoosier Pass lay along the course of the Great Divide, that great coiling, looping, buckled, and broken spine of mountain peaks and ridges that meanders like a swag-bellied backbone of stone from British Columbia down through New Mexico and Mexico, all the way down western South America, until the mountains collapsed into the permanent fury of the storm-tossed seas off Tierra del Fuego. Along the ridges of the Rocky Mountains, the Great Divide separates not only rivers and valleys, but oceans. Had a fleck of ice or a splash of rain fallen on the bench of stone where I lay stretched out in the high country autumn sun and dripped down the eastern flank of the mountains, its journey would have taken it eventually to the Missouri River, down the Mississippi to the Gulf of Mexico and the Atlantic Ocean. Had it by chance trickled down the western face of the stone, down the western face of the mountains, its future would be mixed with the waters of the Colorado, the Snake, or the broad Columbia rivers and, finally, the deep cold waters of the Pacific.

I sat up, spread a map against the smooth bench of rose-colored stone, traced with my finger the course of the Great Divide, which on this map was a bold blue line that followed, more or less, the ridge line of the Rocky Mountains from British Columbia, eventually snaking onto the high peaks of north central Colorado, then turning sharply east at Rabbit Ears Pass, gaining Parkview Mountain and the peaks of the North Park Mountains, and tumbling south and west along the Front Range, down through Rocky Mountain National Park, jutting south again, down past Silver Plume and the great stone eruptions of Grays Peak and Mount Evans, both rising more than fourteen thousand feet, their icy, jagged summits looking like abscesses, open wounds against the hard blue sky, then falling south and southwest, along Bald Mountain, under my bench of rose-colored stone at Hoosier Pass, where it jerks slightly north to Tennessee Pass before following the saddle of the mountain ridges south again, twisting along the great toothed spines of the Sawatch Mountains and the dramatic valley of the Arkansas River, down onto the backs of the La Garita Mountains and the corrugated peaks of the San Juan Mountains before going with the bend of the high country into northern New Mexico.

A cold blue shadow drifted over the map while my finger followed the Great Divide as it crawled along the high ridges of the more than sixty mountain ranges that make up the Rocky Mountains. Fairplay's history, its fortune and fate, are linked to three of them—the Mosquito Mountains, the Front Range, and the Sawatch Mountains to the west, dominated by the highest peak in Colorado, Mount Elbert (14,433 feet). Fairplay is on the eastern flank of the Great Divide, just below where the Divide crosses Hoosier Pass and claws its way toward the high peaks of the sprawling Sawatch Mountains, which seem to drift among the hard-bottomed clouds and sharp, icy alpine sunlight like rafts of lost continents.

I looked down the pass to the east as far as South Park, the rar-efied, thin mountain air stinging my throat, sending a cold shud-der through my lungs. From the rocky saddle of the pass, the valley looked like a vast bowl of earth and meadow, river and stone, a bowl layered in shimmering veins of light, light of end-less textures, intensities, and colors, so that every stone and bend of river, every aspen and pine and the broad expanse of mead-ows, seemed for a long moment to be only contours of light and shadow, a landscape of illumination.

I thought of the mountains I had known and lived among and loved, the low-slung Ozarks and the worn-out, eroded, hardluck Great Smoky Mountains, and every image and thought I hauled up from memory to mind was gilded and traced and marked by endless ranges of light—this same light, the light seeping over the craggy mountain ridges of this high country valley. Mountain light. At once glowing and edged, soft and hard and brilliant, clear, brooding, flashing off every surface, bursting in vast plumes off the river that cut through the valley, and off the ridges of the mountains in the distance.

I rubbed the stones Kiwi LaReaux had given me, held them in my open hand, and each one seemed to ignite in the hard bright mountain sunlight sparkling like a sky of rutilant countersuns.

What was it Kiwi LaReaux had said as she handed me the stones, as she pointed back toward the cold stone pinnacles of the Sawatch Mountains?

"Manna from Heaven."

I spent the rest of the afternoon on that bench of rose-colored stone on the pinched crest of Hoosier Pass, looking west from the Great Divide where the Sawatch Mountains crowd the moun-tain sky with a chaos of snow-packed peaks. I sat among icy stones, Arctic light, and cold, luminescent shadows, feeling slightly adrift, in the overwhelming embrace, once again, of oro-genesis, mountain building, plate tectonics, the great geologic dance of the earth's continents, which are sliding about on groaning crustal plates like children on fresh ice.

The earth trembles as though it were made of viscous gelatin.

Continents move. Mountains move. Everything moves. Constantly. If it's eternity you want, do not seek it in stone or earth or water. All is process, and the process is a continuum of motion and possibility. What is, moves:

Hearts beat.

Atoms throb and warble and pulse.

The years roll on and on.

Waves of convection currents rising from the earth's thick, boiling, liquid core keep the crustal plates in motion, probing in almost imperceptible jolts about the planet like nonstop geologic bumper cars.

What we have catalogued, mapped, and named as nations and hemispheres and continents and oceans are actually no more than heaps of geologic debris, the junkyards of time.

The Rocky Mountains are such a heap, the refuse of orogenesis, particularly the great upheavals of the Laramide Revolution, which itself was part of the Laramide Orogeny, a period of mountain building that rattled the earth more than a hundred million years ago.

By late afternoon the high ridges in the distance had disappeared behind the gray bellies of passing clouds, making the mountains look like dark shards of stone strewn excrescently about the sky, the slagheaps of the planet's history, another of creation's interesting boneyards, a leviathan cairn with every stone an oracle. The oldest, some reaching perhaps a billion years back through the flow of time, speak of great, tumultuous cycles, of upheaval and erosion, and land flooded and drained of rich, warm, shallow seas, then wrenched and folded as the incipient Atlantic and Indian oceans widened, precipitating the breakup of the great single landmass of Pangaea into what would eventually become North and South America, Eurasia and Africa.

And ancient seas rose and fell, drained from the land, and what were the ancestral Rocky Mountains were eroded smooth, and

the sun rose and the moon set without measure or documentation for two hundred million years, a geologic instant or two, a great sigh before the next great upheavals began, about forty-five million years ago perhaps, a collision that would last millions of years and haul the Rocky Mountains into the brooding skies. The last of the great inland seas drained from the land, leaving behind dense clots and deposits of sediment that would harden and settle into layers of sandstone and shale. Even through cool Miocene dawns and bright Pliocene afternoons, the land lurched and flinched, thrusting the smoldering mountains even higher into an endless sprawl of perfect blue skies.

From the crest of Hoosier Pass, on the back of the Great Divide, I looked out over the Laramide Revolution's handiwork, its debris of fact and mystery, the scoured, jagged ridges of the Sawatch Mountains to the west, luminous vales of snow blowing from the fitful, disjunctive summits, while behind me the Mosquito Mountains seemed in contrast to roll across the sky, a rock latticework of eroded plains carrying the ancient seabed sediments, lifting them on broad stone shoulders into the high country light: swollen summits, distended bellies of stone. Unlike the sharp, hard, angled sunlight glinting off the wrenched peaks of the Sawatch Mountains, the light spilling down the bunched, tuberous, bowed ridges of the Mosquito Mountains was soft, the color of melted copper, like the light sweeping across the endless silences of the Arctic tundra.

Sunsets off the Mosquito Mountains silhouetted peaks that looked like rows of worn, yellowed, rotting molars, while the same sinking sun gave the gutted ridges of the Sawatch Mountains the look of row upon row of shattered jaws crowded with splintered incisors. Long ago, erosion scraped the sedimentary layers away from the high peaks and ridges and summits, leaving stark cores of exposed Precambrian basement stones—marrow and stalks and hearts and bulging shafts, fractured peaks and crowns of granite and gneiss and schist: rocks that were once part of the ancestral Rockies, stones that warmed in the sun before life on the planet first stirred.

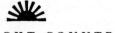

Many geologists believe that the Laramide Revolution has yet to end, that it still trembles through these mountains. The upheaval goes on. Standing on that bench of stone at Hoosier Pass along the Great Divide, watching clouds the color of blood drift across a fading sky, a sulphur moon on the rise, this I can say: more trembled than the constant wind. To the north, in the high peaks of the Front Range, drift glaciers still creep and moan, advance and retreat. Even at great distances, sometimes you can hear them deep in some blue-black mountain night, their cracked-backed groaning heavy on the wind, like the sound of skulls being ground in the bottom of a vast rough stone bowl.

Colorado is true high country. All of the great peaks of the Rocky Mountains, the fifty-four peaks that are above fourteen thousand feet, are found here. From my stone bench atop Hoosier Pass aside the Great Divide I could see four of these dramatic slabs of uplifted stone, their summits cut deep into the darkening sky— Mount Evans and Grays Peak to the east beyond Breckenridge, out toward Silver Plume; Mount Lincoln over my shoulder to the southwest, flooding Leadville with a dark sea of icy blue shadows; and Mount Elbert to the west, the crown of this mountain landscape, its cold, ragged, brutish, unforgiving summit deep in snow, draped with dark clouds, their edges colored coral pink in the moon's flat, dead light.

Just before twilight, what light remained in the sky appeared to melt and wash over the far edge of the horizon, which flamed with drained reds and bruised purples. I looked down the valley, down past Fairplay, where lights clicked on here and there, giving the place the look of a tangle of half-burnt-out Christmas lights. Beyond the town, the valley gave way to shadow, forms stitched in crepuscular light, except for the wide bows and bends of the river, which was a seam of emerald light. To the west, along the high ridges, thick bladders of light slouched down the backside of the mountains until there was only the soft moonlight and the river, which suddenly looked like a great ribbon of pale silver blue light lifted by a black wind, sliding easily through the valley.

To the west, a rattling, icy wind came off the Sawatch Mountains, a great sigh pressing over the high country, beyond intellect or reason: time's own wagging tongue, the universe's common idiom, living language. Kiwi LaReaux heard such a wind weeks later as we watched the sun set from nearby Western Pass. Swami Bill was down on the highway trying to sell Kiwi's latest batch of T-shirts, carrying the message SAVE THE HOLY LAND, FREE TIBET to a busload of tourists from Phoenix, Arizona.

"You know what it's saying?" said Kiwi LaReaux. She was watching the horizon hemorrhage bloody light and listening to the wind's symphony of sighs. I was watching the wind in her lovely red hair.

"Who knows," I said.

"It's a wind with a message, a message from the souls of the departed," said Kiwi LaReaux.

And this is what I whispered into her beautifully freckled ear:

"Maybe this is the wind's message? . . .

"Everything comes and goes."

"Maybe so," said Kiwi LaReaux smiling shyly.

On that first night, though, after waiting for the sky to burn down and the moon to rise, I drove down off the back of Hoosier Pass to Fairplay, took a room at one of the town's two hotels, ate, and crawled into bed. Sleep came easily, gobbling up the fading pain in my head. That night the old shivering dream of the black fish did not come, nor has it come to me since that first night in Fairplay. The nights now bring other, kinder dreams. Among them is a dream of the river I had seen at nightfall from atop Hoosier

Pass—that folded, looping river of shimmering, pale, silver blue light.

For months I kept going back to Fairplay, happily squandering my time in the great sprawl of South Park and along the reaches of the Middle Fork of the South Platte River and the high mountains that embrace the valley. South Park, the smallest of Colorado's three great high country valleys or parks, covers more than nine hundred square miles.

As for Fairplay, it is a town of about four hundred souls, including two full-time lawyers.

Fairplay got its start as a mining town. Many of the miners who had hurried into the mountains after gold was discovered ended up at nearby Tarryall, the first gold town in the valley, where they quickly found out that all the easy claims had been staked and bought up.

Eager for what they considered was their share of the valley's wealth, a swelling number of miners pulled out of Tarryall and set up their own town. It would be a place, they vowed, governed by common decency, where every man, no matter his luck or circumstances, would get a fair deal, an even chance.

They decided to call the place Fairplay.

Being human beings, the miners who founded Fairplay quickly bought up all the most promising gold claims. After all, this seemed to them like the naturally fair and right-minded thing to do. Even so, the town grew and the townspeople continued to pride themselves on their keen sense of fair play, even Jim Reynolds, who quickly discovered that the best deal of all was not in mining gold but in stealing it. The good people of Fairplay greeted the town's first church with reverent prayers and hosannahs, and when the minister suggested that the town might be playing less than fair, a group of the town's most selfless citizens shaved the minister's horse.

The only monument of consequence in Fairplay is the Prunes

Monument, built not to honor God or gold, state or nation, but a burro that spent most of its sixty-three years toiling in the local gold mines for oats and water.

The Prunes Monument is truly fair play. Indeed, the town seems to have a soft spot for the heavy-burdened. Not far from the quiet admiration of the Prunes Monument, among those enjoying the eternal rest and peace of the Fairplay Cemetery, are Shorty, another likable, long-suffering mining burro, and his companion, a dog named Bum.

Everyone in Park County sooner or later ends up in Fairplay. It's the county seat. And what a seat to watch for the first pulse of pale morning light slipping down the mountains and on to the broad meadows and listening to the soft purl of the river in the distance and to a chilly autumn wind rattling among the aspens, their cadaverous yellow leaves spiraling to the ground. The ridge along Weston Pass forms a natural boundary between the woods of the Pike and San Isabel national forests, while Route 9, after gaining Hoosier Pass, climbs into the wintry hubris of Colorado's ski resorts, places like Breckenridge and Copper Mountain and Vail, where Colorado learned long ago that snow is a far greater treasure than gold, that there were unspeakable fortunes to be made simply by charging a hefty fee for letting people be children again and play in the snow. Indeed, recreation in Colorado is business, and business is booming. People rush to Colorado, all of them willing to pay to play in these mountains, to hike, walk, and bicycle through the high country, fish, raft down cascading mountain rivers, and camp in alpine meadows in the clear, cold, hard sunshine.

As it turned out, Fairplay was a town I could not have passed up, even if Odell Euclid had been wrong and it had harbored a whole symphony of accordion players. Any town that admires hardworking burros and dogs is as good a place as any for a man to test his luck, examine his fortunes, maybe even change his fate. Too, there was the high country, and in the near distance that river of pale, silver blue light. So I kept going to South Park and to Fairplay while letting the lovely Dr. Mutzpah's prescriptions reverse my depression's black chemistry. My head emptied of everything save that which had endured and so seemed worthwhile—all those pieces of wild country and layered sunlight and the fast-moving water of high country rivers, wild fish, and the few friends that had somehow stayed with me.

In Fairplay, after weeks of running into each other, Kiwi LaReaux, Swami Bill, and I became close friends. Eventually, I told them how I had managed to show up in Fairplay, how I had fallen from grace, been bounced out of one paradise after another. The morning I told them about my previous life, a life that now seemed so long ago and far away, we were spending a splendid autumn morning off County Road 787 between Alama and Mount Boss, wandering about the haunting trees of the Bristlecone Pine Scenic Area. Kiwi LaReaux believed the trees were bathed in perfect auras, that they glowed like flames of pure burning oxygen. Too, the place was a favorite tourist stop. Easy pickings for Swami Bill, who set up his portable card table in the parking area, piling it high with what he called "socialist magic," great and harmless trinkets, wares cheap enough for anyone to afford—singing crystal bowls, rain sticks, music spheres, cosmic OM tuning forks, and Swami Bill's boxed set of subliminal self-help tapes.

Kiwi LaReaux and I walked among the ancient pines, bent and gnarled and twisted by the unyielding press of weather and time. Kiwi LaReaux told me that bristlecone pines are among the oldest living things on the planet. Up on the high rounded shoulders of the Mosquito Mountains, the ancient trees are drenched for months at a time in a sharp-edged, cold Arctic light.

Kiwi LaReaux told me that the bristlecone pines spoke to her.

"And what do they say?"

"The same thing over and over again," said Kiwi LaReaux.

"And what's that?" I said.

"Time flies," said Kiwi LaReaux.

"Time flies."

Swami Bill joined us. His apple green monk's robe wrinkled in the wind, and the stuffed parrot on his shoulder shuddered, listed farther to the right. I talked openly and freely to Bill and Kiwi LaReaux about my depression, my headful of bad chemicals, and about my comings and goings, how I had come to show up on the highway to Fairplay, about my room on Colorado Boulevard, Mi Oh and the Now & Zen Restaurant, Odell Euclid and *Colorado Living,* the life and death of Dr. Truth, and my days with the lovely and kind Dr. Lilly Mutzpah, how the anti-depressant medication she prescribed was cheering up my brain's brooding chemicals, easing the pain.

Swami Bill's eyes widened at the mention of Dr. Lilly Mutzpah. It seemed he had a distant cousin who was a patient of hers.

Swami Bill's distant cousin was Velveeta Cheese.

Small world.

Bill told me that he had talked to Velveeta Cheese after the shock treatments and that Velveeta Cheese had told him exactly what he had told me, that the inside of his brain felt like a vat of melted honey. Velveeta Cheese had told Swami Bill something else—that the shock treatments made him want to change his name.

To what?

Cheese Whiz.

Suddenly, Swami Bill began frantically working the wires under the sleeve of his apple green monk's robe, so that the parrot on his shoulder began flapping about as though it had been struck either by lightning or sweet lunacy.

The parrot screamed and squawked. Swami Bill put his hand over his mouth so I would not see his lips move.

Bill jumped in front of me, so that I was staring into the par-

rot's red glass eyes. Dingy blue-green feathers twirled in the air.

This is what the parrot keep screaming in Swami Bill's cracked voice:

"OLLIE-OLLIE-OXEN-FREE!

"OLLIE-OLLIE-OXEN-FREE!"

After that first weekend beyond Kenosha Pass in the wide stretches of South Park, watching cool autumn sunlight fill the valley, spill over the ledge of the Mosquito Mountains; after that long and wonderful day up on Hoosier Pass, up along the Great Divide; after that evening I spent watching the Middle Fork of the South Platte River as the valley went black and the river went on glowing like an endless seam of pale silver blue light; after all that, when I was back in my room on Colorado Boulevard, I would wake every morning and crawl out of the blue sleeping bag and stare out at the peaks of the Front Range in the near distance and wait for the morning to take hold, set fire to the sky.

And every Thursday afternoon I would sit in Dr. Lilly Mutzpah's office, in that deep soft black chair, and talk and steal glimpses out of her seventh-floor windows and think of the valley beyond the mountains and the river and its bright water. Dr. Mutzpah would catch me smiling and I would tell her about Fairplay and the mountains and the river and the great blind trout in the wide gleaming pool of the river. I told her about the wonderful Swami Bill and his parrot and the heartbreakingly beautiful Kiwi LaReaux, and how my depression, after I had hauled it up in to the high country, along the river, up there in that relentless country of light and shadow, had eased, let go.

The pain was gone.

The first time Dr. Mutzpah caught me staring out the window at the mountains and smiling, I was not thinking about the river or the blind trout. I was thinking about something Kiwi LaReaux had said to me.

"All these mountains," said Kiwi LaReaux, smiling shyly, "are leaking cosmic amounts of invisible pure crystal healing energy.

"Really . . . And everyone that comes up here ends up getting some kind of harmless metaphysical buzz on. And it's legal and it's free.

"But you gotta breathe deeply."

SWEET HOUR OF PRAYER

When lost in the woods, travel downstream. When
lost in the astral plane, travel toward the light.

—KIWI LAREAUX

The week before I first
walked down to the Middle Fork of the South Platte River, I
climbed Mount Elbert by way of the Black Cloud Trail. I left the
Twin Peaks campground before dawn, walked through cold, dark
stands of aspen and lodgepole pines, ghostly gray and bone white.

By dusk, on my way back down from the summit, just above the
timberline, I walked into a crush of thick and icy glaucous clouds
where it was snowing hard. I kept walking, making my way down
the mountain, out of the clouds and the whirling snow and back
into the woods, where shadows drifted like pale blue smoke
among the Engelmann spruce and white firs, Douglas firs, and
twisted, ancient bristlecone pines. Beyond the woods, tattered
mists of indigo light rose off the blue surface of an alpine lake.

Mount Massive's ragged stone spine tore great black gashes
into the heavy layers of clouds, and I could see deinotherian
plumes of blowing snow spilling off the mountain's summit, a
jagged ridge that looked like the rusted-out hulk of a crosscut
saw, its broken and eroded stone teeth rising above fourteen
thousand feet.

Both Mount Elbert and Mount Massive are located in the vast sprawl of the San Isabel National Forest, which covers more than a million acres in south central Colorado.

While I was up on the crest of Mount Elbert, I stood shivering in endless yowling winds and whorls of snow. The thin, cold air burned my throat, clawed at my lungs. In every direction, the Sawatch Mountains were pressed against the sky like enormous gondolas of implacable stone moored in swales of brooding, gray-black clouds.

That long moment on the summit of Mount Elbert was cold and sunless, and as I looked out over that sky of dark brittle stones and roiling clouds and melancholy light, I kept thinking of the river and its valley beyond Weston Pass, remembering how it had glowed at twilight like a ribbon of silver blue light as I watched it from a bench of stone atop Hoosier Pass, along the Great Divide.

Later, as I hiked along Lost Creek in the upper reaches of Pike National Forest, which covers more than a million acres of high country east of Weston Pass in central Colorado, I was still thinking of the river and the valley, even as I stopped to watch bighorn sheep move easily and gracefully up along the rocky slopes and crags, the spines and stone menageries of the Tarryall Mountains. Swami Bill and Kiwi LaReaux were with me. In the distance the scoured rock face of Mount Evans wrinkled across the blue sky like a scar of stone. We had just hiked back from Lake Abyss, where we had watched the sun rise, watched the cold autumn mountain light drip down stones and onto the surface of the lake, its waters suddenly a plasma of deep blues and bloody reds.

Swami Bill was telling me he couldn't climb Mount Elbert again.

"The parrot can't take the altitude," he said earnestly, stopping to retie the piece of black electrical cord about the waist of his apple-green monk's robe.

"Really . . . He goes loony in that thin air. Spits every twenty feet," said Swami Bill.

"Spits?"

"Yeah," said Swami Bill, his eyes, one green and one blue, shooting a quick glance at Kiwi LaReaux.

"Thanks to Ms. LaReaux," explained Swami Bill. The parrot overheard her telling me that when spit freezes before it hits the ground, the temperature's already at least ten degrees below zero.

"By the time we reached the summit, he'd spit more than the entire roster of the Chicago Cubs on opening day. Then he stopped," said Bill.

"You want to know why he stopped?" said Kiwi LaReaux shyly, her lips forming a slightly menacing grin. Small streams of yellow sunlight eased down the wild curls of her long, red hair, down her white linen shirt, the top three buttons left undone, revealing an elegant neck, a smooth, white throat. Kiwi LaReaux never wore makeup of any kind, as if to underscore that she had nothing to suppress or to hide.

"His poor little eyes froze and cracked," said Kiwi LaReaux, her smile widening.

"It was so sad. He was blind for days until Bill finally found an abandoned doll at the Denver Goodwill store that turned out to be a suitable organ donor, a doll with perfectly matched rosy red glass eyes."

After walking back from Lost Creek to the Goose Creek campground, I crawled into the little blue tent and slipped into the blue sleeping bag, slept until well past noon, dreaming only of the river and the great valley. Inside the little blue tent, tucked beneath my backpack and a growing, unruly heap of clothes, was my George Maurer fly rod, one of the three fly rods I had not had to sell.

West of Hoosier Pass, the Middle Fork of the South Platte River coils down the eastern flank of the mountains, spilling over shoulders of stone, down through the heavily shadowed forest below the timber line and into the valley of South Park, where it cuts through broad meadows, its banks often sunk below berms of tall grass, so that the only evidence of the river is the sunlight flashing off the moving water and a rising susurrant wind.

The river meanders loosely through the valley, an intricate labyrinth of bends and loops as deeply coiled as a nautilus shell. Deep pools of glinting water mark each bend in the river, which give way to stretches of faster water tumbling over a chaos of stones, refracted sunlight coming off their eroded black backs in bursts of pulsating light.

As it moves through the valley, the Middle Fork of the South Platte passes through several reservoirs, including the Eleven Mile Reservoir and Spinney Mountain Reservoir, near the little valley town of Hartsel, not far from Fairplay. Outside of Hartsel, there is a small bridge over the river. I crossed this bridge a dozen times before stopping, pulling off the highway. At first, I left the fly rod in the car, watching the river from the bridge before walking along its damp, grassy banks.

It was early morning when I first walked that stretch of river below the Hartsel bridge. The great earthen bowl of the valley was just filling with sunlight. The river seemed a solid, hammered, sizzling silver glare, an incandescence of wild, stroboscopic light.

If the valley of South Park and the Middle Fork of the South Platte River are no longer true wilderness, both the valley and the river remain edged with wildness and all that wildness portends: relentless potential and possibility and expectation, surviving remnants of a time when the valley and river and the surrounding mountains were undiscovered country—shaped only by the press of time and of history, by the wind's relentless, cold howling, by atavistic light—and the river, a wide vein of moving water, its sound carried on the wind, was a timeless hymn to beauty and solace, change and impermanence.

Often, I would walk along the river, sit among warming stones half sunk in the deep, cold, blue-green water, sleep tucked in the thick grass along the banks, the sun low in the autumn sky, so that the day's light always seemed to be cascading over the distant ridges filling the valley like a flooding tide, a tide of infinite colors and textures.

And for days and days, even though I carried my fly rod, I did not fish.

Sometimes, just before dusk, I would meet Swami Bill and Kiwi LaReaux back at the Windy Ridge Bristlecone Pine Scenic Area on Mount Bloss. Kiwi LaReaux would be up among the bristlecone pines on Windy Ridge, while Swami Bill stayed behind, seated at his portable card table in the parking area, hawking Tibetan crystal malas made in Mexico to cheerful, delighted, smiling tourists.

"What do the pines say this evening?" I would ask Kiwi LaReaux as I walked with her, eager to steal a look at her beautiful green eyes and watch as the day's lambent sunlight made her long, red hair glow as softly as candlelight.

My question always brought a shy smile and the same whispered answer, the words almost quivering in the wind.

"Time flies."

Standing on the Hartsel bridge, I stared for a long time at the river as it moved across the meadow like a tongue of green light. The highway to Hartsel was empty, save for me standing there on the bridge.

I was smiling and couldn't seem to drain the smile from my face.

This was the message the repaired wiring in my brain sent to every bone and muscle and nerve, to every weary cell that is me: It is good to be in the company of a mountain river again. It is good to be along moving water, a river imbued with wildness.

I walked down off the bridge and along the river's broad banks, sat among an ancient eruption of stones and decided not to eat the sprout sandwich Kiwi LaReaux had made for me. Instead I dozed, fell into shallow pockets of sleep and liquid dreams, dreams of water—waters warm and waters cold. Waters luminescent and waters translucent. The pull and pulse of great seas, the press of high mountain rivers. Waters calm and waters tossed and rent. Waters wide and waters deep. Plunging falls and thrashing rapids and single drops of water, each one a wheeling microcosm trembling with protozoic life.

Eventually, I sunk into a sleep as wide and deep and quiet as death, the kind of sleep I sometimes come clawing out of sweating pure black desperation, like a drowning man flailing his way to the surface for one last gulp of air. It is as though the brain is seized for an instant by some frightful aphasia, and for an eerie moment everything seems strange, as though, while in sleep's black hands, I have been suddenly dumped in some alien land, as though I had been completely paralyzed, was nothing more than a thought trapped in a corked bottle, uncertain of who I was or where I was. During such moments, I feel the planet drift and me along with it, and no longer do I ache for any one place, any one great good place to anchor mind and blood and soul. The blood knows more homes, more worlds than the mind can even imagine. Lying there among those warm stones, struggling to break out of sleep's coffin, for some reason I remembered that over breakfast Swami Bill had introduced me to a truly rare social phenomenon: an intact American family, all living in the same place, within ten miles of each other.

Think of that.

Father, mother, children, grandparents, aunts and uncles, nieces and nephews all living cheerfully together in the same town. By comparison, my family, like most American families these days, is as scattered as the particles of a smashed atom. Father in Arizona. Mother dead and buried at Arlington National Cemetery in Washington, D.C., a privilege accorded her as the wife of an American soldier. Aunts and uncles living in New Orleans and in Helena, Arkansas, and farming watermelons in Mexico. Sister in Pennsylvania. Grandmother in Shreveport, Louisiana. Elias Wonder, my great-uncle Albert, and my grandfather buried in the rocky red earth of the Ozark Mountains. Nieces and nephews sprinkled from Buffalo Gap, South Dakota, to the Andes mountains of Peru. And so on.

When my head cleared, I looked over at the river, the shimmering water moving inexorably downstream. I dipped my hand into the water at the edge of the river, felt its current press against my fingers, and closed my eyes and let the meadow and the mountains pour over my senses, fill my head—let the river, its bright green waters, carry me away, beyond the cramped and ponderous boundaries of belonging.

I walked along that stretch of the river below the Hartsel bridge until late afternoon, the sky a single great blue dome of sunlight until, to the west, beyond the ridge line of the mountains, the first reds and purples of sunset seeped into the sky. There was nothing between the river and meadow and the distant mountains but endless sheets and veins and layers and pillars of light, undisturbed and unbroken, not even by a bird on the wing, a tremble of wind, or the first shadows of dusk shuddering out from among chaotic heaps of dark stones. At the edge of a pool, in a small bend in the river just above the bridge, I saw a small trout rise, gulp down an insect on the surface, then quickly disappear, sink down into the pool's deep green shadows. A dimple of disturbed water, the only mark of the trout's rise, its presence, widened into a series of concentric circles of water, each ring a corona of refracted, resplendent silver light breaking in turn against the undercut bank.

I watched the pool of pale green water for an hour, but the trout did not rise again. I sat in the cool meadow grass above the pool, where the river arched into a wide bend, watching dull blue-green shadows wrinkle across the surface of the pool, and other trout rose, the trout of yesteryear, the trout that move through the rivers and streams and creeks I have experienced, known and stored in my memory, rivers that move through my mind and imagination. The rise of the trout in that small pool along the Middle Fork of the South Platte River stirred my old addiction for trout rivers, for wild water and trout that demand such water and will live in nothing less. During my days and nights along the South Platte, I discovered that not only had my depression not tempered my longing for wild water, fast and bright trout rivers, it actually seemed to have intensified it. Just the sight of that rising small trout released splashes of adrenaline into my blood, sent a cold, crackling buzz up and down my backbone.

The river junkie lived on, uncured.

Thank the gods. There was that familiar tightening of the throat, that vague tremble of the muscles in my arms and hands, at the temples, my palms going white and cold, that same inexplicable smile involuntarily shaping my lips and face, that proverbial bloat of amorphous, recondite content swelling in my gut.

I ask a lot of wild water and trout. Too much. More than they can give. Human beings, it seems to me, are desperate to make the natural world dance to whatever tune buzzes in our big brains. We want the earth not only to mirror but somehow fulfill our needs, our yearnings, our desires, to assuage our shortcomings, ease our fears, justify our faith. I have often spoken of how my obsession with wildness, especially wild mountain rivers, seems somehow, however temporarily, to reestablish whatever ancient connections there might be between me and the good earth. My addiction to moving water, to mountain streams, to trout rivers, has more to do with mystery and illumination than absolution and salvation. Angling gives me an excuse to wade into such water, into the world as it is, the inexorable push and pull of life's continuum, the participatory universe, life experienced instead of implied.

Jazzed on the narcotic of wild water, my brain happily makes the connections, splices whatever is fundamental in me—essence of blood and flesh and bone—to the earth, wires me accordingly. Process is reduced to its simplest terms: an act of faith, beliefs beyond chemistry, a dance with magic and mystery. And it's all free and harmless.

Some addiction!

My days and nights along the Middle Fork of the South Platte

River let me know that the connections between me and this average, lonely blue earth, all those ancient bonds, some lost, others broken and frayed, still linger like a dream in the brain, in blood and bone.

The evolution of life, all life, has left heaps of details and signs, clues, pieces, shards, everything but absolutes: truths solid and sure, uncontestable reassurances and meaning, undiluted understanding. So I throw a wolf's pelt over evolution's cold, dispassionate shoulders, put an ancient drum in its hands, a shaman's glint in its colorless eyes, but even so evolution has no myths to soothe me, no message of solace or of meaning. Nonetheless, human beings cling to the curious notion that we are somehow the darlings of evolution, the chosen ones, life's ultimate expression. However, human beings are no more a wonder than the common housefly. The greatest wonder of life is that there is life at all, because whatever life might be, it is certain that it is not the result of reasoned, predictable, inevitable progress, but of a matter of the improbable, the vastly improbable. The earth is as it is simply because this is the way things have turned out. There are surely countless other contingencies that would have worked just as well, even better. Evolution's debris speaks its own language, a tongue that tells a story not so much of change but of constant divergence, awesome diversity and complexity spun from a limited number of threads. Evolution's details mark life as a mostly botched enterprise, few triumphs amid the clutter of dead ends, failures and extinction. Failure, evolution clearly shows, is much more common than success. Life's history is a tale of random stochastic successes and staggering imperfections such as human beings. Our mammalian ancestors got lucky, that's all, survived the staggering mass extinctions of the late Cretaceous and Permian periods. By the close of the deadly Permian years more than 90 percent of all the species then eking out a living on the earth had slid into extinction's one-way oblivion. The mammals that would turn out to be our ancestors were not among them.

Lucky us.

Evolution's signposts through time and history tell us something else, something reassuring, that extinction is nothing personal.

No matter what our big brains tell us, we are coincidental, a one-way, one-time expression of life. Whether we go on, or fail and slip and slide down into extinction's dustbin of failed experiments, of this we can be sure—human beings will never be repeated, nor will dolphins or trout, grizzly bears or glowworms. One life per species. Every living creature is truly a wonder simply because of its being here at all. Everything is a lucky coincidence. Nothing about the evolution of life was preordained, especially human beings. We too are just another lucky coincidence. Scientists interested in the fits and starts of evolution often like to imagine what might happen if life could somehow be hauled back to the instant of the Big Bang, be allowed to start all over again. Would the outcome be the same?

Not a chance. It seems there is absolutely no reason to believe that life—the history of life, the continuum of history as we understand it—would repeat itself. The alternative possible outcomes are infinite, but none among them would find me lying in a cool, grassy, high mountain meadow in Colorado, near a bend in the Middle Fork of the South Platte River, watching a deep river pool of pale green water, waiting for a trout to rise up toward the surface, toward the sunlight.

Angling, for me, is about a lot more than fishing. It is one way of sinking into the press of time, into the current of all the moments that ever were, are, or will be, thinking, as the river's current tugs at my calves and thighs, about such lucky coincidences as wild water and trout and me, the awkward mammal with his big brain and evolving, menacing consciousness, casting for rising trout, for those dim memories and worn connections to everything that was and is, the world of imperfections and luck and successful accidents, fortunate divergence. Here I was along yet another mountain river, wading into the cold, bright water and the earth's bounteous continuum, grasping for old ghosts, harmless and innocent and reassuring myths, ancient virtues, lost gods, and remembering that life knows nothing of our big brains, our notions of morality and justice, honesty and love. Life favors no creature, trout or bird or insect or human being. If it favors anything, it is persistence. So far, our greatest success is not the microchip or the electric light, the polio vaccine, quantum physics, toothpaste in a tube, or the Patriot missile system. Rather, it is our ability to survive, if only barely, by the skin of our teeth, even though our big brains and evolving consciousness keep piling on the evidence that, so far, human existence is a history of the miserable, the embarrassing, and the ridiculous.

As I say, I am a hardcore junkie for wild mountain rivers. Every fix makes my brain as happy as a clam, brings with it not only a splash of hard and cold and honest absolution, but a moment of pure belief: that wild water abides.

The sky beyond the mountains was a smear of maroon light across darkening clouds, and I walked back to the bridge, back to my car, and drove back through Hartsel, past Fairplay, and back to Denver. While I drove, I kept stealing glances at the yellow-green meadows and the river meandering through them, looking, as the sun set, like a broad current of electric silver blue light.

That Thursday I told Dr. Lilly Mutzpah how happy and content my formerly soured chemicals had become, how the pain had eased, how I had become as happy as a mooncalf, how I no longer felt awkward as a duck waddling through sand dunes.

I told her about the mountains and the broad autumn meadows, about Swami Bill, about the heartbreakingly beautiful Kiwi LaReaux, about the river and the small trout that rose in the pale green waters above the Hartsel bridge.

"How do you feel about all this? . . . What do you make of it all?" asked Dr. Mutzpah, who had stopped scribbling in her notebook and was looking at me, her eyes wide and bright, her lips curled in a delicate but professional smile.

"The meadow was warm," I said.

"The river was fast and its waters cold. Swami Bill has a stuffed parrot on his shoulder. Kiwi LaReaux has lovely green eyes and haunting red hair."

"Well, well," said Dr. Lilly Mutzpah.

"Well, well."

And Dr. Mutzpah closed her notebook and said to me what she so often said to me.

"There, there," said Dr. Mutzpah.

"There, there. . . .

"Well, so you've met a real live swami, have you? In all of my years of practice, I can't say I've met even one. So, tell me, has the swami any words of enlightenment?"

"No, but his parrot has," I said.

"The same ones all the time.

"OLLIE-OLLIE-OXEN-FREE!"

Swami Bill's parrot kept yelling "OLLIE-OLLIE-OXEN-FREE" in Swami Bill's crepitating voice for the same reason that Odell Euclid was always saying, "Roll out Jeremy," or that Dr. Lilly Mutzpah so often leaned close to me saying, "There, there . . . ," as I sat in the deep warm folds of that black chair in her office.

"OLLIE-OLLIE-OXEN-FREE" was Swami Bill's way of commenting, through his stuffed parrot's vanished yellow beak and dead, cherry red glass eyes, on how silly life can be, how fragile human beings are. It was his way of coping with life's regular doses of torment and misery and pain. Whenever he met another human being, no matter the circumstances, Swami Bill would shake that person's hand generously. Then Bill would cover his mouth with one hand, work the parrot's wires with the other.

As the parrot flapped its dingy wings, it screamed:

"OLLIE-OLLIE-OXEN-FREE."

"Pass it on.

"Pass it on."

Almost every human being knows the phrase, remembers it

from his childhood days of endless play and games. It is what one child would yell out when the game was over and everything was okay, when everyone was safe from being tagged, chased, noticed, tormented, ridiculed, tricked, safe from being IT! Whenever you heard "OLLIE-OLLIE-OXEN-FREE," it was the all clear. You could come out of hiding, stop being afraid.

Swami Bill and his stuffed parrot with the cold red eyes were sounding the all clear, too, letting grown up human beings know they could let go, stop hiding, come back out into the sunshine.

I sunk deep into a bean bag chair on the floor of Swami Bill's and Kiwi LaReaux's double-wide trailer in the Holistic Motor Court, Ashram & Coin Laundry in Boulder, getting ready to drive over Kenosha Pass and into South Park, as Swami Bill flopped down into a frayed, plum purple naugahyde easy chair festooned with colored beads and popped open a bottle of Czechoslovakian beer. He had taken off his apple green monk's robe and was wearing a pair of marigold orange walking shorts, his ubiquitous pink flip-flops, and no shirt.

Swami Bill had a faded china blue tattoo on his sagging hairless chest. The tattoo was a large, simple cross. It looked like this:

Swami Bill saw me staring and told me about the tattoo. He had been a combat chaplain's assistant with the 1st Cavalry Division in the Vietnam War, long ago and far away. Bill had volunteered, joined the army after graduating from high school in Parma, Ohio, a town, he said longingly, which had no hotel, no daily newspaper, and no map of itself to help out either those trying to get in to or out of Parma.

The 1st Cavalry Division was Muldoon's old outfit.

Small world.

Swami Bill told me that since he was an atheist, since he believed in no single supreme being or creator of the universe, he made a perfect combat chaplain's assistant.

It was Swami Bill's job to usher dead and dying boy soldiers into heaven.

"I was supposed to make sure," said Swami Bill, "they all got into Christianity's heaven, but pretty soon I just let them go to whatever heaven they wanted. I told them whatever they wanted to hear, harmless little fibs that would make eternity a little more comfortable.

"Some wanted harp music and pearly gates.

"They got it.

"Some wanted to know if their lives had mattered at all.

" 'Of course,' I told them. 'Of course.'

"Some wanted to know if they had died in vain.

" 'Of course not,' I told them. 'Of course not.'

"They wanted to know if they had died for freedom and justice, for democracy, for America right or wrong.

" 'Of course you did,' I told them.

"Some wanted to hear angels and the choir invisible.

"I hummed gently in their ears.

"Some wanted a heaven of Fords and Chevys, Pontiacs and Porches, all fast and new and paid for.

"They got it.

"Some wanted women, especially the really young ones who got it before they had had a chance to get laid. So I gave them women, forever young—and willing for all eternity.

"Some wanted green fields and blue skies and cool winds.

"I gave them all of it, endless acres of empyrean firmament.

"Some wanted resurrection, another chance.

"They got it.

And to each of them, to all those young, shredded and shattered pieces of human meat, Swami Bill told me, he leaned close and whispered childhood's all clear.

"I said it to everyone," said Bill, "to monotheists, polytheists, cosmotheists, henotheists, zootheists. Catholics and Jews, Baptists and Methodists, Lutherans and Mormons, Muslims and Lamaists, agnostics and Zoroastrians, nonbelievers and believers in God, hoodoo, Jina, Mary Baker Eddy, Lao-tzu, Alpha and Omega, tamanoas, and the Great Spirit, Yen Lo, gnomes, Pan, and Vidar.

"I just leaned close and said it real soft and clear.

"Ollie-ollie-oxen-free.

"They could let go. It was all going to be okay.

"Okay."

Kiwi LaReaux was lying in a white rope hammock that hung like a great open cocoon between the two big windows that looked out from the living room toward the coin laundry. Her red hair was tied back off her neck with a single piece of blue ribbon, and the flush of her cheeks was the color of rose mallow.

Bill's parrot was propped up in its nest of wires on the deeply cracked and creased naugahyde couch. It was staring at me with its red deadpan eyes.

After Vietnam, Bill told me, he tried a great many occupations, including being a madman.

"I sold instant salvation door to door," said Swami Bill, smiling. "It came in a little packet. All you had to do was add water. When it started selling, I went sane and quit."

The soft sunlight coming through the trailer's front door framed Bill's face, its deep lines and wrinkles looking more like the marks of memory than of time.

Swami Bill talked on, his voice rich and plangent.

He told me that for years he had lived off beer and peyote buttons, hoping the combination would bring either visions or a good night's sleep.

"For years," said Swami Bill, "I was just so very tired."

He said that one day he found himself sober and straight and sitting at a small, dimly lit table at the Yin & Yang Club in New Orleans' French Quarter.

When Bill woke up in the Yin & Yang Club, Kiwi LaReaux was performing. She worked there nightly as a metaphysical stripper.

Bill remembered that she was dressed in silk lounging pajamas and a wide-brimmed summer straw hat with a single neon blue tropical parrot feather stuck in it.

Bill told me it took a couple of shows before he figured out, by watching the crowd, that the idea was to try to mentally undress Kiwi, imagine her naked.

"I couldn't get past the first button of her silk lounging pajamas," said Swami Bill.

Bill told me he sat at one of the dimly lit tables at the Yin & Yang Club every night until 4 A.M. for a week, sending Kiwi LaReaux telepathic messages through the strobing black lights, messages that kept getting lost in the astral plane.

"I sent out vibes and rays," said Swami Bill, "even beams from a flashlight I bought at a drugstore. Finally, I just sent her a note, invited her to my table for a drink.

"What's it cost?" I asked her when she sat down.

"What ya got?" she asked.

"Time," I said.

"Time's good enough," she said.

Bill was smiling as he told me that Kiwi LaReaux was as beautiful now as she was all those years ago when she walked out on the stage of the Yin & Yang Club. She taught him how to meditate, to accept his fate, that time flies, that Tibetan merchandise always sells, to eat raw vegetables and fresh fruit, that a fat bank account and a healthy mutual fund were the surest paths to Zen. Real estate, Kiwi LaReaux told Swami Bill, makes the karma glow a radiant and healthy blue-and-orange.

Eventually, Kiwi got Bill hooked on rapture and bliss and con-

tentment, all of which were legal and far less expensive than peyote buttons. Bill and Kiwi bought the butter yellow VW and
headed west, ending up in Boulder, where they bought a piece
of land, set up the Holistic Motor Court, Ashram & Coin Laundry.

It was Kiwi who decided on Boulder. She told Bill she had
been receiving, long-distance, its tempting, alluring, soothing,
ethereal tintinnabulations over the psychic airwaves for years.
That's why she had been working at the Yin & Yang Club, letting
its desperate patrons sitting in the ghostly black lights imagine
the holy land beneath her silk lounging pajamas. Kiwi LaReaux
was socking away most of her weekly wages for a pilgrimage to
Boulder, a town she firmly believed was built on top of the
largest natural radiating crystal power on the planet, a power so
urgent, so elemental, that each year hundreds of promising and
enterprising soothsayers, consciousness raisers, creation scientists, transcendental parapsychologists, lamas, witches and war-
locks, gurus, and roshis flocked to Boulder, joined the already
swelling population of crystal gazers, astrologers, clairvoyants,
gastromancists, holomancists, I Ching peddlers, numerologists,
ornithomancists and scatomancists, pyramid pushers and penta-
gram sellers, augurs of pre-existence and no existence at all, legions of those who had been abducted, experimented on, and
dumped back to earth by disappointed aliens, and those who had
been raised by Big Foot. Every street in town was crowded with
the disheartened and disaffected, the lost and the befuddled,
beggar bowls in their hands, each one hungry for karmic solace
but willing to settle for a change of luck.

Once in Boulder, Kiwi LaReaux worked as a clairvoyant. She
sat in the big room that would later become the coin laundry, sat
behind thick black curtains, sat there in the darkness, dressed in
a Shinto robe. Whenever a customer came through the curtains,
Kiwi LaReaux would quickly pop a wintergreen Life Saver into
her mouth, grinding it hard so that her teeth gave off tiny eerie
green phantasmal sparks.

As she swung lazily in the wide web of the white hammock,
Kiwi LaReaux said she told all her customers the same thing. She

told them in an urgent whisper to close their eyes, then open them. The time that passed was only that of a blink. And she would tell them that in that same blink of an eye everyone on the planet would be dead and gone and forgotten. Kiwi LaReaux looked into her customers' futures and told them that time flies and they had better make the most of the tiny instant they had before the lights went out. Kiwi also told me that for an extra $20 she would lead them on transcendental sightseeing tours of their past lives or divine the meanings of their troubled sleep, warts, moles, and carbuncles.

Meanwhile, Bill found work in Denver digging graves with a backhoe. They took in two stray cats, named them Higan and Shigan, which is Japanese for all kinds of things, like here and there or heaven and hell.

Neither Bill nor Kiwi spoke Japanese. I later discovered that a friend suggested that they name their cats Higan and Shigan. The friend's name was Mi Oh, the beautiful hostess at the Now & Zen Restaurant.

Small world.

It was Kiwi who came up with the name for Bill's stuffed parrot.

Saddhu. Holy man.

Saddhu accompanied Bill everywhere. He was even present at meals, perched precariously on the edge of a bowl of wooden nuts and wax fruits.

Swami Bill and Kiwi LaReaux often let me stay in one of the three tiny bedrooms in their double-wide trailer. Whenever I stayed over, I slept in Saddhu's room. I got the bed. Saddhu rested wired to a tall, green, plastic tree. On the night table in Saddhu's room were two books, side by side—a new edition of the Gideon Bible and a copy of *The Teachings of Buddha*. Jesus, Buddha, Saddhu and I got along well together. We all slept soundly.

It was while digging graves with a backhoe in Denver, Swami Bill told me, that he made the great discovery that the dead can go right on being heard loud and clear beyond the grave. He made a bundle investing in talking tombstones. For a price, the

dying could arrange to leave a taped message behind in a tape player built tastefully into the tombstone of their choice. The tape player is powered by solar energy so there are no batteries to change, no need for long extension cords or inconvenient electrical outlets. Too, the weatherproof speakers were handsomely disguised as stone. A discreetly placed red button turned the hidden tape recorder on and off.

Swami Bill told me he got out of the talking tombstone business when a seventy-two-year-old woman paid $5,000 in cash to tape an eternal message to her husband or to anyone else who happened by her grave and pressed the little red button on the top of her tombstone.

This, said Bill, was the little old lady's message:

"Remember what that hog-faced minister said fifty years ago? Till death do us part. Well, if you've got your hearing aids in and are listening to this, then they've thrown the dirt on my face and the contract's null and void. Expired. Finished. Pull up your pants, button your fly, for Chrissakes. Tuck in your shirt. Go home, old man. Soak your teeth. Vacuum the floors. Wash the dishes. Pick up your own dirty underwear. Leave me alone. Can't you see I'm trying to get some rest here."

Swami Bill took the bundle he made in talking tombstones and invested it in Tibetan merchandise. Each weekend, he and Kiwi LaReaux packed up the butter yellow VW, loaded it with boxes of Swami Bill's collector's edition of self-help cassette tapes ("*The Ashrama Chronicles*. Also Available on CD. 90-minute tapes, each full of subliminal messages intermingled with silence and whale songs, birdcalls and tropical rainstorms, the sounds of oceans and mountain rivers, symphonies of storm and wind and the desert's profound silences"). Months later, after my job at *Colorado Living* in Denver folded, I again found myself and my belongings back inside the Toyota and on the road, heading out of Colorado, searching for work. Swami Bill and Kiwi LaReaux gave me a set of Bill's tapes, a little something for the long, lonely, open road. I listened and listened.

On that October afternoon as we sat around the double-wide trailer getting ready to drive over Kenosha Pass and down into the valley of South Park, on that day before I first saw the big and beautiful and dyspeptic brown trout rise out of the green-blue shadows of a great pool of the river where it flowed out of the Spinney Reservoir, Kiwi LaReaux was sipping seductively on a bottle of colorless ginseng ginger ale.

Kiwi LaReaux was shy. She spoke little. Most of her communication seemed to come more by way of allelochemics than conventional language. To me, she seemed some rarefied mix of chemistry and quantum physics, a mysterious smile on her face and a simple necklace of soapberry beads about her elegant neck. When she moved, she seemed to leave poignant but invisible traces of herself lingering on the wind—in the grass, in violet shadows and bright sunshine, a smell, a sound, a lingering motion stitched in endless ranges of sunlight.

Sometimes she would walk with me along the river. As I fished, she would wander out into the meadows. I used to turn from the water, see her in the near distance, her long, red hair caught in a sudden press of wind, the day's light flashing off her perfect green eyes.

She never spoke of home or of family. Swami Bill told me, the leer on his face underscoring the irony he wanted me to grasp, that her father was a fabulously wealthy, devoted and beneficent conservationist back east who had made his money in mining plutonium and deciding which pieces of charming and beautiful rural, small-town America would become toxic-waste dumps.

Not surprisingly, Kiwi LaReaux tended to dismiss ecology and conservation, all the hoopla about saving the planet, as so much bunkum. She believed the so-called green movement was nothing but more human hubris and dangerous meddling, that humankind's new concern was not for the fate of the planet but for the fate of humanity. The earth would survive, she would say, no matter what people did or did not do. Earth, after all, had survived disasters and catastrophes greater than human beings could even imagine. It would survive humanity as well, its greed and pretense, its ruinous touch, its ignorant attempts to master the earth, its misplaced belief that human beings were appointed by the Creator of the Universe to be the stewards of the planet, the shaper of its fortunes and fate. The earth, said Kiwi LaReaux, had gotten along fine without human beings for millions of years and it would continue to go on and on with or without us. Behind the fervent pleas of ecologists and conservationists is a deeper plea, said Kiwi LaReaux, a tragic appeal not for the survival of the planet but for the maintenance of the so-called good life that human beings have spent centuries exploiting the earth to achieve and maintain.

Kiwi LaReaux would say that the earth would go on and on until the sun, a minor, average, and all-too-mortal star, burned out. She would walk quietly along the river to where I was fishing, casting gaudy, fraudulent trout flies onto the bright moving water, and sit along the bank. Smiling shyly, she would tell me to blink and then welcome me to another world, fresh and new, every moment wrinkling with possibility.

On the morning I first saw the big brown trout rise up out of the deep water of the pool along the river below Spinney Reservoir, Kiwi LaReaux did not ask me to blink. Instead, she was shaking her head and laughing. Sitting in the cool, tall grasses along the riverbank, she told me that Bill had been a writer of significance when she first met him at the Yin & Yang Club in New Orleans. Swami Bill wrote under the pen name of Chester Bopp and for years churned out harmless original paperback fantasy and science fiction novels. She said that his most famous book was a novel about a parallel universe, identical to Earth in every way, except that in the story's parallel universe, human beings had unprotected sex, and it was safe and wonderful and nobody ever suffered or died. The worst thing that might happen to these other human beings, as they took as many lovers as they pleased, made love madly day in and day out, was either exhaustion or boredom.

"Talk about Fairyland," said Kiwi LaReaux, a soft laugh escaping from behind her shy smile.

The name of Swami Bill's most famous novel, by the way, is *Come and Get It*. It has been out of print for years and years, and these days is as rare as common decency. As things turned out, I would later find a copy of Bill's novel. Actually, Woody Moos found it while picking through a night's haul of garbage almost a year ago. Woody Moos was still a member of the crew of county garbage truck No. 2 then, along with me and Cleopheus and Hamadullah and Thallus. Woody Moos had not yet been fired for stealing a still-warm smoked turkey. Moos found the catsup-stained novel in a bag of soiled diapers and empty Spam cans. During our break, Moos took out his penlight and read to us. Near the end, one of the book's main characters, an honest and lovable whore from Idaho who is still young and beautiful and healthy even though she claims to have made love to more than two thousand male human beings of various colors, creeds, religious affiliations, and economic circumstances, tells the novel's narrator, Chester Bopp, that the most beautiful passage in the English language, save some Bible quotes and Shakespeare's work, is this:

"Get 'em in, get it up, get 'em off, and get 'em out."

Whenever Kiwi LaReaux told me about Swami Bill's life as a writer, his life as Chester Bopp, whenever she told me about the novels he wrote, she would often stop to smile and giggle and laugh.

"What else can a person do?" said Kiwi LaReaux, smiling shyly.

Human existence being what it is, mostly failure and humiliation and bewilderment, preposterous and nonsensical, Kiwi LaReaux did what she had to do to get through each day's new onslaught of poverty and injustice, drug addiction and suicides, murders, crib death, hunger, homelessness, and cold sores, gum disease and madness. She laughed.

I laughed right along with her.

What else can a person do, I would say.

"Call this number," said Kiwi LaReaux, laughing as she handed me a folded tarot card with a toll-free number written on it.

I called.

The telephone number she had written on the small, folded tarot card was for the Tantric Hotline. I would later learn that the Tantric Hotline was yet another division of Swami Bill Enterprises, Inc.

The Tantric Hotline had the same message, the same piece of advice, for every weary and confused caller.

When I called I recognized Kiwi LaReaux's voice, like a light breeze caught in a gallery of wind chimes. On the taped message, Kiwi LaReaux told callers that in order to accomplish all things, everything from contentment to rebirth to bliss, first they each had to accept these great and simple truths of life.

"Paddle your own canoe," sighed Kiwi LaReaux.

"Forgive and forget.

"Fish or cut bait."

There was room on the tape for callers to leave their own personal messages, if they wished, if they had one. You were supposed to wait for the beep . . .

Before the sound of the beep, however, Swami Bill's crackling baritone came on.

This is what Swami Bill had to say to those callers of the Tantric Hotline who had miracles to report, wisdom to impart, blessings to give, advice to offer, goods to pawn.

"If you think you have found or learned the meaning of life, the Way, the Path, Enlightenment, Oneness, Otherness, Sameness, the physical home of the soul, and so on, please press the pound sign and one of the operators with our other line, the Revelation Hotline, will be glad to help you. Meanwhile, remember, dear callers, there is only One Way: a little more common decency, please. A little more human understanding and respect if you can spare it. More kindness, more propriety, more decorum. Give every human being a break and you will find yourself on the road to paradise. Take care, dear callers.

"Good luck to you.

"Good luck to us.

"Good luck to everyone."

BEEP.

No matter how she spent her days in South Park, either along the river or in the valley or up in the mountains, Kiwi LaReaux always made sure that she was back at Swami Bill's side by dusk, as the colors drained from the sky and the moon rose. Just at sunset, Swami Bill would set aside the day's commerce, get up from his portable camp chair, his parrot suddenly flapping madly on his shoulder. Bill turned toward the western sky, the mountains reflected for a long moment in his eyes, one green and one blue. There was a change in his voice, a shift from sales pitch to jessant threnode. Beyond the distant mountains, the edge of the sky seemed on fire, and Swami Bill would turn and invite everyone to join him in what he called his Sweet Hour of Prayer.

To Swami Bill, being an atheist meant only that he had not met a supreme being to believe in yet, not that he did not believe. He believed in the mountains, in the fiery twilight sky, in the rising shadows, the howl of a coyote on a distant ridge, in the chilly wind, in the river and in the valley below, in free enterprise and thrift, in Kiwi LaReaux and in his new idea of piping insect repelling frequencies of sound over commercial radio stations. One station had already signed up. Just think of it, Swami Bill told me, bug-free picnics and hikes and barbecues, baseball games and camping. Just keep the radio on, turn it up, point it toward the insect hordes. It was the latest human miracle, bugless rock 'n' roll.

Kiwi LaReaux would sit on the card table, the day's fading light glowing in her red hair, in her luminescent green eyes.

A cold wind came off the mountains. Near the summits, the great snowfields shimmered in wrinkled spectrums of light, Mexican opal, iridescent oranges, boiling pinks, primal reds, diluvian grays. Sometimes there was a raven on the wing or the rattle of trees shuddering in the wind. Swami Bill smiled, watched the sun set as he leaned against his portable card table piled high with purbas, Thangras, pocket pujas, cobalt blue malas, brilliantly colored prayer flags handmade by the nuns of Lobsering, India, FREE TIBET bumper stickers, chod drums, saffron and sandalwood, nagi and raw musk incense, yellow Katas scarves, booklets on self-massage, on chanting your way to immediate wish fulfillment and macrobiotic cooking, and cassette tapes of Kiwi LaReaux singing a selection of earth songs.

Swami Bill's Sweet Hour of Prayer, though, was mostly a private affair. Bill said little. He did not fold his hands or bow his head, but always stood looking at the dome of fading daylight and smiling as pale blue shadows drifted across his face. Once, well beyond Hoosier Pass, not far from the Frying Pan River, just as Swami Bill had turned to watch the sun set, to begin his Hour of Sweet Prayer, an elderly woman from Boise, Idaho, who had a face that looked like a boiled potato and who had just bought a boxed set of Swami Bill's self-help tapes along with a cassette of *Holistic Hymns and Primal Melodies* performed by Kiwi LaReaux and the Ashrama Jazz Band, went milk white, dropped her bag of tapes, fought off a case of the hiccups long enough to ask Kiwi LaReaux what was going on. Had the Swami gone mad? she wanted to know. Was it a vision? Indigestion? Could she get a heavy discount on the crystal singing bowls? And Kiwi told the old lady about the Sweet Hour of Prayer, how, to Swami Bill, it was sort of a holistic Happy Hour and that anyone could join in and take part.

"What should we pray for?" asked the old woman from Boise. She was part of a group that had paid for an eco-adventure, and she wanted to make sure she got her $4,000-worth of earth experience, even if it meant dropping to her arthritic knees in prayer in a parking lot in the mountains of Colorado.

Kiwi LaReaux was smiling shyly. "Anything and everything," she said.

The old woman let loose of her lightweight aluminum walker, clasped her gnarled blue-and-white hands together, and prayed mightily that Social Security would hang on until she died.

A couple from Salt Lake City asked God for a child and a winning lottery number.

An aging Vietnam veteran prayed out loud that the phantom feelings he had had for years and years, feelings that lied to him and told him his blown-off arms and legs were still part of him, attached, pink and healthy and ready for action, would stop, go away. He prayed to feel no more than what he had, stumps.

I do not know what Kiwi LaReaux prayed for, or if she prayed at all. Swami Bill told me that she prayed for the souls of the departed, for everything that was, is, and will be, for more and more common decency.

I will gladly tell you how I spent every Hour of Sweet Prayer.

I prayed that Kiwi's perfect green eyes would never turn blue.

My mother's eyes were green, pale green with flecks of hazel and cinnamon. By the time the tumors in her brain killed her, her eyes had gone blue—vivid blue, crystal blue, wild blue.

My great-uncle Albert died of brain cancer, too. Before his eyes went deadly blue, they had been a soft, almost liquid brown.

Months later, after I had cleaned out another desk, packed up the Toyota with my shrinking heap of stuff, as I headed over the mountains of the Front Range for the last time, headed south and west toward northern New Mexico, I slipped in the first tape of Swami Bill's *Ashrama Chronicles*. I listened to the tapes all the way to New Mexico.

The tapes' subliminal messages were anything but subliminal or even subtle.

At random moments during the tapes, Swami Bill's stentorian voice would come welling up, cheerfully drowning out singing whales and chirping birds, the resonance of mountain waterfalls and the melancholy moan of sudden summer thunderstorms, overwhelming cascading rivers and yowling winds, the roar of ocean waves breaking against shores of stone, and the heavy organic breathing of tropical rain forests.

And suddenly there would be just Swami Bill's voice, or rather Saddhu, the parrot, speaking in Bill's voice, repeating some word or phrase over and over again, saying the words with an aching tenderness and earnestness.

"Paddle your own canoe.

"Forgive and forget.

"Easy come, easy go.

"Let go.

"Fish or cut bait."

At the end of the last tape, Swami Bill's voice rises above the crack of lightning and the roar of rolling thunder, and while the storm goes on and on, Swami Bill recites these words written by Chuang Tzu in about 3,000 B.C.

Consequently: he who wants to
Have right without wrong,
Order without disorder,
Does not understand the principles
Of Heaven and Earth,
He does not know how
Things hang together.

And there followed a long moment of silence, then Swami Bill's voice again, as soft as a sigh.

"To all of you,

"OLLIE-OLLIE-OXEN-FREE!

"Pass it on.

"Pass it on."

RIO DE LAS ANIMAS

Here by the river,
Drink and bathe thy limbs,
Or cast thy net, and surely
It shall be filled with fish.

—EGYPTIAN BOOK
OF THE DEAD

Kiwi LaReaux would later tell
me that Swami Bill's Sweet Hour of Prayer was more than a spiritual Happy Hour, more than an hour of joy and hope and jazzy
ecstasy for all human beings, believers and nonbelievers alike.

Kiwi LaReaux told me that Bill was using the Sweet Hour of
Prayer to piece together a new religion. So far, Swami Bill's new
religion was a work in progress and had only working titles.
Among them, said Kiwi LaReaux, was the Church of Common
Decency, the Brotherhood of Fair Shakes, the Communion of Tol-
eration, the Dignity of Kindred Souls.

Kiwi LaReaux also told me that Bill had already decided on
many of the new church's creeds. She whispered them, smiling
shyly.

"Live and Let Live."

"Grin and Abide."

"More Grace."

"Pay As You Go."

I am responsible for one of the harmless creeds that are part of
Swami Bill's church in progress.

Here is my contribution:

"More laughter."

That is what my mother said to me often the week before she died, as the tumors in her brain went about killing her.

I like to think that whenever my mother smiled and said "more laughter," as the tumors in her brain hauled her in and out of reason and in and out of time, what she meant was simply that human beings could get through a lot of life's most ridiculous and humiliating moments easier if they laughed more. I like to think that what my mother was telling me was that laughter could ease the pain and the loss, the sorrow and regret, that it could make our brains and chemicals, for a moment, as happy as clams, that laughter was one thing that could make the years go easily by.

"More laughter," said Kiwi LaReaux. "I like that. I like that a lot." Kiwi LaReaux thought about it for a moment and decided to add my contribution to the creeds of the Church of Common Decency, the Brotherhood of Fair Shakes, the Communion of Toleration, the Dignity of Kindred Souls, between "Live and Let Live" and "Grin and Abide."

"More laughter," sighed Kiwi LaReaux.

"A lot more," I said.

"A lot more."

Over a dinner of sweet-and-sour chicken, shrimp fried rice, and Mongolian beef at the Now & Zen Restaurant, on a cloudless night in early November, Mi Oh suggested to Swami Bill that whenever followers of the new religion met or gathered, they should greet each other like long-lost family rather than worshipers, that they should dance and sing, bang drums, hug and shake hands, whistle a happy-go-lucky tune.

Mi Oh was wearing her tight, sybaritic, licorice red hostess dress, the one with the embroidered gold dragon that undulated across her breasts.

Swami Bill pushed aside the plates of sweet-and-sour chicken

and Mongolian beef, the bowls of steaming shrimp fried rice, and shook Mi Oh's delicate small hand, kissed her on both warm, smooth cheeks, hugged her and her dragon close, tight against his apple green monk's robe, whistled a happy tune, clapped and chirped merrily, took hold of her and danced her around the table, rolling his bright eyes, one green and one blue, smiling wildly, while overhead the little bells hanging from the ceiling trilled, sounding like the rush of a distant spring creek splashing over smooth stones.

While Swami Bill and the lovely Mi Oh greeted each other like long-lost family and sang happy-go-lucky songs, I watched the wet reflection of the table's red paper lanterns in Kiwi LaReaux's green eyes and thought of the big brown trout I had seen weeks before in the swift water just above a deep green pool in the Middle Fork of the South Platte River below Spinney Mountain.

It was early morning when I first saw the brown trout. I had been fishing the river below the Spinney Mountain Reservoir since dawn. The brown trout were still on the move, leaving the lake's deep, cold, dark water, entering the river to spawn.

It had been a good morning. I had hooked and released three trout along a single long chute of fast water near where the blue-green river tumbled over shoals of eroded stones and into a large pool of olive green water. From there the river arched gently into a wide slack-jawed bend that eventually gave way to a series of loose, generous coils of faster water and quiet, long runs where shimmering shadows wrinkled across the surface of the river.

Where the river's current edged out of the deep pool, spilled over a dark spine of smooth stones, the water was the same blend of blues and greens as the Gulf Stream, while the deeper water of the wide pool wore the meadow's fall colors, a glinting cloak of muted blues and soft greens and, at the edges, where the intimations of the meadow and mountains rolled on the surface of the water, the decayed yellow of spent jonquils.

The first trout I caught along the river was a small cutthroat. I was fishing well below the pool, along a run of fast water. I felt the trout before I saw it. It struck with a ferocity that left me trembling and gasping, smiling and laughing, all at once.

Why? Because my ruinous addiction to mountain rivers and wild trout had endured, was as wonderfully disastrous as ever. I was hooked as deeply as the trout. Hooked, for a passing moment, to its world, the natural world, the good earth, the press of life in a rush of swift trout water in that high mountain meadow. For a junkie there is nothing like the moment his addiction is fed, momentarily downed in the glow and flush of satisfaction, fleeting fulfillment.

I worked the small cutthroat trout more with the line than with the fly rod because I wanted to feel its every move, its every twist and shudder, feel its uncompromising wildness, the fly line as conductive as copper, jazzing every muscle and nerve and bone with fish and river, the wind in the meadow, the great blue autumn sky. Each time the trout flinched, I worked the line, as if I were almost consciously trying somehow to stitch the moment into my senses, into the folds of my memory—a moment forever alive and vital and immediate.

Bringing the cutthroat trout near, I carefully removed the tiny wet fly from its jaw, watched it as it hung for a long instant in the shallow water, its smooth back a smear of liquid colors, neon yellows and glaucous greens, the distinctive red slash on its lower jaw gleaming like a fresh wound.

I could feel the smile on my face.

Contact.

Connection.

It was good to be so thoroughly and shamelessly hooked again.

Contact and connection. That is what my passion and need and obsession for mountain rivers, for wild water and wild trout is all about—the deep ache to be joined again, even if for a passing moment, to the natural world, that part of life in which everything is whole and united, mountains and rivers, trout and human beings.

To the good earth, as I keep saying.

Home sweet home.

I took a careful step from the edge of the ragged shoal of dark stones and into the shallow river down below the deep green pool, where the river looked like loose loops of rope coiling through the broad meadow. The river's current was swift, and the surface of the water seemed a storm of flaring, coruscant light. The water pulled hard against my hip boots, and I could feel the cold river against my skin. I stood there for a long time as the river carried me out of depression's wasteland.

I cast my line again and the river rolled on and on.

If I was thinking at all, it was only of the cutthroat trout, the river and meadow, the hulking mountains in the near distance. I hesitate to burden this trout or any trout with statistics, the banal hubris of weight and measure. The more statistics, the less wonder, at least for me. Statistics have a way of reducing a trout's allure, stripping away its mystery, and I am hooked more on mystery than on size, more on wild water and mountains than on poundage. It is where a trout can haul me that I tend to remember, not angling's hardware or fly-fishing's techniques. It is the flash of a trout's flanks, the alchemy of its shape and power and color, its nature and wildness that I memorize, not its length and weight.

There were two more cutthroat trout before noon, each one an amazement: a living expression of the river, the deep mountain valley, an amalgam of habitat and sunlight and water, mystery, biology, and organic chemistry.

I did not measure them, or guess their weight, take their photographs. I cannot recall what fly I took them on, except to say it was one they liked.

But I can tell you where they hauled me.

Back and forth and in and out of time.

Even to the edges of the universe.

Some trip.

It always is.

And I can tell you what it felt like when that trout struck, when I hooked it and it hooked me, what it feels like every time.

It felt exactly like the first time, the first trout, when I was a boy, years ago and far away, in other mountains, along another cold, fast, bright mountain river, a river marked by a limitless mingling of sunlight and shadow, endless mixtures of time and life and history. That first trout was a moment of undistilled sensation—simple, honest joy, uncomplicated happiness, undiluted experience, a moment beyond intellect and explanation, a feeling sweeping through blood and bone and flesh like a sudden rush of wind.

I was smiling and laughing. My brain was as happy as a clam. Perhaps it was remembering, as the trout struck, that world before consciousness, that raw, wild, and ancient world, deep and complete, which included human beings, that world beyond the angst of embarrassing self-consciousness.

I was lying on my stomach in the cool, soft, yellow-green grass, below the bottom edge of the deep green pool in the bend of the river below Spinney Mountain, thinking of that first trout, that first wonderfully ruinous trout, caught when I was a boy, long ago and far away, in the deep dark waters of Karen's Pool on Starlight Creek.

I was living with my grandfather Emerson and my great-uncle Albert and Elias Wonder, the full-blooded Sioux Indian that everyone in Mount Hebron thought was a madman, everyone but me and Albert and Emerson. I thought then exactly as I do now—that Elias Wonder was the sanest human being I have ever known, even if World War I had left him with a brain full of mustard gas, even if he had been struck by lightning three times, even if he never wore shoes and kept on trying to die until he succeeded, dying in his sleep of complications from a common cold.

If Elias Wonder were alive today, every time I saw him I would, as a founding member of Swami Bill's new church, the Church of Common Decency, the Brotherhood of Fair Shakes, the Communion of Toleration, the Dignity of Kindred Souls, greet him like long-lost family, with songs and hugs, a happy-go-lucky dance and handshake.

I dug Elias Wonder's grave. It was wide and deep. His body was wrapped in blankets. We lowered Elias Wonder's body into the freshly dug grave with ropes. It took all three of us.

Death is heavy.

And then I shoveled all the rufescent dirt back into the dark hole and stuck a simple white handmade wooden cross at the head of the grave. All the while, Albert played his harmonica, a low-down, weary-souled tune by the Mississippi Delta bluesman Robert Johnson. The sound was like a storm yowling across the land, groaning down the eroded ridges of the worn-out Ozark Mountains.

Albert finished playing, put his harmonica in his shirt pocket, and said, "Good-bye, Wonder. Happy Trails."

After we buried Elias Wonder, Albert could not find the truck, could not remember where he'd left it. It was down below the cemetery, in the cool shade of a stand of oak trees, right where he had parked it.

What Albert did not know, what none of us yet knew, was that there was a tumor in Albert's brain nibbling away at his memory, killing him slowly, one memory at a time.

We buried Albert near Elias Wonder.

Good-bye, Albert. Happy Trails.

A year later, Emerson died in his sleep. He was buried near Albert and Elias Wonder.

I did not dig his grave and bury him. When I finally did get back to the mountains, I visited the old cemetery, found Emerson's grave.

Good-bye Emerson, Happy Trails.

That first trout, the trout that rose from the depths of Karen's Pool, came up from a chaos of half-submerged, slick, moss-covered, gray-green stones near the head of the pool, left me trembling and smiling and laughing and inexorably hooked, addicted before I had even felt its full weight or seen its dark eyes or the blush of colors on its back. That trout left me breathless, then left me yelling, the shouts coming from deep in my belly. That trout filled my senses, my mind and imagination. When I finally saw it, it seemed like some strange blend of faded sunset and rising shadow, night winds, cloudy moonglow and vague starlight.

That trout was a brown trout.

So was the trout I saw rise in the deep green pool below Spinney Mountain along the Middle Fork of the South Platte River, where I lay in the cool, tall, swaying meadow grasses watching its shadow: a thick, watery adumbration wrinkling down in the green water, a heavy, lumpish silhouette hanging at the edge of the river's current. I imagined its blunt head pointed upstream, its tail constantly twitching, its muscles rippling along its back and flanks.

Every quiver of that silhoutte was as alluring as that of a dancer framed in shadow.

As shards of gray clouds drifted across the green surface of the pool, softening the light, the dense shadow rose slightly, an eloquence of motion, its outline like that of some caliginous pigboat or a black bladder of leaking air. Once the clouds had passed, the instant the day's rouge of sunlight again claimed the surface of the pool, the shadow would quickly vanish, sink deeper into the green water, down beyond the sunlight's hot glow, its glint and glare, and lie on the bottom, its soft belly against the rounded black stones, lie there still as an omen, a dark presence: finned dybbuk, gilled Masan, more mystery than fact, as much a product of the imagination as of the river, phantasm-cloaked vital flesh.

Just at dusk, as the sunlight bled from the sky beyond the valley and a cold wind rattled down the subfuscous flanks of the mountains, the fish's dense, dark shadow appeared again, threaded out of the deep water, rose, this time to the near edge of the pool, where twilight's first shadows crept out of the tall grasses and across the pool's surface.

The trout's back arched suddenly, broke the surface, showing its lines, efficient and graceful, practical and elegant. Its colors were a living geography of river and pool, meadow and mountains. In the fading light, it glowed in layers of colored light—the warm gold of melted honey, the pale green of the meadow, the deep green of the pool, the blue-green of the river's current just along its back, its belly the yellow of spent aspen leaves, its head the beryl green of early twilight. Its flanks and dorsal fin were marked by a chaos of irregular splotches, black as the mountain peaks ribbed hard against starless skies. Each spot looked like an eclipsed sun ringed with coronas of amber or sulfur yellow, burnt orange, the deep red of crushed poppies.

Salmo trutta.

Brown trout. Slack-jawed and swag-bellied. Moody, sullen, pig-headed, arbitrary, paranoid, aggravating, antisocial, suspicious, erratic, eccentric, mercurial, morose, splenetic, churlish, fractious, ill-humored, wary, excitable, psychotic, pixilated.

Mad as a hatter.

A piscine depressive.

A trout evidently down with a case of the meat bucket blues.

A fellow sufferer.

Small universe.

The brown trout in the deep green pool of the Middle Fork of the South Platte River was the descendant of immigrants.

So am I.

So are most Americans.

Brown trout did not arrive in North America by way of the Age of Fishes, evolving out of the warming, basal, organic waters of some primordial sea. Instead, they arrived by boat in the 1880s, passengers aboard the ocean liner *Werra,* which docked in New York City.

There were eighty thousand brown-trout eggs carefully packed in special crates converted into cool, aqueous nests. The eggs were small and gummy, chilly and opalescent. The eggs had come from Germany, a gift to an American, Fred Mather, from Lucius von Behr. Von Behr had befriended Mather at the International Fisheries Exposition held in Berlin. Von Behr told Mather about the wonderful trout of German streams, brown trout, and invited Mather to fish with him.

To Mather any invitation to go trout fishing sounded like an invitation to paradise. He accepted and quickly developed a ruinous addiction for brown trout.

Mather wanted desperately to share the joys of his shiny new obsession with brown trout, his exhilaration, with his fellow American anglers, so he accepted von Behr's generous gift, and the eggs were loaded on the *Werra* and crossed the Atlantic, rising and falling rhythmically with the sea as they nuzzled in their comfortable nursery in the ocean liner's dark, chilly, cargo hold.

Once ashore in New York City, the brown-trout eggs did what many immigrant families did when they set foot in America, another paradise, the land of opportunity. They split up.

Some of the eggs ended up in the Long Island Fish Hatchery run by Mather. Some ended up in the Beaverkill River in the Catskills, a river already renowned for its native brook trout. The rest traveled north and west to Northville, Michigan. The survivors were eventually set loose in the nearby Père Marquette River.

Which became North America's first brown trout river.

Home Sweet Home.

Later, the German brown trout were joined and mixed with their black-spotted cousins imported from Scotland, the Loch Leven brown trout.

Germans and Scots.

Some gene pool.

Family.

If they had been human beings and members of Swami Bill's religion in progress, the Church of Common Decency, the Ministry Brotherhood of Fair Shakes, the Communion of Toleration, the Dignity of Kindred Souls, they would have greeted each other like long-lost family, with smiles and dances, earnest embraces, and happy-go-lucky songs.

My own gene pool is swimming with contributions from the Welsh, Irish, and Scotts. Somewhere in there, someone arrived in America, in paradise, in the land of opportunity, with a whopping case of depression, of the meat bucket blues, and passed it along.

Passed it along.

Brown trout have become veteran travelers. Maybe there is some chemical in them that generates wanderlust, a trait not shared by some of their kinsmen, especially the cutthroat and wild brook trout.

Since their arrival aboard the ocean liner *Werra,* brown trout, of one variety or another, have been successfully, if not willingly, introduced throughout most of North America. Originally, brown trout ranged only from the streams of the Mediterranean Basin north and east to the Black Sea, to the cold streams and lakes of Norway, even to the cold dark wild waters of Siberia. These days, however, brown trout can be found from South America to New Zealand, from North America to parts of Asia and Africa.

Brown trout are survivors. What have they done to survive?

Whatever was necessary.

What do they require to survive?

What they have always required: water still edged with wildness, water not yet completely commercialized or compromised by the press of human beings and civilization, even though brown trout are more tolerant of both than are most other trout.

Not that brown trout like change. Rather, they are able to survive it, to absorb and adapt to most of it, even if only moodily, stubbornly.

Brown trout hang on, in large measure, because they are at once fiercely opportunist and tenaciously ecumenical, being able not only to survive but to thrive in a wide range of water conditions. In that water which best suits them and is rich in food, isolation, and solitude, brown trout can grow into true piscine behemoths.

Statistics, again.

How big? More than thirty pounds. A lot of trout. But, then, any brown trout is a lot of trout, a significant fish. How big was the brown trout in the deep pool of green water in the Middle Fork of the South Platte River below Spinney Mountain?

Big enough.

I did not see the brown trout or its substantial shadow again for two days.

After its exit from the Spinney Mountain Reservoir, the river bends and loops lazily through the valley for three miles before flowing into Eleven Mile Reservoir. Between the two reservoirs, where the river runs unmolested, there are trout, plenty of trout—rainbows and cutthroats and leery brown trout. Although I fished this bright serpenting ribbon of river for almost three months, spending every weekend along its banks from dawn until after nightfall, I do not think I covered more than half its length. Indeed, there were days when my journey along the river did not cover two hundred yards, the trout rising hungrily in sunlight and shadow to feed on aquatic and terrestrial insects.

Where it was wide and swift, the river was often no more than two feet deep. I fished these long runs of river first, early in the mornings. I carried everything I needed in my shirt pockets, including a handful of various tiny trout flies tucked safely into waterproof matchboxes. There were mussed emergers and blue-winged olives, rumpled blue duns and blue quills, endlessly tempting woolly buggers, each looking gut-shot and half dead.

Brown trout, including the old brown trout in the deep green pool below Spinney Mountain, are piscivorous. They eat other fish, even other brown trout. It is nothing personal.

They are also carnivorous. They will eat just about anything that comes along, including crawfish and mollusks, including frogs and their relatives, including small members of my own tribe, mammals. Baby birds and mice sometimes fall victim to brown trout.

Bad luck.

Lousy fortune.

A brown trout that is not eaten by sculpin, dace, darters, kingfishers, other trout, including its mother, and survives three years is more than mature. It is old.

The brown trout in the deep green pool of the river below Spinney Mountain was such a trout.

Old.

And sightless. Blind.

I did not see its eyes when I first glimpsed the trout's dense shadow rise briefly in the deep green water of the pool, near the undercut bank where the meadow grasses were tall, lush, yellow-green, and swaying gently in the autumn wind.

Neither did I notice the trout's eyes when I hooked it for the first time, as it took the wet fly and went deep, and easily broke the tippet and left me kneeling in the tall grass below the pool and smiling. Neither had I seen its eyes when it rose to the surface of the pool as rafts of sunless clouds drifted across the sky, throwing a caul of shadow over the pool. The big brown trout rolled on the surface, its back and flanks flashing arcs of dazzling color, colors in motion that illuminated the deepening twilight.

I first saw the brown trout's blind eyes just at sunset, in the blush of early twilight, the sun fading intimations of light—tapers of maroon and orange and coral pinks, flambeaus of indigo and cerulean. I had been fishing the river upstream, below the pool. The evening wind was calm, hardly more than a chilly sigh against the skin, and the mountains appeared crouched in lavish layers of purple shadow.

I cannot recall now what fradulent temptation, what tapestry of feather and fur and colored thread I cast upstream and across the river, dropped on to the surface of the water where it spiraled for an instant like a spent insect. A rainbow trout took it instantly, swallowing it whole—feathers, fur, colored thread, and hook— throwing itself into the air, twisting its body violently, a spray of glistening water coming off its silver head and tail, dripping from the sanguine smear along its flanks. As the rainbow trout twisted in the chilly evening sunlight above the surface of the river, I imagined it there in midair to be a wrinkle in time.

I brought it near, let it go.

The three miles of the Middle Fork of the South Platte River be- tween the Spinney Mountain and Eleven Mile reservoirs are strictly catch and release. I release them twice: once in their na- tive water and once in the wild rivers of light and fast water that have shaped the country of my memory and imagination.

Minutes after I released the rainbow trout, I had fished my way back to the lower reaches of the big pool of deep green water, a distance of perhaps fifty yards.

I sat and rested on a small hump of wet, cool grass below the pool. Each blade of grass was encased in a liquid sleeve of glis- tening dew and diaphanous light. At that spurtive instant every- thing appeared candescent—the widening evening sky, the river, the sprawling meadows, the ridges of the distant mountains, even the edges of single stones.

Everything.

Even the blind eyes I was suddenly looking into, the sightless eyes of the big brown trout that was suddenly at the far side of the pool, in shallow water, near the undercut bank, near the sur- face, at the edge of the river's blue-green current, where it gave way to the pool's deeper, slower water.

Opaque eyes. Umbral, sunless pupils, the color of curdled milk. Withered gray-blue cataracts had claimed both eyes, so that they looked like murky distant galaxies floating at the edge of some marrow black universe.

And yet, as the twilight took hold, as the last of the day's sunlight receded, dissolved into wide rivers of thin colored light on the shoulders of the darkened mountains, shimmered on the surface of the deep green pool, the blind trout's eyes, around the cadaverous pupils and in the moist, sloe black tissue of the conjunctivas, sparkled with particles and waves of light. Its sightless eyes pulsed with points of incipient light, glistening microbic light, amoebic, germinal light, all of it glowing in the damp, evanescent universe of that trout's blind eyes that shone like a darkened cathedral illuminated only by the radiant flames of votary candles.

The trout's eyes still gathered light, held light the old trout could feel but could not see. Before the cataracts took its sight, left it blind, the brown trout in the deep green pool of the river, like all brown trout, had had remarkable vision, eyes capable of focusing, at once, on objects both near and far. The brown trout had seen its world clearly by night as well as day, in detail, as completely, perhaps, as any creature can. The old brown trout, as I learned, however, had lost its sight, not its vision. As the days passed, as I watched it and fished for it, crawled on my belly through the meadow grass to steal a glimpse of it, it seemed to me that the trout saw its world as clearly, in as much detail, as it ever had, not by seeing but by touch, feeling the river constantly against its flesh. What the trout had once seen whole, it now felt whole and alive and moving through every cell, so that it had become, in a way, the river and the meadow, valley and mountains, every wind, every slant of sunlight, every touch of shadow, that whole bright country. It moved as the river moved, moved with its ebb and its flow, its coming and going, as the highly sensitive cells along its lateral line flooded the trout's world with low-frequency vibrations and absorbed their echoes, the living river etched in inaudible sounds and dim electrical impulses, silent

throbs and pulses, every detail translated into sepulchral resonances.

The old brown trout sank back slowly into the deep green water, rose again near the top edge of the pool, where a long chute of swift water splashed over a ledge of pinched stones before giving in to the deep pool's green waters. I shifted slightly in the damp, cool grass, raised my head a little, hoping for another look at the brown trout and its blind eyes that were bowls of tissue absorbing light and color and shadow.

The trout felt that unnatural shift of weight which was me on the river bank, a sudden alien tremble of ground, and turned, vanished, leaving only a tear of colored light that had leaked from its blind eyes, mixed inexorably with the river.

I had seen that light, that color before. In Albert's eyes, in my mother's eyes, in Dr. Truth's eyes.

No matter when or where I fished the river, ultimately I found myself back at the pool of deep green water below Spinney Mountain, casting my line onto its still waters or just lying in the tall, cool grass below the pool where I could watch and wait for the blind brown trout to rise, wait for its melanistic shadow to wrinkle at the edge of the pool, a seam of blue-black water, hope for some glimpse of its blunt head and slack jaws, its blind eyes flooded with light below the ragged, milky edges of its cataracts, a chaos of light that was both mysterious and bold, marked with hints of moon glow and iridescent coronas and translucent halos, all of it edged in a haunting, wild blue light, wild blue earthshine. As I stared at those blind eyes, those pools of reflected light sizzling with streamers of Bailey's Beads, the black flames of witch fires, the pure green flames of St. Elmo's fire.

All of it leaking out of the corners of a brown trout's blind eyes.

Where the river was deep, I would walk down its grassy banks, wade into the cold water, cast my rumpled flies along the edge of the current, let them sink below the bright surface, drown as naturally as possible. The cold and irresistible river pulled at my calves and thighs, and dawn spread across my hands and arms and face, a veil of chilly sunlight and pale blue shadows. And I let myself drift in those veins of basal light between ultraviolet and visible light, the light where life began and where it hangs on, where life is as much residue as essence, where it is as much by-product as product, where life emerged not inevitably but by chance, coincidence, lucky accident, that range of light where life dances on the edge of entropy and deletion, cancellation and oblivion.

Lucky us.

Casting my line over the bright river at dawn, I let concentration dissolve and thought of the first rainbow trout I had taken along the river, how it leapt, hung for an instant in midair, its body wrenching violently, desperate to break free from whatever pulled against it, how when it jumped that last time, just in front of me, the spray from its silver head and back soaked my face. Later, up on the grassy river bank, dozing in and out of sleep, under a warming autumn sun, I thought of the sudden feel of the cold river on my face and imagined that the sensation was something like anhydrobiosis: that condition where some seed of life waits suspended in heat and drought, armored against time as it patiently waits for the touch of water, salvation. It resists everything but water and when water comes, the seed cracks, squirms to life.

Something deep in me cracked and squirmed to life as the cold spray coming off that jumping trout soaked my face, something deep, something that had been shut down, suspended, had gone cold and inert. Something was moved, revived. It was an odd moment, like being caught in a rare instance of conscious myoclonus, every muscle and nerve jumping and twitching. As I dozed in and out of sleep there in the cool, damp meadow

grasses by the river, under the warming mountain sun, I could feel myself smiling again and thinking that if depression can darken the soul, so, too, can its passage deepen it.

I told Kiwi LaReaux about the rainbow trout and my muscles' wild, involuntary dance of excitement as the trout leapt and doused me with cold river water, that feeling of revival, of squirming to life.

Kiwi LaReaux did what she always did. She smiled shyly.

Whenever I was along the river, fishing its bright water, I let myself go, emptied my head, let the moving river soothe my ache for contact and connection, ease my heart's ancient longing for its legacy of wildness.

My little fly rod would twitch and I would follow, willingly, as though it were some some kind of low-rent divining rod. It led me off the banks, out of the yellowing late-autumn meadows and into the river's cold, blue-green current, sinking me not in sense but in sensation, pulling me down to a lower consciousness, that place of mind that was whole rather than fragmented, wet and organic, ancient and elemental, before it was anything else. And the river pulled me down, past Zeus and Kronos, past Uranus and Allah and Jehovah, Indra and Brahma, down past every god, to the honest company of the first progenitors, earth and sun, wind and water, day and night, things diluvian and protoplasmic, mysterious and magical, that soft fold of flesh where there was spirit before there was reason or intellect, that time when a human being's need for dance and wonder was greater than his need for murder, conquest, and domination.

Moving water. River water. Wild water. The earth's pulse: life's cante jondo, its inviolate hymn, its oldest lullaby.

The rhythm of things that ebb and flow.

Come and go.

I took another cutthroat trout from the long chute of fast water below the green pool. I saw the trout rise and strike, saw the distinctive red gash on its lower jaw. Under the trout's relentless pull, the little fly rod bent, and I bent with it, feeling the trout through line and rod, feeling it in my fingers and hands and arms.

As I stripped in the slack line, beads of cold river water trickled down my hands, and my memory stirred. The skin is memory's first storyteller, its shaman, the tireless accumulator and connoisseur of touch and feel. What lives moves and what moves leaves its mark, its feel, its touch, its trace. More of us is left on the wind than at Heaven's gate.

Often, as I fished the river below Spinney Mountain in the valley of South Park, a cold wind would come off the mountains, rattle down the valley and across the river, and I would look out over the tall, swaying, yellowing grasses of the meadow, and in that shuddering membrane of wind and sunlight, shadow and mountain, was certain that I saw some lingering impression of Kiwi LaReaux walking through the meadow, along the river, her long, wild, red hair pulled back off her freckled neck with a single blue ribbon, her presence remaining, alive on the sweet-smelling wind, becoming some metaphor of motion, of sunlight and mountain, of bright river and high country meadow.

Life is like that, I think, always leaving hints of itself wherever it passes. Years ago, in a shallow cave at the mouth of Seminole Canyon, which is a long-dead tributary of the Rio Grande River in the seemingly endless sprawl of west Texas, I spent hours staring at petroglyphs on the cave's walls, drawn with simple paints made of the earth's own colors by ancient man, ancestors of the American Indian, who hunted these once wild, bountiful plains thousands of years ago.

As the hours passed, I found myself drawn back, again and again, to a single small petroglyph drawn low on the cave wall, about as high as a young boy can reach. The petroglyph was not of lost gods or shamans or honored beasts. It was the tracing, in earth red, of a hand, a human hand. And that hand seemed to speak a common tongue, seemed to be saying what human beings seem desperate to say in one way or another,

"I lived.

"I was here."

I reached through time and history and touched that handprint traced on the shallow cave's wall in Seminole Canyon, placed my hand against its outline.

It fit. A perfect match.

It was a haunting sensation. As I pressed my hand against the outline of that human being's hand traced on the cave's wall thousands and thousands of years ago, I was sure I felt that hand press back.

The tug of wild water, the handprint of ancient man, a chilly wind against the skin, the feel of sun on the face and neck, the intimation of Kiwi LaReaux in the meadow, along the river, a body of wind and shadow and grass rather than flesh. Sensation. The touch of things, the feel of things. Implications of shadow. Possibilities of moving water. Nuances and allusion of grass and earth and stone. The skin is more than wrinkled and awkward hide, weak and imperfect flesh. It is a membrane, one so jazzed and wired that it seems like some exiled fold of the brain, capable of much more than cataloging stimuli.

Life's a rub that soon eats to the bone. Skin is the meal it dines on. Skin is buffer and protection and flash point, where life is either sloughed off or hauled into memory, where experience lays down its purple scars, just as living takes its toll. At least twice a day, the first two layers of skin die and are replaced. The dead cells fall away; the life they felt stays, part of the flesh's ongoing narrative, a geography pocked with life's every breath and bruise, every emotion, the stink of fear and failure, the blanch of love, the infrequent blush of success, marks of landscape, leached dreams, faded desires.

The beat-up skin of the blind brown trout in the deep green

pool of the river is such a living map, as well, an almanac of scales and cells and thick flesh that quavers with the details of the trout's own history, a story of river and pool, mountains and meadow, sunlight, wind, and shadow. So, too, is my skin an aging geography of flesh, a chronicle of my own comings and goings, memory's quarry. Muldoon's faded china-blue tattoo cut into my left arm. Scars pink and violet, some bleached white, meander across my hands and arms and chest, scars seared into flesh and into memory.

The beautiful wild brown trout that rose out of the dark waters of the Rio Grande River near Taos, New Mexico, is stitched in scar tissue across the top of my left hand. So, too, is the scorpion that stung me as I read by lantern light in an abandoned adobe hut in Terlingua in Texas' vast Big Bend country. That was when Terlingua was still a ghost town, before its now-famous chili cook-offs brought it back to life. When the scorpion stung me I was reading a novel by Joseph Heller. Come to think of it, I was reading Heller or Vonnegut or Annie Dillard the night the mosquito on Cochino Grande Island, off the coast of Honduras, dropped its load of malaria into my blood, when I felt the tarantulas in my sleeping bag scurrying up my naked legs and belly. The tarantulas were as frightened as I was.

Some of the pinched, thick, ragged scars on my hands and arms come from grenade shrapnel, the flesh's record of the instant that Norwood pulled the pin on the perfectly preserved World War II Japanese hand grenade in the crystal clear waters of a lovely stream beneath the lush jungles of Okinawa.

On the palms of my hands are the deep, wrinkled marks of William Marley Bubo's hand line and the memory of that night the big tuna took the fresh bait, that chunk of pearl white bonita belly, and went deep, hauled Bubo's handmade wooden canoe out beyond sight of the islands, beyond the white skeleton of the reef, and into the deep, dark water. And all the while fever burned in my brain and took me in and out of time and in and out of endless worlds, and along the horizon was the yellow

shower curtain Bubo used for a sail, a yellow sail that glowed in my fever like a rising sun.

Below my right elbow is the smooth, deep pocket of sewn skin where even hair will not grow anymore. I thought the hole was the mark of some exotic tropical skin ulcer until a doctor in Salt Lake City, Utah, cut it open, widened it, went in and scraped the muscle and tendons clean of pus and infection. He said I had something called marine tuberculosis, an infection the doctor said I probably had gotten from years and years of handling fish. Apparently there are more ways for fish to get under a man's skin than I had ever imagined.

The skin at the back of my neck, my face, my arms and hands, all of it is now permanently dark, holding the remembered light and heat and color of the sunrises and sunsets I have known, all all those countless ranges of mountain light flashing off the bright, fast water of wild rivers, cold winds, blistering winds, dead black winds. These days, just the feel of sunlight or a wind off the mountains, rising off the surface of moving water, a coyote's yowl in the distance, late at night, as county garbage truck No. 2 creeps down these worn-out Alabama mountains, a grind of breaks and gears, stirs my skin's corpus of memory, its strange menagerie of life's details, and I will give way to one of them and fall into memory's rich and warm embrace, ride the wind and starlight to some river that meanders through my mind and imagination, full of the trout of yesteryear, like the brown trout in that deep green pool below Spinney Mountain along the Middle Fork of the South Platte River.

These days, as I haul myself on to the back of county garbage truck No. 2, it is not unusual for me to ride the winds and starlight to some fine memory of wild country and trout. Before he got fired for stealing a smoked turkey off a lady's grill the night before Thanksgiving, Woody Moos was on the back of county garbage truck No. 2 as well, deep in his own memories, sobbing gently into his slimy green muffler, singing sweetly and sadly the song he sang every night:

Row, row, row your boat
Gently down the stream
Merrily, merrily, merrily, merrily,
Life is but a dream.

Kiwi LaReaux asked me only once about the latticework of scars on my hands and arms.

What did I tell her?

Only this: They are a ragged map of aging flesh, the wrinkled, sunburnt red geography of how I got from there to here, from here to there.

I was fishing about a half mile below the pool on the river where the blind brown trout lay sunk in the dark water, near where I had first seen streams of light and color drip from its sightless eyes.

Kiwi LaReaux was walking in the meadow along the river, her long red hair loose, looking like small jets of flame probing the afternoon sky's tapestry of spent yellows and bruised violets and deep blues.

Swami Bill had driven over Hoosier Pass to Breckenridge to drop off an order of one hundred silver amulets. They were tiny leak-proof bottles, each guaranteed to hold a healing drop of water from the Ganges River.

Holy water.

Millions and millions of down-and-out, luckless human beings, people afflicted with every kind of misery, physical and mental, travel to India, to the banks of the Ganges River, to sink themselves in the river, hoping that the river will do for them what life fails so miserably to do—wash their troubles away.

Kiwi LaReaux had a whole sack of the tiny silver amulets. She knelt by the river, sunk them in the shallow, translucent water.

"*Which* river doesn't matter much," said Kiwi LaReaux. "As long as it's water that's alive, water that's come from the mountains, with magic left in it."

Actually, Kiwi LaReaux called the Middle Fork of the South Platte the Rio de las Animas. The river of souls. She called every river Rio de las Animas, even the Ganges.

Swami Bill's tiny silver amulets, guaranteed to hold a magical drop of the Ganges River, held instead a magical drop of the Middle Fork of the South Platte, or the Gunnison, or the Frying Pan.

When he was a combat chaplain's assistant in South Vietnam, Bill had ushered the dead and dying into whatever vision of heaven they desired, yearned for.

As Swami Bill, cofounder, president, and CEO of Swami Bill Enterprises, Inc., he was still doing pretty much the same thing, giving people what they were desperate for, whether it was a tiny silver amulet of holy water from the Ganges River or marvelous bargains on singing crystal bowls, music spheres, his inspired, homemade cosmic OM tuning forks.

He gave them magic, heaven, paradise, nirvana, Never-Never Land, the magic of faith and luck, and it was all harmless and heavily discounted.

After Kiwi LaReaux had filled the tiny silver amulets, she dried them off in a blue fold of her pastel dress, held them in her open hands, each one gleaming. As she walked back up the river, she stopped, dropped one of the shining silver amulets in my shirt pocket.

"Here you go," she said, smiling shyly, "an unused wish.

"But I already know what you will wish for," she said.

"More laughter."

"A lot more," I said.

Kiwi LaReaux kept close to the river as she walked, close to the River of Souls. Beyond her, beyond the river, Swami Bill's butter yellow VW was at the rim of the meadow, shimmering in the light like some watery reflection of the sun at the edge of the horizon. Long after Kiwi LaReaux had gone, the wind smelled of her, held the wild color of her hair.

And I cast my line again and shed another million more skin cells. Even so, the smell and touch of Kiwi LaReaux lingered in wind and sunlight. The surface of the river was a glowing reflection of darkening skies and sunlight that made the mountains look as though they had been blasted out of the brooding sky, out of massifs of shadow and blood black light.

The skin keeps its own vault of memory, an anthology or florilegium, a miscellanea of experience traced upon flesh: deepening lines at the corners of my eyes, the curious wrinkles cut across my forehead that rise and fall like cheap venetian blinds with every thought and emotion, turn and tip of the head; my corpus of smiles and grimaces, my accumulation of shrugs and gestures. The nerves in my skin lie in wait, anticipating nothing, expecting everything.

While I fished the long loop of the river, as twilight seemed to leach fading sunlight even from the surface of stones, the muscles of my faced worked my mouth into a half smile, my skin's way of letting me know that it is content, that it is feeling just like my brain, as happy as a clam.

I worked the long elbow of shallow water until nightfall, casting just above the arch of the river, letting the fly drown slowly in the silver blue water, be gulped down below the surface, down into the current's dark throat.

A luminescent stream of crimson light suddenly broke through night's incipient shadows as they crept out of the low mountains, rose from the grass, slouched through the valley. Like bloody tears, the light poured briefly over the meadow, over the river, its surface looking like a wall of liquid fire. The light touched my skin, slid down my arms like a splatter of red rain. I knew those layers of skin crowded with their delta of blood vessels, millions of cells, hundreds of sweat glands, weary follicles, millions of twitching receptors and legions of Meissner's corpuscles and Pacinian corpuscles, nerves that feel more than stimuli, more than pressure, that feed on more than air and wind and river, heat and cold, pain and pleasure, love and hate, fear and mean-

ness, skin that feels even the weight of presence and intimation, the touch of the earth, the press of life's infinite details, even the traces of a day's last bloody light.

The light against my skin did not seem so much to dissolve and give way to night as to drain into my pores, giving my skin a momentary radiance, warming me to the bone. Somewhere in the sunburnt wrinkles of flesh and skin, a shard of crimson light remained, a warm and vital memory long after the light itself had been strangled from the widening night sky.

Living has a way of lingering on the skin which accepts or rejects it, interprets it, kills it or nourishes it, devours it, takes life in and passes it along.

Passes it along.

Standing in the chilly shallow water, I reeled in my line, watched the light quavering high up along the flanks of the mountains. It was the kind of light that gave the slower sections of the river the slow, heavy, thick look of heated mercury. Even through my waders, the river was cold, like an edged blade against my calves. The wind had come up, full of bird song and the splash of the river over dark stones.

Wild water, the continuity of mountain rivers, mimics time, seems at once constant and ephemeral, directed and directionless. Moments along a river come without implication, without topography, boundary, history, so that every moment is whole and inexorably bound to every other moment that is or was or ever will be, like a sting of haptic sensation—which is the almost inexpressible flood of experience reduced to essence, perhaps the mind's way of reducing life's chaos to images of light and shadow and familiar forms. In that sensation is every sensation, the history of life, even before we feel it, experience it, know it. Even before I ever saw a mountain river or stood along one, or fished its wild, cold waters, it seemed that such rivers, such water had always flowed through my blood and bones. I was born

hooked, just as some drunks are born alcoholic, hooked long before the swooning rush of that first drink. Perhaps it is simply some error of DNA, an awkward gene, quirky chemistry, flawed biology, some chromosomal mutation. Zap, you're an addictive personality. The question left hanging is what it will take to soothe the addiction. For some it's alcohol. Others soothe the rattles with drugs of one kind or another, or food, or gambling. There are as many addictions as there are versions of paradise.

For me, it's mountains and wild rivers and trout. Even the thought of high country gives my heart and head a buzz, makes my skin, the whole silly sack of it, two yards square, superficial epidermis and deep dermis, go flush, warm, and every cell tingle. Dead skin sloughs off continually, leaving me in a dim dust of keratin and pheromones. Dead skin cells are flat, empty husks. What they have felt, what they have experienced is siphoned through the pores, down through biochromic layers of skin, pigments brown and yellow, reds and purples, where it is tasted by nerves, forgotten or embraced and passed along to that undiscovered country of the brain, to that isolated, lonely fire that is the incomprehensible mysterium of mind and consciousness, memory and imagination.

SEVEN

NIGHT FISHING

The universe is infinite in all directions.

—EMIL WIECHERT

~~~~~~~~~~~~~~~~~~~~~~~~~

As I watched the blind brown trout rise, dusk deepened into twilight, a yellow moon shouldered its way above the distant mountain peaks, and the surface of the pool looked as smooth as brushed black velvet.

I was still kneeling in the cool meadow grass. The wind was as soft as a sigh on my skin as I watched the night sky trace itself upon the silky surface of the water, where tiny pools of moon glow and earthshine trembled like flames of candlelight. In the distance, the broken peaks of the mountains had become hulking shadows in night sky, while beads of emerald light leaked across the blue seam of the horizon, throbbing against the coming night.

As the stars rose, filled the night sky, so too did they fill the surface of the dark, slick pool of water, so did they rise on the blind trout's glistening, muscled back as it broke the surface of the pool, its elegant shape looking like a tear of black silk soaked in an Arctic mist. And its blind eyes were twin moons: milky pools of reflected light, the flicker of dim shadows, things known and unknown, undiscovered, uncharted, premundane, while on its penumbral back was the entire sprawl of the night sky in minia-

ture, even the flickering shadow of the mountains and the bright river.

The cool touch of the wind reminded me of other such cool night winds, the cool, sweet-smelling desert winds coming off the Chisos Mountains, down past Marathon and Alpine, down in the Big Bend country of west Texas. Such a wind was blowing across the Big Bend country, rattling every window of the Hotel Querencia south of Marathon, the first night I saw Dr. Raul Yarp steal up the stairs of the hotel, an argentine slouch hat pulled down tight over his gray eyes, a telescope tucked carefully under his skinny, sunburnt arms.

It was well past midnight. Yarp had on a pair of cracked and dusty roan cowboy boots. Bleached white socks were pulled up to his bony, sallow knees. White boxer shorts flashed beneath his blue bathrobe. Around his thin, heavily wrinkled, leathery neck hung an enormous pair of black binoculars.

My room was on the third floor of the Hotel Querencia. Dr. Raul Yarp tiptoed up the creaking wooden stairs that lead from the third floor, up another half flight of stairs to small blue door with a bronze door knob, which opened out onto the wide, flat roof of the hotel.

I heard the creaking wooden stairs and opened my room's door just in time to see Dr. Yarp turn up the stairs, up toward the small blue door that opened on to the roof. It was the hat I recognized—the folded and bent argentine slouch hat discolored by sweat, the whole thing covered with a patina of caliche dust and splattered vestiges of sudden desert thunderstorms.

It was the same hat I saw each morning at breakfast and each evening at dinner in the hotel's small restaurant on the main floor, across the wide, spacious lobby that was furnished with furniture made from mesquite wood, its walls decorated with colorful Mexican sombreros studded with immense rhinestones, beautiful handwoven blankets of red and yellow, blue and black, antique ranch tools, and paintings of leathery cowboys and nervous cattle dwarfed by vast sun-blasted mesas and red-rimmed mountains and the passionless west Texas blue skies.

The hotel's restaurant was so small it did not have a name. There were maybe ten tables crowded close together, so that no matter where you sat you could claim some portion of the view from the restaurant's great windows, which looked out on to the highway that passed through town and disappeared in the dust and wind and uncut sunlight into the land's thorny vastness, the mountains in the distance seeming to drift on animated waves of heat like walls of volcanic stone bubbling up from black-blood seas.

Across the highway was an uncertain flock of small stucco houses, white as bleached bone, their wooden shutters moaning in the perpetual wind, tended to by a small, pearl-white-stucco church, a small, greening copper bell hung high above its double oakwood doors. The entire front of the church was covered in tile, as blue as the near mountains drenched in twilight's desert blue shadows. On the wall of blue glaze was a lovely life-size painting of the Virgin Mary, her delicate white hands outstretched, her head slightly bowed, her blue eyes appearing to look down to a little fountain made of blue tiles that had been built at her feet and out of which trickled a constant small stream of cold blue water.

Holy water.

That is what Dr. Raul Yarp would later tell me as he set up his cracked telescope on the roof of the Hotel Querencia, pointed it up into Big Bend's great dome of desert night sky choked with stars and constellations, planets, and galaxies: more of creation's slag heaps, signposts of time, traces of paleolight forever probing the universe.

The little church across the railroad tracks from the hotel and its mural of the Virgin Mary beckoning from the wall of cool blue tiles, her delicate white hands outstretched, seemed to invite every passerby to rest at the small fountain, drink from its pool of cool, blue water.

Dr. Raul Yarp called the fountain the Virgin Mary *tinaja*.

A *tinaja* is an uncommon piece of paradise in the desert country of Big Bend. A *tinaja* is a rare natural spring, a pool of dark, mineral-stained water.

Water, again.

Tangles of Christmas lights had been happily, cheerfully, bliss-fully, hopefully strung from the church's brass bell to the fountain of blue tile, so that, when they clicked on each evening in the hour after twilight, the Virgin Mary and the little fountain and its pool of blue water were tucked inside a protective grotto of twin-kling lights—red and green, blue and white.

Some nights I could look down from the roof of the Hotel Querencia, as Dr. Yarp trained his eye on the fabulous sprawl of the desert night sky, and see that same sky reflected in the little pool of blue water at the feet of the Virgin Mary, just as I would later see the whirl of the Colorado mountain night sky drift across the shining back of the blind brown trout as it rose up out of the deep green pool of the river, while the daylight bled from the sky and the night rose up from the mountains in endless shades of mingled blues and blacks.

Every morning and evening, as I ate in the hotel's dining room, I would see Dr. Raul Yarp's folded and bent and dusty cowboy hat because, as it turned out, he was the cook, and from any table in the small restaurant you could look up and see that hat bobbing up and down, rushing to and fro, just above the raised opening between the kitchen and the dining room, as the two waitresses shouted orders to him.

"Number 2, double the beans, Yarp!"

"Yarp, heuvos rancheros, kill the sun, and hash browns!"

"Yarp! More fajitas!" And so on. Morning, noon, and evening.

Often, when the small restaurant was full and busy, when Rosa and Maria, the two young sad-looking Hispanic American wait-resses, shouted orders in rapid succession, all I could clearly hear was "YARP YARP YARP!"

It sounded like a small dog barking harmlessly.

Dr. Raul Yarp had been the cook at the Hotel Querencia, he would later tell me, for more than three years. And for more than three years, each night, after the last of the pots and pans had been scrubbed and set out to dry, after he had hung his stained cook's apron on the nail by the backdoor to the kitchen, he would go to his room behind the kitchen, strip off his sweat-drenched T-shirt, his faded blue jeans, put on his blue bathrobe, tuck his beloved telescope under his arm, slip out the door and up the stairs, tiptoe up past the third floor to where a small blue door opened onto the roof of the hotel, onto the breathless expanse of the Big Bend night sky.

The night I first saw Dr. Raul Yarp sneaking up the staircase of the Hotel Querenica, his cracked telescope under his skinny arm, I had been roaming the Big Bend country for a week.

It was my fourth trip. I kept coming back, easing down into the indifferent solace of the country's immensity, giving in to its inexplicable temptations, its mysterious appeal.

I drove south from Odessa, down through the Permian Basin, down Farm to Market Road 1053, west Texas rushing by the car window in vast sepia-colored chunks, everything burnt brown and parched reds, shadeless under an oceanic blue sky, the wind hot, shadows thin and thirsty and comfortless.

Down past Fort Stockton, the town looking like a scattering of bones bleaching under the desert sun, with every deepening mile the country defied boundaries, limits. Even the idea of measured distance seemed somehow inappropriate, fatuous.

Below Marathon, where miles mark time rather than measure space, is Big Bend National Park—more than eleven hundred square miles of stone and thorn, arroyo and volcanic mountains, the scratch and claw of upland desert and the cool pine forest in the high reaches of the Chisos Mountains, life spare and harsh and unadorned, practical and fiercely opportunistic, hunkered down in dessicated seeds and dusty roots, panting softly in the windless shadows, adrift in the warm, thick, brown waters of the Rio Grande, coiled down under scorched stones, burrowed down in the dust and cracked earth, waiting.

Even so, among its purple, hard red, and cinder mountains, all that volcanic slag, that chaos of crags and buttes, talus, bajadas,

rimrock and calcite ridges, there are perfect sanctuaries of light and form and shadow, of deep, uncorrupted quiet.

The national park alone is bigger than the state of Rhode Island, and west Texas seems to just go on and on, like some eerie sea of rock and sand, sunlight, wind, and sky. Farther south on Texas Highway 818, more than eighty miles beyond Alpine, is Terlingua and a few other small dusty backwater desert towns that shimmer in the land's sizzling layers of light like chimeras of edged sunlight and dust and animated heat.

Terlingua used to be an interesting ghost town. Its name comes from the three languages that were spoken there—Comanche, Spanish, and English.

The first time I ended up in Terlingua there was no lingua at all except the scurrying of beetles, the hiss of snakes, the sound of nighthawks on the wind. It was still a dead town, full of ghosts and a moaning, constant wind. Human beings had abandoned Terlingua when it stopped being a prosperous mining town, when the outside world lost interest in turning the cinnabar found in the nearby sunburnt mountains into great pools of commercial quicksilver.

So the last occupants packed up, moved on, and Terlingua became an interesting ghost town. On my first trip into the Big Bend country, I spent a wonderful night in Terlingua. I was driving south from Alpine. Alpine, by the way, was once Murphyville, Texas, until the townspeople decided that Alpine sounded more exotic, interesting, and commercially appealing.

By the time I got to Big Bend it was nearly midnight. Even so, the whole country radiated with the day's heat, looked a deep and flawless blue-black under a full moon shining like a slab of polished jade. It was too late to camp inside the park, so I pulled over in Terlingua, hiked up an old caliche road to one of the small roofless, windowless, doorless adobe huts gathered tenaciously on a rock-strewn hillside near the town cemetery, which was not abandoned, but full.

No vacancies.

All that was left of the adobe hut I bedded down in were the stone walls and the packed-dirt floor. I unrolled the blue sleeping bag and crawled in, and the brilliant desert night sky seemed to sag into the hut, press softly against my chest and the hut's stone walls glowing in diffuse whorls of starlight. I could not sleep and just kept staring up at the night sky, tracing constellations, riding the great white parabolas of shooting stars as they flamed across the sky, stark white and faded red, each as transitory as a flash of summer lightning.

A cool wind came off the mountains, filled the abandoned huts, each one with its own peculiar plaintive sigh, lament, like the sound of sudden remembrance or yearning, mingled with the howl of coyotes on the move, the scuffling sounds of mice and kangaroo rats—all residents of Terlingua that had stayed on, hung on, even thrived, including the scorpion that stung me.

The fault was mine, not the scorpion's. Sometime during the night I rolled over, stretched my right arm across an open copy of a book I had been reading by lantern light. Annie Dillard, maybe. Or Joseph Heller or Kurt Vonnegut, Jr.

I cannot remember which and am only certain that a book was open and the scorpion that stung me was one with literary interests. It was resting or reading or hunting there in those soft white paperback pages when my arm showed up.

ZAP!

For hours I was the madman of Terlingua, on my hands and knees, crawling between its stone walls glowing bone white in the bright starlight, murderously slapping and pounding, crushing and grinding every inch of the abandoned hut's dirt floor, a flashlight in my teeth, my canteen in one fist, a pocket knife in the other.

The scorpion's sting?

It left me nauseous, with chills and shakes, a mild hallucination or two, the most interesting of which was the view from the hut's doorless doorway: the desert vibrating in a melt of menacing blues—a blue wind coming down off blue mountains, blue shadows dancing across the face of a blue moon, blue waves of heat radiating off glowing blue stones, under which were huddled

beautiful neon blue scorpions. In time, the whole landscape seemed to burn down into a landscape of liquid blues: smoky blue creosote and edged blue yuccas, lechuguilla, prickly pear, ocotillo, sotol, blue veins of selaginella, the resurrection plant, ascending up marbled blue canyon walls. The blue desert was the earth laid clean, ascetic and reptilian, a body of blue flesh, raw, relentless beauty, flesh of sunlight, heart of stone.

Terlingua is not a ghost town anyone. Opportunity did what it is never supposed to do: knocked again. The last time I passed through Terlingua, I noticed there was a new roof on the hut were I first stretched out under the Big Bend's haunting night sky, where the neon blue scorpion stung me, where the desert wheeled through the night in a whorl of blues.

There was a sign up on the caliche road near the cemetery that had this to say to Terlingua's growing number of visitors:

SLOW, PLEASE. DUST ATTEMPTING TO SETTLE.

I followed Dr. Raul Yarp up the stairs of the Hotel Querencia, out the small blue door that opened onto the roof.

After Yarp set up his cracked telescope, pointed it up at the night sky, he reached into the pocket of his blue bathrobe and offered me a handful of tamale-flavored Slim Jims.

"Desert soul food," said Yarp.

From the roof of the hotel, to the east, were the crouched ridges of the Dead Horse Mountains, while the heavily crenellated peaks of the Santiago Mountains crowded the near western sky. At twilight, shadows coming off the Santiago Mountains looked like antediluvian creatures rising out of the moon glow.

Between these mountains, from the roof of the hotel, I could see the highway fall away into the Big Bend, looking like a pale, nervous, fragile seam of light slowly enveloped by the deepening night, disappearing among hillocks and marrow red mesas, sun-blasted buttes, immense walls of eroded stone. Dust devils danced on the night wind, in and out of the fading sunlight, like black angels. In that light that lingers beyond sunset, somewhere beyond Burro Mesa, beneath the edge of a young, pale yellow moon, twilight crept out of the purple mountains and smelled of storm, of revelation.

I spent days in the Chihuahuan desert collecting relentless ranges of light and color, walking the Grapevine Hills, looking for shadows out on Tornillo Flat, resting in the lush, cool shade of Pine Canyon, chasing the sunrise at Boot Spring and Laguna Meadow. During the long hours of the desert sunset, I would sometimes hike up on to the South Rim of the Chisos Mountains, six thousand feet above the economical desert. The Chisos rise so suddenly, so abruptly that they truly look like abandoned islands in a burnt-out sea of sand and dust.

Up in the Chisos Mountains, those cool, green islands rising out of the desert's lean, hot winds, on a cold desert morning I watched a mountain lion slouch down through the heavy morning shadows of Glen Canyon.

What woke me was not the mountain lion or the rising sun, but the racket of a handful of Colima warblers in the trees near my blue sleeping bag. When I sat up I discovered the cause for the birds' urgent protests: a small knot of elderly women standing perhaps fifty yards from me, staring at me and the Colima warblers through a dazzling array of binoculars and monoculars and spotting scopes. Some of the ladies were busy scribbling away in small, colored notebooks. One was apparently recording my every move as well as the warblers' every move, on video tape. Every few seconds the ladies, in unison, would raise their arms, frantically wave their hands at me. As they told me later, after the warblers had had enough and flew off deeper into the trees, they were trying politely to tell me to shove off. They were not interested in me or in my behavior as a human being loaded and primed with depression. They were interested in watching and recording and taking notes on a far more interesting life form—that of the Colima warbler.

The ladies were members of a bird-watching club from Buffalo, New York. They had driven all the way to Big Bend, then hiked up to the South Rim of the Chisos Mountains looking for a rare species. A writer wrapped in a blue sleeping bag, his eyes bloodshot from spending the night watching ghost lights glow on and off, off and on, among the distant Rattlesnake Mountains, was not what they had in mind. They had come all that way to get a look at the rare Colima warbler.

The warblers were everywhere up on the mountain. To me they were as common as the cold, unemployment, depression, or paradise.

The members of the birding club from Buffalo, New York, explained to me, sweetly, kindly, that their waves were meant to drive me off.

Instead, when they waved, I waved back, madly, smiling a big toothy smile like they were long-lost family. If it had been a year later, and had we all been members of Swami Bill's church in progress, the Church of Common Decency, the Ministry of Dignity, the Brotherhood of Fair Shakes, the Communion of Toleration, we would have greeted each other with more than waves. We would have danced and shaken hands, embraced and sung happy-go-lucky songs.

There are nights when the desert mountains of the Big Bend country radiate with ghost lights—ethereal flashes, ephemeral arcs, wandering sepulchral bursts of light, capillary blue, corpse green, waxy yellow, visceral red. A Comanche ranch hand I met in the restaurant of the Hotel Querencia told me that the ghost lights are the souls of the dead peacefully drifting about the cool winds and blue shadows and warm stones of the mountains.

Desert country reminds me, always, just how slight is the margin between the living and the dead.

The Comanche ranch hand told me that the souls of the dead

glowed so beautifully because they were in paradise.

There are so many.

Yarp talked and talked while he spent his nights on the roof of the Hotel Querencia, looking through his cracked telescope for hours, wandering like a disembodied pilgrim through the maelstrom of stars and constellations and planets and galaxies strewn across the sky, doomed always to see the universe not as it is, but as it was. The night sky's light marks the passage of things, not where the universe is going, but where it has been, the shock waves of the Big Bang. Dr. Raul Yarp watched its debris hurling through space, toward that edge of first darkness and first light.

While Dr. Yarp loved the Big Bend country, his passion was the desert's night sky, the universe's history written in an infinite topography of light, paleolight, fossils of light.

The stars, Yarp told me, reminded him nightly that among the many things a human being cannot do, despite his big brain, despite his faith and convictions, despite his intuitions and dreams, despite his beliefs and awareness, is to matter, matter at all.

That is a human being's deepest and most ancient fear, Yarp told me, that he does not really matter.

For a creature that did not matter, Yarp worked desperately to find something that did, and each night he would tiptoe up the staircase and out onto the roof of the hotel to meet his mistress, his soft, supple, mysterious lover, the night: sweet-smelling, deeply beautiful, frightening in its countless shades of darkness where there was nothing to seek and everything to find, more to feel than understand, a whole undiscovered universe beyond the touch of beliefs.

Illumination.

Each night that I followed him up the stairs, Yarp would set up his telescope, pull up the folding metal chair he kept on the hotel's roof, then open the small picnic basket he would bring up from his room off the kitchen, a basket filled with Mexican beer, paella, fresh warm tortillas, cheese, tostados, and a mixing bowl of his own salsa, which he called the Devil's Smile. Its sweet avernal smell, he said, came from the barbecued peppers he used. And we would eat and drink in the cool desert night, Yarp cursing the full Comanche moon for obscuring his view of the stars, the dim glow of distant galaxies, other worlds.

Yarp was always turning toward me in the darkness and saying, "In the beginning was darkness.

"All was night."

I met Dr. Raul Yarp in 1989, during what would turn out to be my last trip to the Big Bend country.

Already the pain in my head was getting worse. I greeted the mornings gobbling down handfuls of aspirin. And the sweat-drenched nightmares had begun, dragging me through endless Munchian landscapes of hopelessness and despair, leaving me in that Stygian sea, melanotic fish rising, my throat constricted, my jaws pried open, throbbing with pain, as from the passage of some silent black scream.

I had talked to my mother by telephone only weeks before. I called her often. We could do for each other what few others could do. We made each other laugh. Somewhere in all that laughing, I told her about my new headaches, the pain in my head.

There was a nervous moment of silence. Then my mother spoke. She was giggling. She was always giggling. Guess what she said?

"Me too."

"What?" I said.

"Headaches. Bone crushers. Mind benders.

"You know what cures them?" she said.

"Megadoses of Jackie Gleason's old television show 'The Honeymooners.' You think you got troubles and woes and pain? Spend an hour a day with the Kramdens.

"Put some Gleason in your head, routinely, hear me?" said my mother. "An hour a day—keeps the brain from knotting up."

I could hear the television in the background, hear Jackie Gleason, Ralph Kramden, threatening to send Alice, his long-suffering television wife, to the moon.

My mother laughed and laughed, was still giggling like a schoolgirl, when she said, in a whisper, as though telling me a great secret.

"Son, you don't have to live blue."

She would tell me that same thing again in a cracked and strained voice the week before the tumors in her brain killed her.

My headaches, as I learned later, were from the depression burning through the chemical wiring in my brain. My mother's headaches, as she would learn in just a matter of weeks, were from the little galaxy of tumors that had been growing in her brain and that would, as they went about killing her, feed on her memory and imagination.

The week before she learned of the tumors in her brain, my mother called me.

She was not laughing. There was no Jackie Gleason and "The Honeymooners" playing on the television, keeping her head free of aches and pains.

"What color are my eyes?" she asked.

Again and again and again.

And I told her.

"Hazel."

"Tell me, again," said my mother.

And I told her, again and again and again.

"No they're not," said my mother, ending the conversation.

"They're blue. Perfectly blue."

When the tumor in his brain began devouring his memory, just before it killed him by and by, my great-uncle Albert had shown up at Karen's Pool along Starlight Creek wrapped in a green

sheet. There was a crown of wild flowers stuck in his tangled gray hair. He paced back and forth on the riverbank above the wide, deep pool, reciting passages from Shakespeare's play *King Lear*.

Albert's British accent was impeccable.

His soft brown eyes had turned wild blue.

There were days when the desert of the Big Bend country quivered in a sheen of blue-and-green light for an hour after sunset. As the sun slouched toward the seared horizon, I drove up into the Chisos Basin, an immense saucer-shaped gabion of eroded rock that has sunk down through the heart of the Chisos Mountains. The high ridges smelled of juniper and pinyon pine, and the leaves of the southernmost stands of quaking aspen flashed in the declining sunlight like light coming off polished gold. Cliff swallows rose and fell with the wind like some mysterious confetti of color and whistle and motion.

I sat in the growing shadows looking out over the Big Bend country through that great eroded tear in the mountains, a window of stone that looked toward the Rattlesnake Mountains and beyond. And the sunlight went on and on and on. On many nights I thought surely it would go on forever. Eternal glow: a country flaming in light, hardened and edged by the sun's merciless constancy, the landscape wearing shadows like robes, becoming some nightmarish mummery, something out of a tormented geologist's nervous dreams—humped lava flows, laccoliths, rock chimneys, craggy spires, anticlines, synclines, calders, faults, volcanic caps and domes, stone extruded, intruded, broken, folded. During the long, slow hours of sunset, the whole country looked like some abandoned caldron of creation, time hammered into history on anvils of stone.

That evening I thought a soak in the hot natural springs down along the Rio Grande might do my head some good. I hiked down into Hot Spring Canyon, down to the river, lay under the cool shade of the trees below the gray-and-red and smoky blue canyon walls, stones pocked with the fossil remains of ancient marine creatures that had thrived in the primordial seas that covered this land millions of years ago. The sky turned the color of faded roses, and I walked upriver to one of the shallow hot springs and sunk myself down into its heavy, steaming water, my feet anchored in mud, my arms stretched out, my head against a warm red stone. Overhead was the immense desert night sky. Andromeda, at the night sky's edge, was a fragile smudge of dim white light.

Andromeda—another galaxy drifting along in the swelling, onrushing universe, and I wondered how long the speck of light I perceived as Andromeda had traveled back through time and space to fill my hazel eyes as I sat there in that hot spring along the Rio Grande River, in a small canyon just across the river from Mexico.

I would see a similar smudge of light once again, by the way, as dim and pearl white as the smudge of Andromeda wheeling through the universe, or at least my mind's version of it. It would leak out, along with all the other fabulous specks and seams, rivers, and motes of light and color and form, from the blind brown trout's eyes as it rose up out of the green waters of the wide and deep pool below Spinney Mountain on the Middle Fork of the South Platte River in the Colorado high country beyond the mountains of the Front Range. When I saw that smudge of pearl white light fall way from the trout's blind eyes, I knew that the depression that had come and gone had left more than it had ruined, soured, tainted, or destroyed.

Including all those nights in the Big Bend country, on the roof of the Hotel Querencia with Dr. Raul Yarp.

Including that night I lay soaking in the natural hot spring along the Rio Grande, absorbing the desert night, not trying to solve the eternal riddles of the universe or grasp the perfect transparency of space, wanting only to sink into the deep solace of the desert, a

land still unbroken, defiant, edged in wildness. The chaos of stars and galaxies and planets in the immense night sky, the press of history and time and space, offers only an ever-deeper mystery, of which we are, everything is, an inexorable part. The hope we are left with, Dr. Raul Yarp told me while we were on the roof of the hotel in the desert night's cool darkness, is that all of this—life and earth and human beings and the universe, and so on—that all of it is, in the end, greater than the sum of its parts.

I kept following Yarp through the small blue door and out onto the roof of the hotel Querencia. Some nights, as I walked up the dark staircase and out onto the roof of the hotel, into the cool blue desert nights, I thought of trout rising in cold, fast water, bright water. Like Yarp, I rose out of my lonely room and into the glowing desert night. The desert sky was my river, just as it was Yarp's lover, his paradise, his Holy Land where nightly he wandered, ever the awed and amazed and ecstatic pilgrim.

"Worlds without end," said Yarp, adjusting his cracked telescope, focusing on some vague nebula, some galaxy of a million billion stars, some planet's silky shine, some constellation's familiar seductive pattern of light. All of it was and had always been fleeing away from Yarp, from me, from this small, blue planet called Earth, from everything since the instant of the Big Bang, a bang so big, so incomprehensible, that from a speck of unimaginably compressed, condensed matter, it would spew out all this, more than I can see, more than any night sky can hold, more than any mind can imagine, more than any awareness can sense, grasp, comprehend. The unbelievably vast was born of the inconceivably small. Out of perfect blackness the improbable astonishment of light, and pulsing in that light and every character of light since was every possibility and every probability, including the awesome improbability of life, of bacteria and elephants and human beings, all of it hurled across the soundless vacuum of space, at the instant of the Big Bang.

The soundless primal scream.

The First Moan.

The First Squirm.

That first moment is still around, as is every moment that has ever been or will be, every moment of the present, the past and the future.

According to Dr. Raul Yarp, they are all up here, drifting in the night. Not just one universe, but many, more than the mind of man can conceive, contemplate, hold.

What is, what was, what would be was out there, out there in the sweet, sweet night.

To that soundless vacuum, Yarp pressed his ear, just as Juan-Chuy had pressed his ear to the waters of Magdalena Bay in Baja.

Juan-Chuy was our guide as we traveled for a week in sea kayaks up and down Magdalena Bay among migrating gray whales.

Juan-Chuy was listening for water music, the songs of the gray whales who had traveled south to the isolated bays and lagoons of Baja to court and mate and sing.

Yarp was imagining the pop and hiss and crackle of radiant energy, the buzz of atoms and subatomic particles and waves, the relentless creep of matter.

Yarp told me there was but one lonely atom per centimeter of cold space. The crowded night sky was an illusion, a wonderful and harmless fantasy. There was plenty of wilderness up among the stars, plenty of space in space, plenty of room for him to roam, lose himself, find himself, look here and there for whatever he yearned for.

And what did Dr. Raul Yarp yearn for, search for among the stars? What the universe offered freely to every human being.

Peace and quiet.

The night's silence, the sound of creation.

In the beginning not only was there night, there was peace and quiet.

As the night deepened, Yarp would put a small pillow on the seat of the metal folding chair he kept on the roof of the hotel and on which he sat as he looked into his cracked telescope and let himself go, traveling among the stars, the visible planets, red-and-white clouds of wheeling nebulas, stars being born, burning cold blue and volcanic red, stars dying, exploding, going cold, collapsing on themselves, reduced to something beyond nothing, a gravity so pure that nothing can escape its pull, not even light: Black holes on the far side of understandable dimension, where things fall apart, even Newton's laws.

Or, as Yarp called Black holes—Night Souls.

Just before dawn, at the edge of night, out of the protean and beautiful blackness, would come the first false dawn, the green-and-blue glow of zodiacal light, flashes of sunlight reflected off clouds of interplanetary dust.

Dust to dust, light to darkness, and darkness to light. Night souls throbbing silently in the blackness, in the night.

Night, the first primordial plasma.

Yarp especially loved the storm-tossed nights, when the Big Bend country became a swirling Wagnerian opera of roiling black clouds, a crush of thunder and roar and slashing winds, the sky a great quavering noctilucent maelstrom of arcing lightning—benzine blue and nacreous white. On such nights the roof of the Hotel Querencia seemed to slip and rock, as though built on some fault of stone.

On such nights, Dr. Raul Yarp lost his bent and folded argentine slouch hat, and his pale gray hair blew wild in the storm. His eyes were bright and wide, and there was a slight smile on his cracked lips and weathered face, while purple flashes of lightning penetrated the lingering double rainbow arched high over the ridges of the Dead Horse Mountains. And Yarp climbed up on the edge of the flat roof trying to see over the distant mountains, wanting to glimpse the earthly end of the rainbow, as he ate pick-

led green chilis from a Ball jar and screamed over the moaning wind of total eclipses, the truths of the sweet night, the perfect seduction of umbras. Meanwhile, the great storm moved slowly south, across the upland desert and across the Rio Grande, down into Mexico, and the sky went black, the moon becoming visible again, a mandala of illumination. Still balanced on the edge of the roof, Yarp was looking through his big black binoculars and telling me that the storm had filled Tycho, the moon's largest crater, with a sea of peaceful blue-white light. Later, in the hour before sunrise, tattered aquamarine and amethyst mists drifted across the desert, hung close to the ground, shredded by glistening needles and thorns.

While such storms passed violently across the desert, Yarp pulled his blue bathrobe tight against the cold, blue desert morning and hurried down to his solitary room off the hotel's kitchen, returned with hard-boiled eggs and another bowl of the Devil's Smile, warm tortillas, and cheese.

I was inside Dr. Raul Yarp's room off the kitchen of the Hotel Querencia only once. He sent me down off the roof for more beer. Yarp's room was a lamasery devoted to the night sky. Star charts hung on every wall along with posters of wheeling galaxies and milky, blooming nebulas. There was one small bookcase near the mattress on the wood floor filled with guides to the night skies. From the ceiling, which Yarp had painted sulfur black, dangled illuminated mobiles, barely stirring in the cool desert wind, of constellations and galaxies and planets.

Yarp showed up at the door as I was staring up at that night black ceiling, the mobiles hung with lengths of thin white twine, dangling just above Yarp's sheetless mattress. His arms were loaded down with leftovers from the restaurant's kitchen. He was thinking out loud to himself, as he often did, wondering about the lives of subatomic particles and waves, correcting himself under his breath of beer and hard-boiled eggs and chili peppers, that there was not so much life among the particles and waves as there was infinite possibility, patterns of probability, the potential for everything and for nothing at all.

"Worlds with out end," sighed Dr. Raul Yarp, a warm golden stream of Corona beer dripping down the corners of his mouth.

Dr. Raul Yarp sometimes trembled as he set up his cracked telescope.

It was not like the residue of trembles that shook and rattled Velveeta Cheese after his series of electric shock treatments, trembles and rattles that still sent spasms through his body when he reappeared in Dr. Mutzpah's waiting room after a long absence. He told me he had been zapped five times. He told me his brain was happy, was always smiling, that the inside of his head felt as warm and luscious as a vat of melted honey.

Yarp's was the tremble of simple and honest excitement, of a human being hurrying to slip himself through a series of tubes and mirrors, transform himself into light, become what he once was: an amalgam of time and space, interplanetary dust, starlight, particles and waves—pure possibility, probability, potential.

That was the night up on the roof of the hotel that Yarp told me that his passion for night and the pull of the universe had cost him his job as a fifth-grade science teacher in Oklahoma.

"I told the little darlings," Yarp said, "that their cells were like stars and that their blood was like the endless night and that in their cells was the history of the universe.

"I told them that God was, like everything else, highly improbable but certainly possible, given the infinite connections and interconnections of particles and waves.

"I told them their flesh and bones were the stuff of stars.

"I told them that in the beginning there was night.

"The school board asked me kindly to pack up my star charts and telescope and my poisonous Satanic beliefs and get out of town, out of Oklahoma."

Yarp told me something else.

It was not his students who turned him in to the local school board. It was his loving wife, Mrs. Julia Spoone Yarp.

She later divorced Yarp and his name, and as the Reverend Julia Spoone founded the Hallelujah Rollers and began touring the country, holding spiritual rollerblade clinics, often with local chapters of Joygerms Unlimited, which called for a world free of "gruff and grumpy grouches."

Yarp told me that his ex-wife and his daughter had become bedouins, that they moved from town to town. Yarp said that whenever he found out where they were, he would call and write.

No one ever answered. After Oklahoma, Yarp gave up teaching. Who could blame him? Or any teacher? Instead, Yarp became a short-order cook and drifted into the Big Bend country, where the night sky was legendary, where every night was a chaos of fact and magic.

To Dr. Raul Yarp astronomy was as soothing as poetry. Across every desert night sky flickered the consanguinity of life.

All day, Yarp dreamed of the coming night as he stirred big, deep pots of beans and fried fajitas, as the aboriginal, tentacular light of the Big Bend flooded in through the restaurant's ceiling-to-floor windows. He swabbed his face with a damp black bandana covered with pearl white diagrams of famous constellations.

"YARP YARP YARP!" shouted Maria and Rosa, and Yarp's crumpled, bent, and folded argentine slouch hat bobbed up and down. Underneath it, Dr. Raul Yarp sipped mescal, what he called night's mother's milk, smiled and waited.

Waited for the night.

Billions of neutrinos, traveling at the speed of light, are buzzing in and out of my big brain as I write these words, as I go about remembering Dr. Raul Yarp and the Big Bend country, here in my small room on top of a worn-out mountain near Jonah's Ridge, Alabama.

It is well after midnight.

Jonah's Ridge, Alabama, by the way, is only a day's drive from Eden, Georgia.

And Eden is just another word for paradise.

There are, as Kiwi LaReaux told me, her beautiful green eyes flooded with mountain sunlight, so many.

So many.

The window of my small room is open wide and there is a cold wind among the hickory trees. It has been two hours since I climbed off the back of county garbage truck No. 2. Tonight, the garbage truck burst into flames coming down the mountain highway. The all-night manager at the Piggly Wiggly saw the speeding ball of lovely orange flames and told us later he thought a comet had fallen out of the night sky. We were riding that comet, the crew of county garbage truck No. 2, all four of us laughing hysterically as the truck, in flames, rolled to a stop at the bottom of the mountain. There is something ridiculously funny about a burning garbage truck racing down a mountain highway on a clear cold winter night, three black men and a white man hanging out of the cab windows laughing uncontrollably.

We put out the fire at Slagh's AutoWash, next door to the Piggly Wiggly supermarket.

Hamadullah fed the machine a quarter; Thallus set it for the wash and wax cycle; and I took the miracle water wand and climbed onto the burning truck, trying to douse the flames.

Cleopheus kept running back and forth to the Piggly Wiggly supermarket for change, more quarters, howling all the way, tears running down his face.

Cleopheus is always laughing. He thinks I am the funniest white man he has ever known.

Putting out the fire that erupted tonight on county garbage truck No. 2 left a thick purple scar on my upper left arm, just beneath Muldoon's tattoo.

When Dr. Raul Yarp saw the tattoo on my arm he smiled and told me how he had made love to a beautiful young Mexican woman who lived just across the Rio Grande in the village of Boquillas, near where the river disappears into the blue-black shadows of Boquillas Canyon.

Yarp said he met the beautiful young woman in the rose-colored rocks above the Boquillas Canyon overlook. Every day at sunrise, Yarp said, she would ride her burro across the shallow river, tie it among the shady trees by the river, and hike to the overlook where Big Bend tourists often stopped to admire the desert from a safe distance. She sold the tourists beautiful pieces of amethyst for next to nothing.

Actually, what she sold the tourists, Yarp told me, was beautiful pieces of worthless fluorite that looked like amethyst. Fluorite was mined across the river in Mexico, not far from her village. It was everywhere. It was as common as caliche dust. Yarp said that her small hut was crowded with potato sacks bulging with fluorite. And each morning she would gather up a small sack and ride across the river, and somewhere in the river the common fluorite became amethyst, rare and valuable.

The beautiful young Mexican woman's name was Belinda.

Belinda, said Yarp, never told the tourists the pretty stones were fluorite.

"She asked them what it looked like to them," said Yarp.

They always answered amethyst.

"They want pretty purple stones," Belinda told Yarp. "So I bring them pretty purple stones."

Belinda took Yarp across the Rio Grande on the back of her burro. They walked side by side up the riverbank, into the village, to Belinda's small hut. She undressed in the hot, heavy shadows. A brown potato sack was hung over the hut's one window.

Yarp told me she was the color of browned butter and be-

tween her breasts was a small tattoo of Saint Mary Magdalene's face, a divine blue tear on her cheek.

Yarp said that the tattoo on my left arm, Muldoon's tattoo, and the tattoo between Belinda's breasts, were the same shade of blue, the color of raw turquoise. Desert blue.

Yarp raised the bottle of mescal and hailed Belinda's perfect butter brown breasts and the wonder of quasar 3C273 beyond Virgo, its light more than a billion years old and still it raced away from Yarp, from me, from earth, from everything, at 340 miles per second, leaving behind its own illusion traced in vague specks of red-blue light. Yarp took a long pull from the bottle of mescal, passed it over, telling me to raise it high in praise, that this quasar was the closest he and I would ever get to the first light, the universe's embryonic glow.

Yarp said that there were maybe twenty-five hundred stars visible with the naked eye, even his mescal-soaked eyes. The greatest telescopes would, in time, perhaps record the receding light of a hundred billion galaxies. Each of those galaxies, said Yarp, might contain from ten to a hundred billion stars.

And still, Yarp told me, smiling, always smiling, it would all fit into the divine blue tear running down the soft cheek of the tattoo of St. Mary Magdalene between Belinda's lovely brown breasts.

"Quo vadimus?" Yarp was always asking, again and again, over and over.

Where are we going?

And Yarp would always answer his own question, telling me that everything was heading for that edge where first light and Mother night were, one, whole, joined.

"Maybe that's heaven," Yarp said softly. "Out there somewhere, where Mother night ends."

About a week or so after my mother was admitted to a hospital in Phoenix, Arizona, with a dazzling array of small tumors eating away at her brain, she had a seizure.

She survived. Later, she told me that while the seizure whacked through her brain, she was whisked off for a peek at the afterlife. This is what my mother told me about heaven, about the afterlife.

"Don't worry," she said, "everything is wholesale. Otherwise, it's all pretty vague."

Small world.

Small afterlife.

The cold desert wind made Yarp smile as he lay there on the roof of the hotel.

Yarp told me he was looking not only at the stars or planets or constellations or visible galaxies. He was looking at the pure blackness between them, among them, surrounding them, all that immensity of space buzzing with the birth cry of creation, the crackle of microwaves, the initial flood of radiation, particles and waves, released that first forty-millioneth of a trillionth of a trillionth of a second after the Big Bang when hydrogen was formed. The universe still bristles with these microwaves, this alluvium of background radiation, creation's residuum, its inextinguishable sigh.

In the beginning there was night and radiation, the afterglow of radio waves and infrared, gamma rays and X rays, and finally the aureate splendor of ultraviolet light. And the universe goes on and on, has gone on and on for fifteen or twenty billion years, tracing its history in a legacy of lingering light.

Raising himself up on one elbow, Yarp suddenly began to sing:

> *Twinkle, twinkle little star,*
> *I don't wonder what you are,*

NIGHT FISHING

For by spectroscopic ken,
I know you are hydrogen.

"Finally, there was light," said Yarp. "Illumination."

Yarp believed that among the great disappointments of human beings was that our first god—Nature—had turned out to be so fragile, so vulnerable.

Just like us.

And so, Yarp said, our ancestors went about looking for other gods, gods that were omniscient and omnipresent, gods that were beyond the rot and ruin of nature, beyond cycles and rhythms, beyond beginnings and endings, gods that could assure us that we mattered, gods that created us in their own image and created the earth and the heavens for us alone, gods that would give us an eternal heaven beyond this world, this universe that is ever swelling, gulping up timelessness as it probes the edges of darkness, this universe and its fearful mysteries, its dark promises, including the death of our solar system and its sun.

"We pray for salvation," Yarp would say, "when deliverance is so near at hand." For Dr. Raul Yarp it was as close as the desert night sky, immediate and ongoing, written in the living and dying stars, at the black heart of Black Holes, in the warm mystery of dark matter, things that are but that cannot be seen.

"Our future, like our past," Yarp would say with a nervous giggle, "lies in the dark."

In the warm dark heart of Mother night.

"More salsa?" said Yarp, as the dark giggle died in his throat.

"Go on, it's good for you. You're a long way from tartufo bianco country."

Tartufo bianco. White truffle, the most expensive fungus on the planet.

As he ate, Yarp told me about the day a magician showed up in the restaurant for dinner. He had driven over from Alpine, where he was doing a week of evening shows at the Alpine Holiday Inn.

The magician went by the name of Edgar the Prestidigitator.

That evening in the restaurant of the Hotel Querencia, the magician performed wonders for everyone in the dining room, including Rosa and Maria and the short-order cook, Dr. Raul Yarp.

Yarp told me that when Edgar the Prestidigitator had finished entertaining the Gomezes at table 2 and the Mr. and Mrs. Henry Oates family from Iowa at table 4, and after he had eaten his dinner of six soft tacos, four burritos stuffed with cheese and onions and jalapeño peppers, chicken fajitas on a bed of steaming rice and refried beans, had drunk a pitcher of sweet tea, a pot of coffee, and eaten a wedge of fresh, warm apple pie, Yarp introduced himself and took Edgar the Prestidigitator up the stairs of the hotel and through the small blue door and out onto the roof. Yarp said he pointed up to the deepening twilight sky, an orange moon on the rise, and said, "Look up, Edgar, at some real magic!"

Edgar the Prestidigitator, Yarp told me, backpedaled away from him, back toward the open blue door and the stairs down to the lobby of the hotel, mopping sweat off his forehead with the sleeve of his black-sequined magician's jacket, yelling back at Yarp as he fled down the stairs that if Yarp wanted to see some truly amazing magic he should get on over to the Alpine Holiday Inn for the late show.

"I'm going to do the clearly impossible," yelled Edgar the Prestidigitator.

"With a wave of my wand, friend, I will teach a common house cat to shake hands warmly and mean it!"

The night Dr. Raul Yarp told me that the earth's future, like its past, was somewhere deep in the night, he brought a battery-

powered cassette player up on to the roof, slipped in a tape.

It was a tape Yarp had found earlier while cleaning his room.

He had dusted and mopped and straightened for an hour, thrown out bag after bag of trash. When he turned to find me standing at the door to his room, he handed me what felt like an empty green garbage bag and asked me to carry it down to the Dumpster outside the backdoor of the hotel.

I asked him what was in the bag.

"The anthropic principle . . . get rid of it."

The anthropic principle is sacred to human beings who believe that human beings are the ultimate measure of all things.

The tape Yarp put into the cassette player up on top of the roof was of the Mississippi Delta bluesman Son House. The recording had been made almost thirty years after Son House had given up singing and playing the blues and vanished. A handful of blues lovers found him years later in Rochester, New York. They put a microphone in front of him, asked him to take up his guitar again and sing.

Sing the blues.

Son House had perhaps the most haunting voice of any blues singer, even Robert Johnson, who was murdered by a jealous husband or boyfriend or lover and is buried in an unmarked grave in a small, nondescript cemetery in the Mississippi Delta.

I told Yarp a story my mother had told me often as we listened to tapes of Robert Johnson and Son House and a lot of other Mississippi Delta blues singers in her hospital room as the tumors in her brain went about killing her. She kept remembering things from her childhood, like the times my great-uncle Albert took her along on trips to Helena, Arkansas. She remembered throwing pennies and nickels into a worn brown fedora placed at the feet of a group of street singers. Blues singers.

Albert played blues harmonica. He was pretty good for a leathery old white man with a ruinous addiction to the Ozark

Mountains, wild trout, and beautiful women.

Albert, said my mother, joined in with the black men, played his harmonica. Later, he told her the men's names.

Robert Johnson and Willie Brown.

Yarp wanted to know if my mother knew she had been listening to heaven's music, to the choir celestial, life's own bruised and battered chords.

I could not say. All I knew, all I could say, was what she told me—that the music made her clap her small hands and tap her small feet, that it made her want to sing.

Sing the blues.

The night we listened to Son House was the night Yarp asked me, for the first and only time, what I did for a living.

I told him about my work, my job as a full-time magazine writer with the Southern Progress Corporation.

He said it all sounded pretty much like paradise.

And it struck me, as he said those words there in the deep blue desert night, that it actually was something like paradise.

Yarp said something else. He said it sounded like I was living the American Dream.

Maybe, I said, washing down another handful of aspirin for the vague pain in my head with a mouthful of warm, sweet, sunny orange Mexican beer.

Much later, listening to him day after day as he spoke from the pulpit of his folding brown metal chair at the corner of Seventeenth & Stout, in downtown Denver, I would hear another doctor, Dr. Truth, go on and on about the American Dream. Day after day, he would tell the uninterested passersby that the American Dream was not wounded or sick, not lost or misplaced, not patiently waiting for better times, not blind and mute, not anything but stone-cold dead.

"Look at me!" Dr. Truth would scream. "Go on, take a look. Take a good look. I'm the American Dream. Have you ever seen anything any deader?"

As he spoke, Dr. Truth would wave a sign he wore around his

neck as he spoke from atop his metal chair. I was in the tiny knot of mildly curious human beings who had stopped to listen to Dr. Truth the day he took the sign from around his neck and held it high over his head, proclaiming it the New American Dream.

The sign was a great square of cardboard. On one side was printed in lovely blue letters:

CONTENTS: SPAM LUNCHEON MEAT. TWO DOZEN 24-OUNCE CANS.

On the other side, the side Dr. Truth urgently waved in the faces of the little knot of mildly curious human beings, written in red-tipped Magic Marker by a shaky hand, was this message.

HOMELESS!! WILL WORK FOR FOOD!

Woody Moos wears a sign that says the same thing, that he is homeless and will work for food. He wears it as he stands at the off ramp of the interstate, near the Galleria, which may be the biggest shopping mall in Alabama.

Since begging is against the law, Woody Moos never says a word. He simply stands there at the end of the off ramp, facing the traffic as cars pull off the interstate heading for the Galleria.

I saw Moos standing there a week ago. It was drizzling and there was a cool wind coming off the nearby hills. Moos had on his yellow rain slicker, garbage-stained jeans, and a pair of bladder purple Doc Martins. His grubby green muffler was wrapped around his neck.

I pulled over and we talked for a while. He told me he had been wearing his sign and standing on the off ramp for about a week. He reached under his yellow rain slicker and into his jeans and pulled out a great wad of frog green dollars. The look on Moos's face was more bewildered than usual.

He was not smiling or singing. He told me that cars coming off the interstate generally passed him up. The drivers simply ignored him, refused to read his sign or look him in the eye.

"But plenty stop," said Moos in a blank voice. "They roll their car windows down long before they see me. They stick their hands out, full of cash.

"I always ask them what kind of work they would like me to do.

"They wag the cash harder, avert their eyes.

"And I keep asking them what they want me to do. And you know what they keep telling me?

"They keeping telling me to take the money and just go away."

Go away.

While Son House's songs, fossils of space and time, played on the cassette player, Yarp again settled down in his chair, moved his cracked telescope to a different section of the night sky, talking, as he worked, talking, as I say, more to himself than to me, saying that perhaps, as the universe matured, got older, the night sky might brighten a little, that the night is so dark, even when glowing with the sloughed-off light of vast numbers of stars and quasars, nebulas, and galaxies, because it is still so young, at fifteen to twenty billion years of age, just a cosmic child.

Yarp liked the idea of spending his evenings with something so young and supple and seemingly infinite in all directions, a universe that was still in its childhood and therefore still full of limitless potential and possibilities, even something as beautiful and mysterious as the tattoo between Belinda's breasts, brown as melted butter.

"I should bring Belinda up here," said Yarp. "The young need to be together."

That night the swirl of the Milky Way arched in the deep, clear, desert sky, glowed from Cassiopeia to Sagittarius like the dust of crushed jewels sprinkled across a bolt of brushed blue-black velvet.

Yarp reminded me that the Milky Way is home to our average planet, our modest solar system. He talked longingly of the Milky Way, its pinwheeling heart, which is a hundred thousand light-years in diameter, how as it follows the push of creation deeper and deeper into space, we revolve in its whirling membrane of stars and planets, black holes and dark matter, its union of space and time, once every 250 million years. It was like being, Yarp said, a grain of sand caught in the belly of a great storm wave.

Dr. Raul Yarp stared at the glow of the Milky Way and said what he often said during those nights on the roof of the Hotel Querencia.

"La vida es sueño."

Life is a dream.

The last time I saw Dr. Raul Yarp it was three hours after twilight. I had gone to up to the roof of the hotel to say good-bye.

Beyond the small blue door that opened onto the roof, onto the deepening desert night, I saw Yarp sitting on his chair, next to his cracked telescope, which was pointed up toward the stars. Behind him, near the center of the flat roof, Yarp had set his big aluminum flashlight upside down, so that it was facedown on the roof. The flashlight had a head as wide as a halved melon, and Yarp had switched it on, so that it gave off eerie, soft yellow auras of light.

Suddenly Yarp got up from his chair and began to dance slowly around the overturned flashlight and its circles of light, its heart of darkness.

Yarp danced on and on, a shadow moving in and out of the soft yellow light, in and out of the deep blue desert night, and as I watched I thought of the ancient Indians in the caves of Seminole Canyon moving around their bright night fire, singing creation songs while one of them dipped his hand in a stone midden full of sticky paints made from the earth, then pressed his palm and fingers hard against the cave wall, leaving his red handprint on the smooth cave wall alive with the trembling shadows of fire and dancing human beings.

And Dr. Raul Yarp danced on and on around the upturned flashlight under the stars, with a bottle of mescal in one hand.

He danced on and on even after the flickering flashlight went dead, danced on under the stars, in the sweet young arms of the deepening night.

In the beginning there was night.

Mother night.

THE MAGIC HOURS

We wish to be angels, not made of meat.

— R O D O L F O   L L I N A S

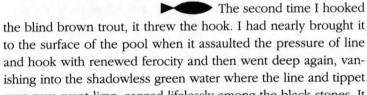

The second time I hooked the blind brown trout, it threw the hook. I had nearly brought it to the surface of the pool when it assaulted the pressure of line and hook with renewed ferocity and then went deep again, vanishing into the shadowless green water where the line and tippet gave way, went limp, sagged lifelessly among the black stones. It was the first days of November, and a cold wind shuddered across the meadow, over the river.

I waded quietly, carefully, to the bottom reaches of the pool where the river narrowed, became shallow. It purled gently as it passed over a shoal of earth-colored stones and fell away into a long chute of swift, bright water that looked like a great blade of edged rutilant sunlight cut deep into the high meadow.

I sat on the nearby grassy bank of the river below the wide pool, bit off what was left of the old tippet, knotted on a spare I kept rolled up in my shirt pocket along with my small waterproof matchbox of trout flies.

I tied on a Griffith's gnat, one that looked like a pinch of burnt orange sofa, and sat there on the bank for a long time watching the morning's thin clouds dissolve, watching the deepening dawn set fire to the distant mountains, listening to the sound of the late autumn wind in the tall grass, feeling the day's chilly wind soft on my face.

At dinner the night before in Fairplay, Kiwi LaReaux had asked me about my days along the river and the blind trout.

I told her what my skin and brain had told me—that they were as happy as a clam, that it was good to be in high country again, along a river, in a country still touched with wildness. I told her that the depression that had been boiling in my brain had picked a beautiful, hopeful, and optimistic place to dump me.

"Kicked from one paradise and into another, huh?" said Kiwi LaReaux.

"I suppose," I said.

We were both smiling shyly over big stoneware bowls of hot chili. The bowls were the white of sun-bleached bones.

A small giggle rose in her elegant throat, and her limpid green eyes beamed in the restaurant's dim yellow lights.

Kiwi LaReaux told me that Swami Bill got the same feeling every time she gave him a Parisian Body Rub.

A Parisian Body Rub, said Kiwi LaReaux, is a massage administered with a thick lather of exotic, sirenic creams and lotions and a necklace of fine, natural pearls.

Kiwi LaReaux learned all about the Parisian Body Rub, I found out, from Mi Oh at the Now & Zen. Two days later, over a double order of Moo Goo Gai Pan ladled over mounds of steaming white rice, I asked Mi Oh about the Parisian Body Rub. It sounded like something else that would soothe my skin's burden of memory and experience and ease my depression's slagheap of sour cells, give me a fresh glow, make me and my brain dance and whistle, and feel happy as a clam.

"Not for you," said Mi Oh.

"And why not?" I moaned with almost tearful disappointment, as the image of having thick, sweet-smelling, seductive oils and a handful of tiny, heavenly, perfectly round and smooth pearls rubbed over and keened into my weary back lingered deliciously in my mind.

"Melted butter, first, then pearls, my gaijin-baby," giggled Mi Oh cryptically.

Trout and women are equally incomprehensible to me, which is probably why I am endlessly fascinated by them both. It only took Mi Oh saying melted butter and my mind tingled involuntarily and my muscles began slipping into libidinous knots, as though on the edge of sensuous cataplexy.

I let the Moo Goo Gai Pan cool and imagined candlelight, silk sheets, Shinto chants, warmed oils, holy lotions, just me and Mi Oh and her red hostess dress, the one slit up both sides to reveal her golden brown thighs, the one with the dragon embroidered in golden thread wrinkling to life with every rise and fall of her breasts. As it turned out, Mi Oh was a trained and licensed masseuse.

So much for imagination.

What I got, by appointment only, was a half hour of what Mi Oh assured me was necessary, holistic pain.

Forget the candlelight. Her office, off the kitchen of the Now & Zen, was a glare of blinking white-hot fluorescent light. From the floor-to-ceiling sound system came not the otherworldly allure of Shinto chants but the latest offering from groups named the Dead Kennedys, Nirvana, and the Butthole Surfers, music that sounded like the amplified, unedited recordings of dental students performing unanesthetized root canals. Silk sheets gave way to antiseptic linens, body-bag green. The room smelled of witch hazel and eucalyptus.

Gone, too, was the hot red hostess dress.

Mi Oh entered dressed professionally in a passionless white nurse's uniform.

Beneath the body-bag green antiseptic linens was not a bed, but one of the restaurant's original kitchen counters, stainless steel and blue cold.

Mi Oh did not even fight to suppress a giggle as I took my place on the kitchen counter. I could feel her breath on the back of my neck. She was telling me about the healthy benefits and many blessings of therapeutic massage, how she was going to press my body's natural trigger points and bleed my dolorous muscles of poisonous lactic acid, rearrange my electrons and protons, pop my neck, straighten my spine, recharge my frazzled energy field, and polish my aura.

She worked only on my back, neck, head, upper chest, and arms. Mi Oh was a whirl of precisely trained fingers and hands, her dark eyes fixed and determined, her beautiful face at times hidden in a eucalyptus mist.

So fast were Mi Oh's hands that the feel of them on my back made me think of a great net of freshly caught fish suddenly tossed onto a ship's slick deck. The feel of Mi Oh's hands was part squirm, part deep rub, part caress. Then, suddenly, her hands would stop and Mi Oh would press what felt like a two-pound ball bearing into specific muscles. The two-pound ball bearing was, of course, Mi Oh's dainty thumb digging into my muscles' trigger points.

Trigger points.

Mi Oh pulled them all. As she did, I began to understand what she had meant when she told me that before the Parisian pearls came melted butter.

Because, when it was over, that was what I felt like—like two hundred pounds of melted butter and a healthy grimace.

With Mi Oh's help I got to the back door of the restaurant where the alley led to my apartment building, my room, my blue sleeping bag. Human dumpster divers crawled in and out of the twin giant garbage dumpsters looking like brightly colored mutant flies buzzing about some aromatic piece of rotting meat.

"Well?" said Mi Oh, a wide, professional, satisfied smile on her lovely face.

"Me oh, my oh," I said painfully.

"Feel better, don't you?" she said. "Now your electrons and protons are properly charged and aligned. Your spine is supple again, your neck straight. Your energy is again positive, not negative. Your aura glows.

"Why, my gaijin-baby," said Mi Oh, "I'll even tell you the secret of life."

Just as Mi Oh gave me a gentle shove into the alley, this is what she whispered into my ear.

"Ten glasses of water a day and plenty of B 50, my gaijin-baby."

Water, again.

After I had hooked and lost the blind brown trout for the second time, as I sat on the grassy river bank below the wide, deep pool of green water for most of the morning, I still felt like two hundred pounds of melted butter, the muscles in my neck and back gushing lactic acid at the thought of trigger points, even at the thought of thick streams of exotic lotions embedded with tiny pearls. So I closed my eyes and felt the warming sun on my face, and even though I tried not to think at all, the blind brown trout was there in the cool darkness of my mind, rising and vanishing in the river's bright water. I let the image carry me past monochronic and polychronic notions of time, into the limitlessness of Darwinian time and Valkyrian space.

River time.

Bright country time.

Soon enough, I raised up out of the grass, took up my little fly rod, tied on another fly, a Clousen's minnow, and walked downriver until I came to a run of deeper, colder water. By then, morning was heavy on the valley, and the sky looked freshly scrubbed, an unwrinkled sprawl of blue that seemed to go on and on and on.

Not only were the valley and the mountains and that stretch of river still marked by wildness. So, too, was that vast blue sky drenched in wildness, especially at twilight and in those blue-black hours of sunrise when that whole country, that great bowl of sky and mountain, meadow and river, glowed in infinite shadings and layers and ranges of light, an illumination even beyond the flash and sizzle of essence, a light that burns down through

the mind and heart, drips into the blood, probes what lingers be-
yond conscious memory.

The high country often seemed a geography of light, glitter
and flare, quiver and arc, every glow and angle and shadow
bristling with revelation, as much as a man might need, all that he
might seek, and of every kind—simple and complex, practical
and magical, worldly or private.

Near noon I came to a pocket of beautiful malachite green water
rippling over a bed of drowned stones. The river was shallow,
and the sunlight refracted off the stones gave the water the look
of a comet's tail, a long, gentle ribbon of flashing light.

I fished the upper edges of the green water, let the fly sink, go
with the modest current, go with the pull of the river. Swami Bill
had told me that fishing was an excellent pastime for perfecting the
meditation instructions he had passed along to me, free of charge.

The power of meditation, Swami Bill assured me, was in the
secret word or mantra he had given me. Actually, I would end up
with a whole collection of secret mantras. Swami Bill was always
handing them out. I could say them, rhythmically, like a chant, or
just think them, run them through my noodle like a happy-go-
lucky song. Either way they were supposed to zap whatever
stress might be coiled about my bones and joints, nerves and
muscles, bring on instant and ecstatic relaxation, transform the
meat bucket blues into holistic bliss.

One of the secret mantras Swami Bill gave me was OM.

"Isn't that an awfully public private mantra?" I said.

Swami Bill had put his hands over his mouth, which meant that
the parrot on his shoulder was about to speak. Too, I had the
feeling Bill was obscuring a widening smile.

"Say it!" croaked the parrot, its balding wings flapping insanely.

"O–M," I groaned.

"No, no!" chided the parrot. "Jazz it up. It's not a funeral hymn.
Say it as though you were a member of Bill's new church and had

just spotted another member and were getting ready to greet him as though he were long-lost family, getting ready to break into some happy-go-lucky song."

"Om-om-om," I sang weakly.

"Faster still," cried the parrot, now weaving drunkenly on Bill's shoulder in a confetti of its own spent feathers.

"Faster still! You're almost there. You're almost to paradise!"

"OMMMMMMOMMMMMOMMMM . . . ," I gasped.

"Faster!" demanded the parrot as its wires broke and it pitched forward limply, wings still flapping furiously.

"OMMMOMMMMHOMHOMHOME—HOMEHOMEHOMEHOME!"

That was my new secret word, my shiny new mantra.

"HOME."

I was singing it in my head like a happy-go-lucky song as I fished the narrow pocket of malachite green water, in between mouthfuls of a sourdough biscuit stuffed with beef and green chilis.

What a catchy tune!

More schemata for my big brain. It cannot get enough, delights in rummaging around in life's stochastic sludge for a buzz, some new feel or touch, some new experience, more and more information. Human beings hunger for life's details because they are curious, and they are curious because they are imperfect, even though they deny their imperfection, many claiming perfection, boasting that they were made in God's image. What god would go about looking as bewildered and embarrassed and ridiculous as a human being?

If it were not for our imperfection, our long, ongoing series of evolutionary pratfalls, if we were indeed as perfect as a microbe, there would not be any need for curiosity. Or modern art. Or the Sistine Chapel. Mozart, the Dead Kennedys, or bottled water. Fly-fishing or the Tantric Hotline. All they are is by-products of human curiosity, human life, which is itself just another unrepeatable evolutionary deviation. Had the Big Bang hurled what became this planet either just a little closer or a little farther away from the average star we call the sun, this wouldn't be the

little blue planet crawling with life, including human beings, who call the planet Earth.

"OMMMHOMHOMHOMEHOME."

Home Sweet Home.

My little SweetWater fly rod shuddered suddenly, the tip bending, forming a delicate arc.

A moment later, I brought the trout, another small, bold and fierce cutthroat, to the surface, where it wrenched violently in the water. I brought the trout near, did what I always do, let it go, watched it disappear, vanish down into the darker water of the current, down among the flashing stones and the morning's indigo shadows.

My little SweetWater fly rod is cane and was made by George Maurer of Kutztown, Pennsylvania. George Maurer and I have something in common, something besides trout and fly-fishing. Handcrafted cane fly rods like Maurer's are often much more than mere fly rods, fishing poles. They are part art, part skill, part magic, part technique, touched with dreams and yearnings and mystery. And all of this in a couple of ounces of cane and hours and hours and hours of exacting, detailed work. Evidently, there is little money in it. Evidently, making cane fly rods by hand is for most such craftsman no more lucrative than a career in liberal arts.

I said George Maurer and I have something in common, something more than fly rods, a common obsession for trout, wild rivers, and fly-fishing.

Trash.

Trash is funding this book, this story about the depression that whirled in my brain, about what it devoured before I got lucky and woke up in Denver, Colorado. This story of how fortune pushed me through a pale blue snow and into the offices of Dr.

Lilly Mutzpah, who had kind blue eyes and told me that depression was one human disease that can be treated and that the soured chemicals in my head could again be happy as a clam. This story of how fortune smiled again and deposited me beyond Kenosha Pass, the mountains of the Front Range, and into the sprawling high country meadows, the great valley of South Park, and the river that meanders lazily through it, the silver blue waters of the Middle Fork of the South Platte, where, in a wide pool of green water below Spinney Mountain, there was a big brown trout in whose blind eyes I kept finding intimations, implications, pieces of my own memory. Trash is also helping keep George Maurer in business as a maker of exceptional handcrafted cane fly rods.

As I write this story now in the summer of 1992, on any night you might pick, you could find George Maurer, the cane rod craftsman, working as a janitor in a school near Kutztown, Pennsylvania, and me, a thousand miles away in the same sweet darkness, on an Alabama mountain on the back of county garbage truck No. 2.

Small world.

While George Maurer spends his nights keeping public education free of clutter, mopped and scrubbed, I am tucked in the cab of the garbage truck with Thallus, Cleopheus and Hamadullah. We all smell like sour milk and orange peels. Some nights I will ride for miles with my head hanging out the window.

And how did a garbage man, a stock clerk at the supermarket down the mountain, and the cleanup man at the shoe factory down in the fuliginous valley, get the bucks for a cane fly rod?

Barter. George Maurer's addiction to trout includes a passion to read every word that has ever been written on trout and fly-fishing. Years ago he wrote me a kind letter suggesting that we make a trade: my lonely little books for one of his cane rods. I wrote Maurer that it would not be a fair trade, that I would be getting too much of value and he would be getting almost nothing of value.

Maurer insisted. It was like offering a junkie the keys to the pharmacy. Who could resist. So we traded, even.

The SweetWater fly rod I have, by the way, is only one of many that George Maurer makes. The model has a name, one given it by Maurer, not me. It is the Starlight Creek Model, named for a tributary of the Delaware River in northern Pennsylvania.

The creek that ran through my grandfather's failed farm in the low-slung, hardluck, hogbacked Ozark Mountains, the creek where I first learned I was an addict for the high country, for mountains, for wild mountain rivers and trout, for the good earth, was named Starlight Creek.

Small world.

I like my little Starlight Creek rod. I like knowing it is handmade, knowing there is so little technology between me and rivers and trout, sunlight and meadow and mountains. I like knowing that the man who made it has got it as bad for wild water as I do.

Common ground.

A friend of mine has pointed out to me that I am a fishing writer whose books do not have an ounce of practical, useful angling advice or information in them.

He is right.

Here is the only practical and useful bit of angling advice I can offer.

Thank whatever gods there are for luck. That, and have fun. Enjoy it. Smile more, laugh more. It's just fishing.

The flanks of the small cutthroat trout that I hooked in the malachite green pocket of water with my little SweetWater fly rod shone like liquid silver.

I reeled in my line and stepped out onto the riverbank, walked upstream, and again was warmed by the feel of the continuity of mountains and river, valley, meadow and sky, the deepening sensation that despite the overwhelming diversity of light and shadow and color mixed into the great earthen bowl of valley and river and surrounding mountains, it all seemed of a piece, a whole bright country spilling over the horizon, a country without margins, full not only of honest wonder, but of pure possibility and exhilaration. And the morning was oddly quiet, the only sound being the trill of the river, a magpie rising on the wind. Where the river turned into a more or less straight stretch of faster water, I eased back into the cold water, cast, again let my rod anchor me to the river and valley and the mountains as my little fly spiraled briefly on the surface of the swift water before being dragged down, down into the mirrored glare of reflected and refracted sunlight coming off the surface of the river, off the yellow-green grasses, off the deep purple flanks of the mountains in the distance.

As I stripped in the beryl green line, slowly, slowly, so that my rumpled fly would more closely mimic a moribund insect, one not quite dead yet completely spent, I was smiling again, thinking about human beings and our extended biological family, our lineage, how most of us blanch at the thought of our cousins the apes and go no farther. I go as far as I can, sinking, finally, down among single cells, living cells. They, too, are part of my extended family. Among my ancient sisters and brothers, parents and grandparents, nieces and nephews, are trees and oceans, turtles and wild orchids, and the swarming microbes.

Life is my tribe.

This average blue planet is home.

I am a failed human being for many reasons.

Aren't we all?

Among my shortcomings is that, unlike so many of my fellow human beings, I have had absolutely no luck in separating or even distancing myself from the natural world, the great living organism that is planet Earth, to which life clings, everything from the biota to the microbiota, though just barely, it often seems. No

matter how solitary it may seem, life is actually a rather wondrous and amazing collective of partnerships, both grand and microscopic, all inexorably intertwined, interconnected, inseparable, from single cells to whales, from fireflies to human beings.

Thanks to organic chemistry and biochemistry, every lonely human being can trace his or her lineage back to primordial bacteria, anaerobes, the Age of Bacteria. Things were simpler then. Fossils of Archean bacteria have been found in the ancient rocks of Labrador and Greenland, near the polar cap, rocks that are more than three billion years old. The history of life is mostly a history of the microbes. There was nothing else for more than two billion years. There would still be nothing else if bacteria had not blundered into all kinds of lucky discoveries. Human beings have built the Sistine Chapel and the atom bomb, car phones and gas chambers, talking tombstones, cities, telephones, and the internal-combustion engine. Bacteria, though, pulled off the greatest magic of all: they learned how to turn poison into energy.

Oxygen was the poison. Cyanobacteria kept fooling around with it, with living, until they stumbled onto what we now call aerobic respiration.

Bacteria learned how to turn poisonous oxygen into the sweet stuff of life.

Think of that.

Not bad for a microbe. And it was just a humble start. Bacteria kept on taking chances, probing every possibility, taking every risk, trying anything and everything. All of the basic chemical processes of life are the handiwork of microbes. So, too, photosynthesis. From the start, it seems, life, too, has been an addict, a junkie for risk, for gambling on every contingency. I am here, everything that is alive is here, mostly because life probes every possibility, takes every chance.

I can be sure of my bacterial beginnings, biochemists tell me, because of the mitochondria in my cells, which is itself a direct ancestor of these ancient bacteria. That they are in my cells has nothing to do with me, has nothing to do with human beings. Rather, I am here, human beings as a species are here, because of them. Life, it seems, is more than interrelated and interdependent. It is one big family, whole and complete and inseparable and drifting through the universe.

One for all and all for one.

Which is exactly what Swami Bill kept telling me.

How microbes, which got along perfectly well by themselves on the planet Earth for billions of years, became giraffes and spiders, wildflowers and human beings, is evolution's story.

And mostly, as scientists keep pointing out, evolution is an ongoing story of failures, imperfections, mutations, luck, and so on. Life, as I said, is an addict, hooked on chance, not on progress but on process, life itself, not on expression or form but on essence.

As a human being, stuck in a life that often feels mostly embarrassing and foolish, it somehow feels fitting to be the product of error and failure, to be an evolutionary blunder. Evolution, as I say, is only evolution and has nothing to do with progress or purpose, which are human notions, the products of our big brains and evolving consciousness, which are, naturally, just incredible, unrepeatable coincidences.

And all of evolution's blunders and failures and mistakes, every expression of life, whether extinct, dying, or hanging on, all those gone and yet to come, have the same biological family tree, more or less, the same extended family.

Not only are we all in this together, there is apparently only one way to get through it, and that is together.

I began thinking about ancient bacteria, microbes, members of my extended family, my tribe, during my long nights in the Denver Public Library. I used to go there every weekday evening after leaving the magazine. At first, my intention was to read everything I could find on depression, the disease that had me by the brain, had evidently had me since conception, was perhaps, in my case, genetic. Another one of life's wondrous blind blunders.

Anyway, I soon learned that the literature of depression is much too depressing.

On some lonely, cold blue autumn night, I found myself

among the library's stacks and stacks of books devoted to biology and chemistry.

I took one down. At random, of course, to keep in step with evolution. The book I took down from the stacks, opened, read from, turned out to be a recent history of biochemistry. Life's family album. It introduced me to my Ur-ancestors, the prokaryotes (monera, one-celled organisms with no nucleus, chromosomes, mitochrondia), and the eukaryotes, the first modern cells, and all those ancient bacteria and their relatives the mitochondria in my cells. Without them, there would be no me. No human beings. No big brains. No consciousness. Anyone feeling blue, looking for some reason for human beings, need look no farther than their own cells and the mitochondria residing there. They are responsible for it all—language, poetry, Hiroshima, the Holocaust, good and evil, god and man, tooth decay, Mozart, the Dead Kennedys and Nirvana and Helmet and why every time I hear their music it makes my teeth hurt.

Mitochondria and I are tenants in the same mobile home, this odd and silly and embarrassing sack of flesh and bone.

What do I give my mitochondria? Room and board.

What do they give me? The energy to do everything from breathing to casting a fly line over bright, wild rivers to thinking about the incomprehensible odds of existence, not just of mitochondria and ancient microbes, but of anything at all.

Anything at all.

Perhaps the question is not does magic happen, but can it happen more than once?

We get along, my mitochondria and I, because we have a symbiotic relationship. We cooperate. Actually, my mitochondria and I are hardly alone. Life goes on thanks more to mutual assistance than to anything else. Life is participatory. This mobile home that is me, this ridiculous sack of skin and bones, big brain and sizzling chemicals, nerves and muscles, is a vast collective, a union, an alliance, of creatures. That is what I learned from all those nights in the Denver Public Library, trying to make sense of the latest news from the worlds of organic chemistry and biochemistry. We are here for a lot of insane and illogical, nonsensical, ambiguous, unfathomable reasons, but mainly because life works, because there is common ground, cooperation, collaboration, reciprocity, mutual assistance, inexorable symbiosis. I have said often that we are in this, whatever life is, together, but that is putting it too narrowly. Rather, everything is in this together, and our fate is as common as our connection to each other. If human beings do not work out, if they turn out to be more bad luck, another failure, a dead end, life will do what it always does: blow on the dice, and roll them again and again.

Human beings, however, are one of life's coincidences that are not much good at getting along. Biochemists shake their heads sorrowfully and point to our big brains and evolving, shiny new consciousness as the troublemakers. We are, as our arrogance tells us, the only creatures we know of that are aware—of themselves, of life, and hence, we are also aware that life is mostly failure and misery, something, naturally, we want no part of. Consequently, we have denied most of our rich and wondrous biologic and evolutionary history and ancestry, our extended biological family, including our fragile planet home. Why settle for the earth, failure and misery, after all, when you can imagine heaven? Why be temporary and mortal, when you can imagine being immortal? Why settle for being a unique evolutionary coincidence (after all, everything alive is unique, so much so that uniqueness is as common as the cold or depression) when you can imagine being the crowning achievement of life on Earth, the chosen children of the Creator of the Universe? And on and on. Given the human condition, it is certainly understandable why human beings, all of us, want so much more, dream and imagine happier worlds, lives full of joy and happiness, other conditions, other circumstances, other lives, why so many human beings are willing to give up their souls just to get off the planet and into a kingdom they believe is being maintained for them by the Creator of the Universe.

Why not?

My grandfather and my great-uncle Albert and Elias Wonder

used to ask the Reverend Conrad Biddle of the Mount Hebron First Primitive Methodist Church many of these same questions, in their own way. Often, the old men and the Reverend Biddle would argue about the merits of religion well into the night. There was no clear victor, ever. Biddle would end up jumping up and down screaming, "Only the Lord God knows . . . only the Lord God knows," then storm out the door, and Emerson would moan, shake his head, and say what he was always saying, that "the earth is enough," and walk out the back door, down the footpath that led to the edge of Starlight Creek. I must have inherited the same frayed gene, because now I find that I am saying the same thing more and more.

The earth is enough.

A harmless refrain. And I keep on saying it.

Indeed, why not? As long as it doesn't do anyone any real harm, as long as it doesn't upset this strong buddy system I've got going with my mitochondria.

Biochemistry was often the hottest topic around the dinner table at Fairplay or back at the Holistic Motor Court, Ashram & Coin Laundry. Swami Bill and his parrot reduced the whole argument to one sentence. It was something else Bill remembered from his childhood, something he and his friends said a lot when he was a boy and the future looked wide open.

"All for one and one for all!" yodeled the parrot, as Swami Bill's Adam's apple bobbed up and down in the thin, translucent skin of his wrinkled throat, Bill masking small sobs by pressing his hand hard against his trembling lips.

Kiwi LaReaux scribbled the phrase down on a napkin and added it to the swelling list of chants and homilies and harmless little creeds that members of Swami Bill's church in progress would exchange whenever they met, just as they would exchange smiles and laughs, handshakes and hugs, and happy-go-lucky songs.

Often, Kiwi LaReaux would recite the church's growing number of creeds and harmless, innocent homilies as she walked in the meadow, near the river, and I could hear her from where I was on the river, wading in the cold, swift water, casting for trout, casting for whatever I could hook, for whatever the river would give.

With the sun low in a sky hemorrhaging with color, Kiwi LaReaux looked as though she was a quilt of shimmering shadow, and her voice would be the only sound on the wind, near and soft, hypnotic, as she repeated the new church's harmless creeds. Her voice was not that of a shaman, oracle, sage, seer, wise man, or prophet; rather, it was the voice of a beautiful female human being.

"More courtesy.

"More humanity.

"More cooperation.

"More equity.

"More accommodation."

And More Laughter. Which is the innocent little creed I gave Kiwi LaReaux. I got it from my mother, who kept saying it as the tumors in her brain went about killing her.

Listening to Kiwi LaReaux's beautiful voice, her innocent little homilies rising on the wind, drifting over the river, I remembered that human beings have gotten something from blind luck that no other creature has, something that will be our rich future or our sad and sour undoing.

Choice.

According to Kiwi LaReaux, magic, too, is as common as the cold, unemployment, and depression.

She was lying on a blue blanket spread out along the river. From where I was fishing the river, the blanket looked like a piece of fallen sky. Kiwi LaReaux had brought a picnic of fruit and wine. Luckily, I had a candy bar and cool root beer in my daypack. She had her Walkman plugged into her ears. She nibbled at an apple, sipped from a bottle of wine, and her head swayed innocently with whatever music was being pumped into her brain. I guessed she was listening to either Mozart or Loudon

Wainwright III, who seem to me to go well with fruit and wine.

I guessed wrong.

She was listening to a band named Nirvana. Nirvana was also one of Mi Oh's favorite bands. She played some of Nirvana's music when she transformed me into melted butter.

Nirvana, of course, is just another word for paradise.

Kiwi LaReaux turned off Nirvana, set her tape player down, took another bite of apple, another sip of wine. Her lips glistened and held the wine's sweet smell. I was telling her about the blind brown trout in the big oblid pool of deep water down below the Spinney Mountain reservoir. I was telling her about how the trout's blind eyes were flooded with infinite shades of color, layers of light, even my old friend Dr. Raul Yarp up on the roof of the Hotel Querencia Hotel in the Big Bend country with his cracked telescope pointed at the spread of the universe across the night sky. That it all leaked from the trout's blind eyes, mingled with the river. That in those sightless eyes, storms of light and color, I had seen so much, felt so much, imagined more. I told her how in those blind eyes flooded with color and light and shadow I had found pieces of my own memory: the color of my dying mother's eyes, gray whales rising out of the dark, cold waters of Magdalena Bay in Baja, Mexico, nudging my sea kayak playfully. And on and on.

Kiwi LaReaux finished the bottle of wine.

"Magic happens," she said, smiling shyly.

Much later—in fact, just last Christmas—Woody Moos, before he lost his job as a member of the crew of county garbage truck No. 2, found a wrinkled purple-and-white bumper sticker in a black plastic garbage bag stuffed with dead daffodils and a brand-new pair of comfortable, bloodstained bedroom slippers. This is what the bumper sticker said:

MAGIC HAPPENS.

Small world.

Woody Moos kept the bumper sticker, stuck it on the back of the truck. It is still there, even though Woody Moos is long gone.

Moos put the bumper sticker directly under another sticker he rescued from the truck's grinding gut of garbage. It was red, and shouted in giant baby blue letters, SHIT HAPPENS.

More than once I found Moos standing behind the truck, staring blankly at those two bumper stickers. He would turn toward me, shrugging his narrow, bony shoulders, repeating the bumper stickers over and over:

"Magic Happens. Shit Happens. Magic Happens. Shit Happens."

Until, finally, he told me this.

"You wanna know something. I don't think there's a spit's worth of difference between them."

As for Swami Bill, he claimed to be wonderfully and equally befuddled by both magic and luck. He did not claim to understand luck, but he is always delighted when it turned out to be in his favor, like when he learned about a new kind of underwear being developed, underwear laced with particles of metallic silver to protect the wearer's sexual organs from unsafe levels of radiation. Bill was able to get in on the ground floor, cheap. Bill could not believe his good luck. Confidentially, Bill assured me that silver metallic underpants would be even bigger than talking tombstones. Every time Swami Bill mentioned the underwear, the parrot on his shoulder would start singing the new advertising slogan Bill had come up with.

"Strut confidently into the new century, friends, wearing your radiation-free BVDs!"

After Kiwi LaReaux polished off the wine and the last of the apples and pears, plums and grapes, she stretched out on the blue blan-

ket spread in the meadow near the river and slept, and I waded quietly upstream another twenty-five yards, tied on the fly I had that came closest to the moment's mix of sunlight and shadow, mountains and valley, wide blue sky and autumn meadow, and cast it across the bright water, let the wind and sky, the rush of the river flood my senses, go on repairing whatever remaining burnt wiring the depression might have left inside my head.

I lived on the days and nights I spent in the high country, in the valley of the Mosquito and Sawatch mountains, the tumbled ridges of the Front Range, as though each moment were some pure anodyne. Mountain rivers have a way of scrubbing the emotions clean. And, as I say, what was left down in my brainpan when I started fishing the Middle Fork of the South Platte River was what had survived, what had endured, what had held on to me, stayed, made the long journey with me from there to here, here to there, out of the sludge of the meat bucket blues and into the high country, into the mountains, into that whole bright country.

I liked hiking into the meadows along the river before sunrise, walking the river as the mountains appeared to drift in dawn's blue-black shadows, not so much fixed stone as wavering strata of light—warm blues, deep purples, ash grays, coral pinks, terracotta, tranquil maroon. Walking down through the meadow, down along the river, I often felt as though I were actually crossing some dim boundary of memory, as though walking into that bright country of river and mountains was somehow a way of cheating time and finding myself, if only for an instant, back in that time and press of wild earth that my bones recall, that my blood remembers, that my cells embrace, that earth that lingers still in the oldest folds of the brain, where the pineal tissue still bristles with each sensation of light. It is a world becoming so distant that more and more it seems more imagined than real, a collection of common vague recollections, dreams, wishes, yearnings, a world more and more of memory, a world, more and more, that exists more inside the mind than outside it.

Among the great charms of fly-fishing, trout fishing, fishing mountain rivers, are the long hours spent looking for fish, waiting for fish, praying for fish, thinking of fish, or simply not fishing at all, at least not for fish. My own addiction to angling is so ruinous because I am a such a terrible junkie for the water and country that wild trout demand. I am like an alcoholic turned loose in a distillery with a truckload of empty bottles. I do not know where to begin, and so I fill my pockets and creel and brain with everything. Sometimes, when a trout does show up, it feels almost coincidental, more blind luck.

It was like that often along the Middle Fork of the South Platte River. Hours would pass without even the intimation of a trout, and it did not matter at all. What mattered was the country—the river, the valley, the mountains, the great domed sky, the light and the feel of the wind, and just the possibility of trout.

The morning that I walked down through the meadow, in and out of time, through all those shimmering strata of light and color, I waded across a shallow neck of water to the far side of the river, and stood there for a long time looking back over the meadow, and dawn seemed to rise out of the river, flood across the land. And Thomas Traherne's little rhyme suddenly broke loose in my head, putting another involuntary smile on my face.

> *Can all the sky*
> *Can all the world*
> *Within my Brain-pan lie?*

As it skipped about my brain, the little rhyme made me laugh. And the wind came up, sharp and cold against my face.

The sun warmed the meadow and the valley, so that by midday even the river felt warmer, amniotic. In its current swirled the microcosm, the meocosm, the macrocosm, tugging irresistibly against my legs. Overhead, the sky was an endless vault of turquoise. And the surface of the river flashed like a polished vein of Mexican opal.

After I hooked and lost the blind brown trout the second time, I made and broke a dozen solemn vows to break its spell, forget it, leave it alone, forget its blind eyes, how I imagined that trout felt the river, how every shift of wind, every rustle of grass, must have traced itself on its flesh, every sound, every vibration a warning, how it survived on the river's touch, its feel, its pressures, and smells, its heat and cold, its contours, the shape of its stones. Daily I would take the oath to ignore the deep green pool and daily I would find myself back on my belly, crawling through the tall meadow grass to the small rise below the pool and raising myself up slowly, slowly, watching for its shadow, some wrinkle of water, any piece of evidence that it was there, in the deep water, those white eyes leaking tiny pools of light down into the dark water.

I did not see the blind brown trout again until the second week of November. It had been a week of storms in Denver, first ice, then snow, then a curious cool rain that came and went for two days before the skies cleared, went blue again all the way to Wyoming.

Over the Front Range, beyond Kenosha Pass, down in the valley of South Park, work crews had finished putting up snow fences along the valley highway. The river ran hard and fast with the recent rain and the low ridges of the mountains glistened.

After I set up my little blue tent, stowing my small bundle of gear, the sky was still flush with soft afternoon sunlight, so I went down through the meadows, down past the reservoir, and walked along the river until I had passed well below the pool of deep green water where I had first seen the blind brown trout, where I had hooked it twice and lost it twice. I kept a good distance from the river and found myself still moving cautiously, quietly, nearly holding my breath. Even so, I was certain that despite every measured, calculated footfall, the sightless trout, if it were in the deep pool or in the faster water either above or below it, could still sense my presence and had already sunk down into the deep, shadowless water along the edge of the undercut bank, lying there heavy and dark as a stone.

Reaching the curl of the river below the pool, I doubled back, moving even more watchfully, keeping hunkered down in the damp, chilly meadow grass, the late afternoon sunlight on my face, my shadow tumbling across the swaying winter grass like the shadow of some passing, wayward, solitary cloud.

By the time I got to the small hummock of earth and grass and stone just below the pool, I was on my knees, as though in desperate prayer.

And so I was.

Let it rise, I prayed.

Let it rise.

There in the chilly grass, among dark stones, I waited and watched the surface of the pool, its smooth surface shuddering under a sudden gust of wind which scattered the sunlight into streaks and fragments of jaundice and aspen yellow, the dark red of raw garnet, methyl orange.

Delicate shadows slipped down the mountains, cloaking entire ridges and folded massifs of stone in diaphanous purple veils. The wind softened, and in that sudden quiet came the sound of the river alone, the sound of water probing its way down through the valley, through the glowing winter meadows.

And I kneeled there in the grass and watched and waited, waited for anything and everything, some feel of water, some creep of shadow, some range of light that might stir the blind brown trout, urge it to the surface of the pool, its thick, undulating silhouette moving through the blue-green water like some slab of twilight, moonish and darkly beautiful.

And move it did, coming off the bottom as the day's light drained from the sky, up from among its lair of slick, dark stones, up from where the water was raven black.

It rose slowly, took on detail, went from implication to fact, a blur of shape and colors, a boil of disturbed water at the surface that soon went calm, and the trout's every move was precise, exact, assiduous, at once exquisite and scrupulous.

From the hammock of grass and rock below the pool, I could see only its smooth back rise and fall, roll on the surface, glow in mists of rich, brooding, flickering sunlight: tinctures of red and blue and yellow and violet coming off the surface of the pool, rising off the river, low against the meadow like clouds.

Where the blind trout broke the surface, the light bristled, ignited like a magnesium flare, and I saw the arch of its thick back held in that light and saturated by it, so that every detail of it, every scale and pattern and color, every mark was drenched in resplendent light. The outline of the trout's back cut a parabola into the light for a long moment, a moment that hung on like a sigh, some breath of impending storm, a heaviness of air and water, fish and river, meadow and mountains, burning in primary colors, the whole valley a fire of colored, incandescent flames, of moon glow and earthshine, as aureoles of lingering-at-the-horizon sunlight melted like cheap candles.

The graceful, elegant arch of the trout's back, as it broke the surface, tracing an arc across the dying light and rising dark, looked like some rising countersun, a shimmering of greens and burnt golds, tongues of orange and bloody reds, neon yellows, and blacks deeper than its blind eyes.

So, the blind trout rose, rising up out of the embers of day, the gathering twilight, the bright, wild, fecund water, a pure autopietic pneuma of river and light, mountains and valley, wind and shadow, the whole bright country.

Dr. Lilly Mutzpah, as I have said, told me she thought, based on the medical evidence she had gathered, that my particular strain of depression was inherited, genetic, a kind of immortal sadness passed along from generation to generation.

I never knew or even suspected that I had the disease, really. Being shy and quiet, pensive, self-conscious, and moody had always seemed perfectly normal to me. My mother, who was shy, quiet, pensive, self-conscious, and often moody, thought it was perfectly normal, too.

And even on the worst days, when the meat bucket blues tore at every nerve, ached in every bone and muscle, there was, for a long time, no pain, no smoldering indication that the chemical connections in my brain were going code blue, until those last couple of years, when often the inside of my skull felt parboiled and every twitching ganglion from my scalp to my gut felt as though it were being continually zapped with jolts of electricity. And even when the pain came and stayed, even after I ended up in Denver, in my little, unfurnished room on Colorado Boulevard, crawling in and out of the blue sleeping bag, lying huddled in its warm comfort for days at a time, soaked in fear and sweat, I still spent hour after hour looking out my room's one ceiling-to-floor window at the folded ridges of the Front Range. Great fields of snow covered the summits, the high peaks. At sunset and sunrise, the snowfields looked like distant pale blue seas. And the depression went on drowning me slowly, the way some crocodiles kill their prey, rolling the kill over and over, dragging it deeper, down into the dark water, beyond sun and shadow, down to its food cache, some rotten log or jumble of stones, and stowing it safely there where it can soften, ripen. Even on such days, the endless play of light and shadow, color and form on the near mountains astonished me.

That is what my strain of depression never drowned completely. Astonishment.

I have always been astonished and amazed by almost everything, especially everything about the natural world, where time is simply time, directionless, the press of things as they are.

Astonishment.

And seeing the blind trout rise again reminded me of other times and moments of pure astonishment that the depression in my brain had almost drowned, destroyed.

I am, it seems, always staring at some body of wild water—river, creek, marsh, cold blue mountain spring, blackwater swamp, saltwater flat, tidal pools, expanse of sea, sprawl of brooding ocean rising and falling against a horizon of blue light, river cataracts, moving tides, yowling falls, bayous and mountain lakes—my head swimming with anticipation. There is no telling what will haul itself up out of wild water.

Like that night in the cabin smelling of marsh gas near Fargo, Georgia. I had ended up there after four days of canoeing through the dark water labyrinths of the Okefenokee swamp, that great bowl of seeping water out of which flow the St. Mary and Suwannee rivers. In the cabin, members of our little expedition had gathered in the soft yellow shimmer of a single lantern as the two little ladies from Indiana cheerfully levitated Mr. Tommy Smott of Sioux City, Iowa.

The cabin was atop a lush green hammock of cypress and bay trees. The light from the single lantern threw nervous, uncertain shadows along the walls. One shadow was rising: the shadow of Mr. Tommy Smott.

Just as Mr. Tommy Smott ascended above the little ladies from Indiana, I stepped outside, walked down to the edge of the swamp's dark water and sat. The wind was cool and sweet, smelling of pungent marsh gas: part natural cyanide. It's a heady smell, like rotting apples.

We had hauled the canoes out of the black slough just before sunset, the sky a solid red blister, as a wonderfully cool wind rustled among great mats of deep green lilies and spadderdock that clogged the edges of the slough. The canoes drifted in the swamp's nearly imperceptible current, and under that sky the swamp's tangled tapestry of sloughs and lakes and creeks looked like venules of black blood. I dipped a tiny net into the tea-colored water, water rich in tannic acid and marsh gas, and hauled up a wheeling constellation of whirligig beetles.

Beetles are like paradise. There are so many.

If you hold whirligigs close, they too smell of rotten apples.

More natural cyanide.

In the little net with the whirling whirligigs was a predaceous diving beetle, a mosquito fish, a fishing spider, a tiny bubble of air fixed pragmatically, professionally, to its abdomen, its simple answer to the Aqua-lung. Near my canoe, on the surface of the slough, a surface gone madder red with sunset, swarms of water striders performed a frenetic, mysterious ballet, an odyssey of pure motion.

And that night, after supper, the little ladies from Indiana levitated Mr. Tommy Smott from Sioux City, Iowa, and anyone else in the group with a sudden need for ascension, saying in their soft midwestern voices, "Now, rise." And it seemed somehow perfectly natural, even believable, under that slice of amber moon crawling up out of the swamp's ripe muck. The wind put a chill in the blood, and I watched the night's stars strewn not across the night sky but across the obsidian surface of the bayou, that perfect mirror of black water, the swamp's constant ooze of water and land, land and water, with no certain boundary to show where one began and the other ended, and I just stared at the bayou in that grip of night for hour after hour, wondering what might haul itself up among those reflected stars. Everywhere on the surface of the bayou were bright constellations of alligator eyes glowing electric yellow, dozens and dozens of them, like miniature suns. Patient eyes, themselves waiting for something to stir, something vital, edible. In time, down the bayou, there was the vague sound of something thrashing in the water, and the eyes, all of them, sank instantly into the dark water, sending small black waves across the surface of the bayou, a shudder that sent a tremble through the island, and the whirligig beetles danced on and on as the moon and stars rose.

Astonishment.

That blind trout rising at twilight, hauling itself out of the darkening water of the river, its back cutting a parabola through the sinking sunlight and into the budding night, seemed for a mo-

ment to eclipse the sun, then be consumed in its brilliant flame, the colors of the trout's back dripping onto the surface of the pool, flashing off its back, blades of red and gold, yellow and green, and it reminded me of another night, as well, a night in Baja, Mexico, among the barrier islands of Magdalena Bay, when Juan-Chuy rolled up his pants legs, walked down the beach and waded into the water, turned his head, bent down, put his ear to the bay's cold, dark, moving water.

It was well past midnight and I could not sleep. Neither could Juan-Chuy. We had been sitting on the beach below the low-slung dunes, listening to the resonant pulse of the Pacific, its blue-black waves breaking relentlessly against the beaches along the ocean side of the island, beaches that looked like fire-drawn seams of silver under the bright, bone white Baja moon.

As Juan-Chuy stood waist-deep in the calmer, quiet waters of Magdalena Bay, he told me that when he was a boy he would sometimes bring his ponga, which he had made, and row and sail it in the bay, along these islands, and eat and sleep and play in the bay and listen to the ocean, which often frightened him, he said, because when he was a boy he imagined that the sound of the Pacific, its black waves against the soft islands, was the sound of God breathing.

Juan-Chuy smiled and kept his ear down in the waters of the bay, listening for different sounds, different gods. He was searching the bay's relentless cacophony of noise for music—the song that would mean the presence of whales.

Gray whales.

For a week we had been among the gray whales spending the winter months in the fecund, isolated, protected coves, lagoons, and bays along the Pacific coast of Baja, Mexico.

Our days were spent in our sea kayaks exploring Magdalena Bay and the long, slender finger of Magdalena Island from below Puerto Magdalena to above Puerto Lopez Mateos and Boca de Soledad. Juan-Chuy kept to his ponga.

I like sea kayaks for the same reasons I like fly rods: for their lack of fuss and clutter, for their efficiency and simplicity, for their practicality, and because they put as little technology as possible between me and the water—the waters of Magdalena Bay.

The nutrient-rich waters of Magdalena Bay and its winter guests, the gray whales, are, by the way, yet more members of my extended biological and biochemical family: living things.

Life is my tribe.

The gray whales spent their days moving in and out of the stone-cold waters of the Pacific, in and out of the calmer, quieter waters of the bay. Often, one would rise near the sea kayak, sometimes only yards away, as though truly curious, spouting giant obloid crests of water into the air, their knuckled backs gleaming black-and-green in the harsh Baja sunlight under a cloudless Pacific blue sky.

So many were there that in time their presence became common, expected. We watched them; they watched us.

Late every afternoon, we would choose some wide, deep expanse of beach on the island's bay side, haul the kayaks out of the chilly water, set up our tents among the dunes, protected from the wind, the night's cold bite. Tent raised, I would climb atop some golden ridge of a high dune that looked out toward the Pacific, beyond beaches heaped with the ocean's debris, a seemingly endless sprawl of brilliantly colored shells and the sun-bleached bones of sea turtles and sea lions and gray whales, albescent, decaying slowly in the Baja's deep heat, under its adamant, olamic sun, a sun embalmed in a hard blue, cloudless sky.

From the high dunes I watched the blue-green waters of the Pacific and the darker, quieter waters of the bay, for hour after pleasant hour. Clouds of fish flashed in the bay, shoals of them, gleaming silver. Pieces of a shattered kayak rolled in the heavy sea where the waters of the ocean and bay mingled in a perpetual low, menacing roar. And if I kept at it, watched and watched, there would be whales breaching, spyhopping, propelling their great hulking bodies out of the bay, rolling in midair, some appearing momentarily suspended, sheets of blue-green water pouring off their massive heads and flanks, giving their flesh the look of wet obsidian.

More big mammals playing in water. Vital water. Zoetic water.

Breaching and spyhopping both strike me as perfectly reasonable and understandable behavior—a whale's way, perhaps, of just having a look around, sampling the air and sunlight, making a splash, getting a few barnacles off its head and back, a whale's way, perhaps, of saying it is here, just as that handprint on the cave wall deep in Seminole Canyon marked the passage of ancient man. Both are ways of communicating, saying, I am here.

A human being leaves his handprint.

Fish click their teeth.

Termites beat their heads against whatever is handy.

Leeches tap.

Frogs croak.

Turtles sigh.

Snakes rattle and hiss.

Whales breach and they sing, fill the oceans and seas with their haunting chorales and madrigals, requiems and solos, cradlesongs and harmonics full of theme and variation, deep-water rhapsodies—yearnings, perhaps, or simply greetings, or the sounds of profound resolution.

How astonishing to communicate by song, to pass the days singing.

Life likes to make noise, sing a song, keep a beat, tap out rhythms.

Ebb and flow.

The rhythm of things that come and go.

Juan-Chuy's skin was the dark brown of Baja at dusk, and all I could see of him as he stood waist-deep in the shallow water beyond the beach, the dark waters of the bay, was his bright eyes and his teeth as he smiled and went on listening to the bay, waiting for the gray whales to sing, fill the deep water and his ears with song.

I asked Juan-Chuy what the song of the gray whale sounded like, what he heard when he put his ear to the waters of Magdalena Bay.

"The sound," said Juan-Chuy, "is like that of a sea gull vomiting up fish bones."

Sweet music indeed.

Just as the blind brown trout was a wondrous, undeniable expression of the river, its pool, the near meadows and mountains, so too was Juan-Chuy a celebration of geographical resonance, that sustaining belief that a man who is lucky enough to be marked by a certain piece of earth, a place, becomes that place. Landscape shapes the man before man shapes the landscape.

Juan was Baja.

Swami Bill was Boulder.

Dr. Truth was anywhere and everywhere, America. The good old U.S. of A.

Many times, Juan-Chuy told me, he had tried to break free of Baja, flee to some other, kinder, more generous part of the world. He ran not to escape Baja, but rather its human history of unbroken poverty and misery.

And always he had come back. Seven times he had left and seven times he had come back, back to Baja's isolation, it wildness, its edged, thorny, sun-blasted beauty. Under its harsh sun, again and again, he finds what he most hungers for—uncorruptible autonomy.

What he needs is there, in the simmer of an almost equatorial sun, in the rich blue ocean and sea and bays. He made a new ponga, a fishing boat, and has saved up enough money for a motor that will let him follow wherever the fish run. He has built a small house on the outskirts of La Paz, and there is a woman in the city, a woman with beautiful black hair and black eyes.

"She . . . how you say? . . . gets to me, like the sea . . . like the fish . . . like the whales," Juan-Chuy said. "The woman has my heart. Baja, the sea, and God struggle for my soul."

The allure of Mexico's Baja is doubled-edged: part haunting dream, part sweat-drenched nightmare, so that what makes the place so tempting also makes it intolerable. Its torment lies coiled within its fascination.

Baja is hard and harsh and unforgiving, implacable, unrepentant, stretching like an arthritic finger eight hundred miles south from its tenuous, star-crossed union with California, to Cabo San Lucas.

Years ago I caught a marlin in the cold blue Pacific waters off Cabo San Lucas.

In a bar in La Paz a man whispered of the great fish in the waters off Cabo San Lucas. I had just given him a crinkled American dollar bill for a drink and some food. He drank and ate and talked of the fish at Cabo San Lucas and drank until the dollar was exhausted. At the airport outside of La Paz, I paid $20 American for a one-way ticket to Cabo San Lucas. The plane was some sort of old propeller aircraft. As it turned out, Pablo, the pilot, was a taxi driver in La Paz who almost had enough hours to qualify for a pilot's license. The plane had six seats. Besides Pablo and me, there were six other human beings and a variety of small farm animals. An hour late, after buzzing a flock of skeletal goats crowded into the meager shade of a single weary stone, Pablo landed the plane. A blue Chevy Nova materialized out of the midday sun: a taxi, the only one in Cabo San Lucas.

The next day, as I say, I caught a beautiful blue marlin and wanted to let it go until the young boy who worked as the boat's deckhand explained to me what a wonderful and kind thing it would be to give the fish to the people of the village, which I did.

As the big boat moved heavily through the blue Pacific, back toward land, past the sea lions sunning themselves on the warm rocks of Los Archos, back toward the docks, he raised little flags to let everyone know the boat had had luck, that we had caught dorado and rooster fish and a blue marlin.

Waiting at the wooden dock was a crowd of women and children. The children kept staring at me as though I were from another planet.

And, of course, I was. I was from the planet on the far side of the Rio Grande, the planet behind the fences and barbed wire and armed guards.

When the small crowd saw the beautiful blue marlin being hauled from the boat, they all laughed and cheered and clapped as though I had brought them manna from heaven.

I did what most Americans do in similar situations when they are traveling in Mexico or Africa or India or almost any place on the planet, I felt ashamed and embarrassed and gave the children every peso I had.

That was years ago, when Cabo San Lucas was still just a dusty, hot, broke and broken fishing village on the road to nowhere.

That marlin always reminds me of the paradox of Baja, that it is a hardluck, burnt-out land surrounded by the Pacific on the west, the Sea of Cortez to the east, deep blue seas fat and heavy with life, with manna from heaven.

Baja is a peninsula, a geologic thread of stone left hanging by the press of plate tectonics, the drifting continental plates. Baja hangs on, a pinched scar of scrub and stone tracing the existence of, the path, of the menacing, patient, and lethal San Andreas fault, which now and then shakes its death rattle up and down California's rotting spine, just to remind it that things come and go.

Come and go.

Early Jesuit missionaries called Baja the "thornful rock." It still is mostly thorn and rock and brutal sun, the kind of unrelenting desert sun that burns a landscape clean, down to its irreducible elements, down to things rudimentary and fundamental, whether it be the life of a lizard or a human being. I noticed this in the way Juan-Chuy spoke, the power and economy of his language, how whenever he spoke it was of what mattered, was for him immediate and urgent, thoughts of sea and fish and land, his boat, weather, whales.

Juan-Chuy told me that in Baja a man's choices were simple: he could go with the land or die trying to go against it.

Baja's honest hostility is the greater part of its allure. It is a place where civilization has yet to make much of an impact. Only the sun and sea and desert abide: the sun and sea and land Juan-Chuy had fled from seven times and returned to seven times. The sun and sea and land and the woman in La Paz with the beautiful black hair and black eyes. Baja, said Juan-Chuy, was a place where family and home, the details of living and dying, were still matters of great importance to everyone.

To the outsider, Baja is an acquired taste. You have to like the edged sunlight and the sea and the desert, at least tolerate not just isolation but insulation: Baja is full of human beings who, for whatever reasons, do not wish to be found, disturbed, located, bothered, noticed.

In a dirt-floor bar on the outskirts of La Paz, a bar that smelled of sweet Mexican beer and urine, vomit and venomous salsa, an American who had been in Baja for more than twenty years told me that there were only two kinds of people he had yet to see drift through La Paz—umbrella salesmen and Jehovah's Witnesses.

Baja, he told me, makes the same pact with every one who comes. You either stay and adapt, pack up and leave, go insane, or die. Baja, he said, does not care which.

"Have a warm cerveza, gringo," said the man, his white cotton shirt stained yellow with sweat. Beads of it dripped steadily from the tip of his nose, down his chin, off the matted ends of his gray hair.

"Come on. Decompress," he said.

"There's less pressure on a man down here, friend. I mean, Baja's beyond laid back. It's the perfect place for anyone fresh out of future plans."

It wasn't until 1973 that a highway, in the modern sense, nearly, was built that successfully navigated the entire peninsula, north to south. Officially, it is known as Highway 1. My friend in the bar in La Paz hailed it as the Road to Nowhere. When I left La Paz, driving north to meet Juan-Chuy at Puerto Lopez Mateos on Magdalena Bay, there was a large handpainted sign just out of town that had this to say to everyone traveling Highway 1, the Road to Nowhere.

NOW YOU KNOW WHAT DEATH IS LIKE.

A salubrious wind came off Magdalena Bay.

Juan-Chuy, waist-deep in the shallow water off the bay, his ear pressed to the surface of the water, whispered that he could hear fish on the move, passing nearby, big schools of them.

An hour after sunset, we had gathered on the beach, around the big fire in front of the mess tent. Juan and I sat in the cool sand eating platefuls of warm tortillas and Baja spaghetti, with a choice of sauces—vegetarian, combustible, and incendiary. There were big bowls of spicy cervica. All of it had been prepared fresh by Juan-Chuy. We ate and talked, and somewhere during the conversation I remember mentioning, as I often do, that I thought the mystery of the earth, the natural world, life, was just as precious as any other wildness, as worthy of protection as forests and oceans, mountains and rivers, whales and eagles, snail darters and wild flowers, that maybe it too was being squandered, being ruined, was endangered.

"How can you protect magic?" Juan-Chuy wondered aloud.

I shrugged my shoulders. "Maybe just by accepting it and passing it along," I said.

Passing it along.

Juan kindly offered to pass along some of Baja's mystery to me, some of its manna from heaven—its sunlight and its indigo seas fat with fish, more fish than a man can imagine, its quiet, the peace of its isolation, its endless blue skies. Its boneyard beaches. Its solitude. Breaching whales. Women with beautiful black eyes and black hair.

He never mentioned a single town, a single piece of human ar-

chitecture, a work of art, a book of poetry, an industry, the cost of living, not even the modern splendor of Highway 1.

Baja: hypaethral, spare, inimical, menacing, endlessly tempting, its beauty as deep as its poverty, its mysteries seemingly safe, joyously insoluble, inextricable.

And in the smooth, dark, shallow waters of the bay where Juan-Chuy kept his ear down to the water, there were forty-ton mysteries in motion, whopping mammals with hearts the size of Swami Bill's butter yellow VW, mammals that greeted each other just as members of Swami Bill's church in progress greeted each other—with a happy-go-lucky song.

While Juan waited for the whales to sing, I sat on the beach, my feet buried in the cool sand, eating the last of the fresh pie Juan-Chuy had baked over embers of coal buried in a shallow sand pit.

There are toothed (odontoceti) whales and baleen (mysticeti) whales. Gray whales are the most ancient of the baleen whales. They have been fumbling and blundering through evolution for more than twenty million years.

Whales are the largest creatures on the planet at the moment. Like termites and cockroaches, marsupials, brown trout, and human beings, they are evolutionary coincidences.

Some coincidence!

Gray whales can grow to forty tons, even though their diet is almost dainty, consisting of tiny marine organisms like krill and amphipods and isopods, which they eat by the ton, scooping them up, straining them through the bristly edges of immense baleen combs that grow from the roofs of their Brobdingnagian mouths.

Gray whales were once as plentiful as ivory-billed woodpeckers.

The ivory-billed woodpecker is extinct. Its evolutionary luck ran out, with a lot of help from human beings.

Atlantic gray whales are gone, too.

In 1946, the International Whaling Commission prohibited commercial hunting of gray whales, and almost thirty years later Mexico made the whales' wintering grounds in the bays and lagoons of Baja a whale sanctuary, including Scammon's Lagoon (Guerro Negro and Ojo de Liebre).

Ironically, or at least coincidentally, Charles Melville Scammons was the California whaler who first followed migrating gray whales to Baja, not to give them sanctuary but to kill them, render them into lamp oil and soap and so on and so on.

The Pacific gray whales hang on, survive, numbering as many perhaps as fifteen to twenty thousand. And they still follow the pull of their blood, migrating each winter more than six thousand miles from the icy waters of the Bering Sea to the isolated bays of Baja. They travel in small pods, or groups of five to fifteen whales each.

Human beings used to move about in extended families or in tribes. These days, however, we tend to drift about in disaffected pairs or wander about the planet solo, lonely and lost, a tribe of one.

The pregnant female gray whales arrive in Baja first, the giant bull males last, all of them eating little or nothing as they migrate, hardly even a scoop of krill. By spring, when they make the return trip to the Bering Sea, many will have lost 30 percent of their body weight, a couple of tons.

While in the deep, cool, quiet lagoons and bays of Baja—Punta Banda, Santo Tomas Point, Coronado Islands, San Martin Island, Magdalena Bay, Scammon's Lagoon—the whales court and mate, and the pregnant females bear and nurse their young.

There is, for a time, sanctuary.

And all winter long there is breaching and spyhopping and lots of singing back and forth down in the deep water.

I watched the gray whales for hours and hours, day after day, watched them come suddenly bursting out of the sea or merely raising their great heads out of the water, their bodies as elegant and functional as trout, titanic yet smooth, completely practical, efficient, no useless options of unnecessary ornamentation like

hairdos or body art. Forty tons and every ounce of it as graceful as a bird on the wing.

That last day, after we had hauled the sea kayaks onto the beach, after we had made camp and begun gathering around the warming fire in front of the mess tent, only a handful of the group wanted to join Juan-Chuy in his ponga, ride out into the bay one last time to watch the sun set and hope for whales.

"You can only see so many whales," said the judge from Los Angeles, who was divorced and deeply disappointed that there were not more single or divorced women in the group. He had traveled south to Baja to court and mate, too.

"I was told there would be available women," he said, staring blankly into the fire, "and what do I get—eight days and nights with a fired electrical engineer, an aging hippie, TV people, some kind of writer, and newlyweds!"

The TV people were from HBO, the Home Box Office channel, which is a wholly owned subsidiary of Time Warner Inc.

The fired electrical engineer was from Boston. He had paid for his eight days of sea kayaking among the gray whales in Baja with his severance pay.

"I thought it would be nice to have an adventure to dream about when I'm back home in the unemployment line," he said.

As for the "some kind of writer," that was me. I was on assignment as a full-time magazine writer and editor then, an employee of the Southern Progress Corporation, which is a wholly owned subsidiary of Time Warner.

Then, my depression was only a vague melancholy swimming in my blood, adrift in my head, down deep in my bones and muscles, as it had always been. I would not find out until I ended up in Dr. Lilly Mutzpah's office in downtown Denver, walking there in a steady fall of pale blue snow, that my depression had been coded in my genes, had been passed along to me at the moment of conception along with all kinds of other codes, including the code that I would have hazel eyes and that I would go bald, by and by.

Although depression is as common as the cold, it is still a difficult disease for most people to understand, accept. It seems too vague to be taken seriously, especially for those who have never experienced it full-throttle. Depressives, I have learned, are deeply embarrassed, ashamed, afraid. After all, when they confess, try to tell someone about this thing—disease, condition, affliction, this black depression, this bleak despair that has them by the throat—the usual reaction is not understanding but misunderstanding, a kind of bewildered disbelief. And why not, I suppose. On the surface, depression, to the unaffected, does seem like an awfully vague and silly, even minor complaint. How can being down in the dumps be a real disease? We expect our diseases to be more empathic, recognizably lethal, dangerous, tragic. Unlike the ravages of alcoholism, which carve themselves so deeply into the alcoholic, depression masks its torments well.

I am proud to say that the company I worked for has a great compassion for alcoholics. Writing and alcohol, after all, are old and dear and destructive friends. Had I been an alcoholic, I would have been shipped off to dry out, been given the opportunity to kick my addiction to drink, come back to work with my breath smelling minty fresh.

But my disease was depression, though I did not know it at the time. My friend the CEO suspected it. But all he was sure of was that I was much too sad and blue to go on working in paradise. Sooner or later depression is just too depressing to be around.

It is true about the newlyweds. They had rushed from their wedding in California to Baja to honeymoon as they kayaked among the gray whales. They too had come to Baja to mate. Every night they would leave the campfire, walk back to their tent among the dunes giggling and kissing and holding hands.

And the judge from Los Angeles would spit mouthfuls of

tequila into the fire, and the flames would claw into the night sky, throwing ghostly shadows against the dunes.

I went with Juan-Chuy to watch one last Baja sunset and hope for whales. I could not see enough of the whales.

Juan steered the ponga from the island's shallow beach out into the deep waters of the bay. The whole immense Baja sky burned magenta, and dusk's ubiquitous cold wind came off the ocean.

Juan-Chuy took the ponga near the boca, the wide mouth where the bay opened to the Pacific, killed the motor, let the ponga drift. Chimeras of bruised purple and red light slouched across the surface of the bay, and no one spoke. The only sound was the ponga rocking gently in the swells until the whale surfaced, was suddenly there, rising out of the silence of water and sunlight, rising just as the blind brown trout would rise in that pool of deep green water of the Middle Fork of the South Platte River. And the light and color I remember of that last Baja sunset would leak out of that blind trout's eyes.

The whale was a young calf, its dark green head just out of the water, its mother below it, as the calf rose, spouting almost playfully, drenching us.

The calf was so near the ponga that I could clearly see the eye it had turned toward us, a milky blue eye that seemed far too tiny for the calf's huge head.

The calf moved closer still, the eye moving back and forth, a curious, tiny, milky blue eye, wondering, I thought, what to make a boatload of gasping human beings: evolutionary newcomers, misfits, troublemakers.

The young calf stared and stared, sinking and surfacing ever nearer the drifting ponga.

Nearer and nearer.

And the big female stayed close always, until she too rose spouting great plumes of seawater into the air that lingered for a moment like an cold, iridescent fog. Juan did nothing—nothing to upset the whales, nothing to annoy them, intrude upon them. The ponga drifted. They watched us; we watched them.

The big female sank down deep into the water, her back flashing endless shades of green and so crowded with gray-white barnacles that it looked an immense stone festooned with lichen. Magnified by the deep, clear, blue-green waters, the female's great wide back seemed to span the boca. Then she rose again, her every movement appearing consciously gentle, as she bowed her back up against the bottom of the ponga, lifting it slightly, letting the wooden bottom scratch the length of her back, then setting it down again upon the water, gently, as if she were aware of our frailty, our vulnerability.

By then I was hanging over the sides of the ponga, my face a blend of fear and astonishment, reaching out to touch the female's massive back, her supple gray-green skin.

Then she sank again into the bay and rose next to her calf, both of them rolling on the surface as the ponga drifted away, the calf, already a ton of mammal, nursing hungrily.

What did it feel like to touch a whale?

Warm. Mammalian warmth.

Just like you and me.

Family.

That night I could not sleep. Neither could Juan-Chuy. We sat on the beach, and then Juan-Chuy waded into the bay and put his ear to the water and listened for the whales singing. Just as he looked up toward me and smiled, just beyond him, out in the deep water where a thin vein of moon glow and starlight wrinkled across the surface of the bay, a gray whale rose, its great back breaking the surface, moving through the water like some rogue wave.

WHOEVER YOU ARE

To bring the dead to life
Is no great magic.
Few are wholly dead:
Blow on a dead man's embers
And a live flame will start.

—ROBERT GRAVES

I finally caught the blind brown trout. It did not throw the hook or break the line. The line held and I brought the trout close, close enough to touch.

It was the second week of December 1990, and it was snowing along the Middle Fork of the South Platte River, all through the great valley of South Park.

It was a soft, delicate blue snow.

The sky over the valley, over the meadow, up among the snow-covered peaks of the Mosquito and Sawatch mountains, had gone gray-black, and in every direction the day was sunless and moody. Rafts of dark, anvil-flat clouds sagged heavily over the high ridges.

The wind off the river was cold, stinging. Below the deep pool, where the river ran fast and shallow over cold, black stones, the rippling water looked like a boil of black blood yet the surface of the deep pool was tenebrous and as calm as a black yawn.

I had fished all morning along that stretch of river below the pool and had had no luck. The day's fortune had brought the delicate, pale blue snow, but no sign of trout.

From among the dark, craggy flanks of the mountains came the wind's crepitated wail: a sound like that of bone being crushed heavily underfoot.

The snow was the same color as Dr. Truth's shoeless feet when he was found dead in an alley in downtown Denver, under a heap of holly green garbage bags.

Truth's dead eyes were open. They, too, had gone blue, cold blue, and there was a bent smile on Truth's frozen black lips, as though death had taken him in midthought.

Odell Euclid and I had seen Dr. Truth just the day before.

He was where he always was—atop his folding, brown-metal chair on the corner of Seventeenth & Stout streets. His eyes were still polychromatic.

He still had his shoes, too, a pair of dirty emerald green slippers. Dollops of blue snow were stuck to the toes of each slipper. The emerald green slippers looked as though they had been made for a giant's feet. Dr. Truth had stuffed them with wads of balled-up newspaper. Alive, his feet buried in his huge, floppy, dirty emerald green slippers, Truth had looked ridiculous, like an unemployed circus clown.

As he spoke, flakes of blue snow melted on Dr. Truth's trembling lips. Truth was telling the steady stream of human beings that passed him by, ignored him, that the milk of human kindness had soured, was in fact bitter as bile. He was saying to each blank, uninterested face, in warm and compassionate shrieks, that the cards of life had been stacked against every one of them, that they had always been stacked against them, that they would always be stacked against them.

Dr. Truth sucked in great gulps of cold air that rattled in his lungs and throat as he yelled louder and louder.

"Smell that, friends!

"Smell it! That odor of rot. Sweet mortality!

"Ahhh, so much for our meat, ladies and gentlemen. Want to know, friends, what survives? What goes beyond the rot?

"Not bone. Not mind.

"Not your smile, not your looks, not your hidden dreams.

"None of that friends! No! No!

"You know what stays?

"Not why you lived, friends, but how!

"The how—that's what lingers. For a while.

"A while."

The next morning, Truth was dead, frozen stiff.

Someone had taken his dirty emerald green slippers.

As the paramedics wrestled with Truth's stiff, icy corpse, finally got it inside a moss green body bag, Odell Euclid took his stocking cap from his head and said, "A moment of silence, please, for Truth's passing."

Later, when I told Swami Bill and his main squeeze, Kiwi LaReaux, about Dr. Truth, Bill said what he used to say to dead and dying boy soldiers when he was a combat chaplain's assistant in Vietnam, as he sent them along to whatever vision of heaven they most desired. He said to them what he says to every human being he meets, what is the subliminal message played loud and clear on his series of self-help tapes, what he said to me, time and time again.

"OLLIE-OLLIE-OXEN-FREE."

Swami Bill asked me if I knew what kind of heaven Dr. Truth had hungered for.

I did not know.

"It doesn't matter," said Swami Bill.

"Whatever it was, he is there.

"He is there.

"Take care, Truth. It's all going to be okay. Everything's going to be fine.

"OLLIE-OLLIE-OXEN-FREE."

Odell Euclid wrote a moving tribute, a touching obituary for Truth, which the magazine refused to print. Instead, Euclid was let go.

Fired.

The week before I caught the blind brown trout in the deep pool of the river, as swirls of delicate blue snow filled the sky, I visited Dr. Lilly Mutzpah for the last time. Ending my weekly visits was a matter of economics. Dr. Mutzpah's medical services had become something else I could no longer afford.

I had seen her each Thursday afternoon for more than three months. I was her five o'clock appointment.

I would miss her. I would miss talking to her, that hour in her black chair's soft embrace in the sad light of late afternoon, as shadows danced over her translucent olive skin, shadows that shuddered like excited black fish. I would miss her kind blue eyes, the view from her office window, the peaks of the Front Range in the distance glowing in countless ranges of light and color. I would miss her soft voice as she leaned close, whispered, "There, there . . . there, there."

As I said good-bye to Dr. Lilly Mutzpah, I remembered that first day when I showed up at her office seeking relief from the black pain in my brain, the despair that tore at my days and nights, as the chemical wiring inside my skull went bad. She asked me why I had come.

I told her I could not remember if Humpty-Dumpty had fallen or been pushed.

Dr. Lilly Mutzaph smiled, took me by the arm, said warmly, kindly, "There, there . . . there, there."

Dr. Mutzpah told me that I was suffering from depression, that it was a disease that I had probably always had, that it was probably hereditary, a melancholy as old as the evolution of human beings. When Dr. Lilly Mutzpah talked about depression as a disease, she often called it Inferno Scatenato.

Hell unchained.

I called it what I had always called it.

The meat bucket blues.

During that last visit, Dr. Mutzpah asked me one last question about the day I lost my job, the day I was fired by my friend the CEO. She wanted to know if I had learned anything from the ex-

perience that might be of value to other workers, to the CEOs of corporate America.

All I could think of to tell her was this—that firings and fly-fishing lessions should probably never be scheduled for the same day, especially if they involved the same employee.

Dr. Mutzpah smiled, failed at holding back a girlish giggle. It was the first time I had heard her laugh. It was a lovely laugh. On that last day in her office, Dr. Mutzpah shook my hand, said good-bye, wished me luck. Her last words to me were these:

"Take care."

And these:

"Oh, and about Humpty-Dumpty. He slipped. That's all. He slipped and fell, and then he got put back together again. It happens all the time."

Which is true. Human beings, it seems to me, are always slipping, falling, and getting back up, moving on.

Moving on.

On that last day, on that last visit, I thanked Dr. Mutzpah for her concern, for her kindness, for being all the king's horses and all the king's men, for caring enough to put me back together again.

I hooked the blind brown trout on my first cast across the dark, smooth waters of the pool.

The fly fell to the surface of the pool, spiraled once in the delicate blue snow that was falling harder and harder, then was sucked down by the river's cold, black current, sank down among the bottom's eroded black stones.

The trout hit the fly savagely, swallowed it without hesitation, bending the tip of my little SweetWater rod into a severe arc. Minutes later, as I hauled it up, the trout looked like some vague nebula coming slowly into focus, a great smear of light and color, form and motion.

The trout seemed like a quaver of burnished golds and dark greens, bold yellows, soft oranges, and brooding reds upon the dark surface. And, suddenly, there were its eyes. Those blind eyes, eyes flooded with shadows. Pupils covered with cataracts as thick as paste.

I brought the blind brown trout near and saw that its eyes carried reflections of the mountains, of the whole bright country, swirling in whorls of delicate blue snow.

My hands trembled as I fumbled with the leader and tippet, with the hook imbedded deeply in the trout's hard jaw.

The tips of my fingers were as blue as the edges of the trout's blind eyes. I could feel the icy river through my waders, through layers of pants and long underwear, and in that cold water was the sharp bite of eons and eras, the push and pull of life and time, restless and relentless. And in that pool of dark, winter river, the wildness fashioned by my mind (of thought and dream, of desire and wish, perception and sensation, of experience, fantasy, and schemata) and that raw, uncut wildness of the river, that whole high country, seemed at that moment inseparable, inexorably the same.

I folded that moment into my memory. Another piece of wild country, of mountains and mountain rivers, of wild fish, to wrap about my flesh and bones. A moment of matter that mattered to me, a moment that was whole and complete, existence perhaps as fully realized as I will ever know it, stitched to every other moment by the rhythm of things, that rhythm that holds true even beyond the limits of meaning.

The rhythm of things that come and go.

Come and go.

Kiwi LaReaux once told me that she kept coming to the high country so that she could gather the essence of things, to listen to the shamanistic chants of the wind, the revelational trill of mountain rivers, the quiet ecstasy of stones. As she talked, Kiwi LaReaux took a small, collapsible pyramid from her day pack, attached its sides, placed it on a flat rock, and set three apples inside.

"To keep them fresh," she said.

"Bill," said Kiwi, "uses it at the trailer park to keep his razors sharp."

Swami Bill and Kiwi LaReaux slept in a tent that was pyramidal in shape.

"Its powers keep one's bioplasm fine-tuned," said Kiwi La-Reaux, "open to everything.

"We got it at a garage sale. Two bucks. Miracles happen. They are as common as paradise."

One's bioplasm, Kiwi explained, was a person's *chi'i*. Their life force.

Kiwi LaReaux believed that a human being's *chi'i,* their life force, is their spirit, their soul, the thing that lasts, that goes on and on beyond the sweet rot of mortality, is the essence beyond essence.

Who knows?

When I first told Kiwi LaReaux about the blind brown trout in the deep pool of the river, she smiled shyly.

"Sounds like a revelation," she said. The night was deep and cold, and there was a lantern outside the tent, around which we were gathered. I watched the reflection of the lantern's soft orange light in Kiwi's beautiful green eyes, quivering there like nervous flames of some primeval fire.

"I'm not sure I'm looking for revelations," I said.

She was still smiling shyly.

"Oh, you don't have to," said Kiwi LaReaux. "They come looking for you."

By then, I was smiling shyly, too, smiling because the pain in my head had gone, because the depression had eased, because the bewildered chemicals in my brain no longer felt like pools of hydrofluoric acid nibbling away at the inside of my skull, nibbling way at my muscles and bones and nerves.

Kiwi LaReaux leaned toward me, touched her fingertips to my forehead. Her fingertips were wonderfully cool against my skin.

Kiwi LaReaux explained that her fingertips were busy checking the health and vitality of the alpha waves zigging and zagging through my brain.

There was a mystery, deep and abiding, that embraced Kiwi LaReaux like the cool blue mists that clung to the grasses of the high meadow, a mystery that I thought must be something like paradise. Swami Bill and Kiwi LaReaux believed that they had been uncommonly lucky, that their life together generated a harmless and innocent enchantment. All either of them wanted to do was share the magic, spread the joy.

Spread the joy.

While Kiwi LaReaux smiled bashfully, pressed her cool fingertips against my forehead, monitored my brain's alpha waves, I noticed that her touch was like her beautiful green eyes, and that she smelled of the river and the mountains, of the meadow, and of jasmine. Kiwi LaReaux's cool touch was one of the many lovely and warm nuances she left upon the silky texture of time.

With the tips of her long, slender fingers pressed lightly against my forehead, Kiwi LaReaux told me that my brain's alpha waves were warm and strong and glowing.

"The misery seemed to have disappeared," she said.

And all I could do was sit there and smile.

I finally freed the hook from the blind trout's jaw. It took minutes. Too long. I could not stop staring at the powerful muscles wrinkling below its glistening flanks, at the wild plasma of colors on its back, at the chimeras of light and shadow slouching across the surface of its eyes.

Looking at those eyes, I felt suddenly as though I had been pulled out of my skin, down through the blowing blue snow, down into the dark winter river, down through those blind eyes into the irreducible press of time. Down in those cold blue blind eyes was something that had renewed the connections of my memory, the flood of my years told in light and smears of primary colors, tides of dreams and desires, loss and pain, loves and small joys, at last fully felt, realized, resolved.

For an instant, in the shallow water where it shuddered violently as I fumbled with the hook, the trout traced its presence in a tremble of wild water. And the hook came free.

In that brown trout's blind eyes, I went on remembering and imagining, went on wheeling through the moments of time's timeless time, even the moments I had tried to push aside, including the moment I walked into my mother's hospital room in Phoenix, Arizona. She was in Pod C, Room 1221, Bed 2 of the Good Samaritan Hospital.

She smiled.

I smiled.

"You're just in time to hear the fat lady sing," said my mother.

I walked to the side of her bed, bed No. 2, bent down, hugged her, and saw that what she had told me weeks before was true, that her hazel eyes had turned wild blue.

The call came on September 3, Labor Day, 1989.

It did not come as I had imagined all such calls come—deep in the night, startling, paralyzing sound, more death rattle than ring, that call whose message you know even before answering.

Instead, the call, from my father, came at about five o'clock that Sunday.

I did not know it was my father at first. It was just the distant sound of someone sobbing. Finally he spoke, in gulps, between sobs.

"Mom . . . has cancer.

"It's in her brain."

As my father talked, I remembered that my mother had told me months before about having bad headaches, headaches she was treating cheerfully and often with heavy doses of slapstick comedy, old television reruns of "M*A*S*H" and "The Honeymooners."

I had talked to my mother only weeks before. She had called again, asking me nervously, seriously, about the color of her eyes.

"What color are my eyes?" she said.

"Hazel," I said.

"No they're not," she said.

"They're blue."

As I would later learn from her friends in Arizona, my mother's headaches and blackouts and dizzy spells were nothing new. She had been having them for months and months, but she never complained until the pain in her head brought tears to her eyes, eyes newly blue.

My mother never said anything to my father. She was like that. Quiet and shy, never wanting to bother anyone, impose, be a burden.

At the time, my father, a retired army colonel, was working as a full-time consultant. He would fly to Dallas each Sunday, spend the work week there, and catch a plane back to Phoenix each Friday afternoon.

My mother, a soldier's wife, stayed at home. She wanted it that way. She would have it no other way. Home, some permanent place that was hers, was all she had ever wanted for a long, long time. Getting one had taken her more than thirty years and more than fifteen moves.

We were military bedouins. We moved every two or three years. The more we moved, the more my mother dreamed of a permanent home, a place she would never abandon, never give up. Years ago, my mother had fallen in love with the Sonoran Desert, and after my father retired, they moved to Arizona.

Home at last.

My mother's passion for the desert burned deeply. She especially loved the desert mornings and the desert at twilight, those

hours of cool blue shadows and the skies on fire, burning as the sun rose and the sun set. Each morning, she would gather up a large bucket of birdseed and walk down among the stunted trees and shrubs behind the house and scatter the seed over the red earth and scorched stones. She swore that the birds gathered each morning in the trees chattering madly in the blue shadows because they were waiting for her and her bucket of birdseed.

And my mother never let them down, never disappointed them.

My mother made it clear to everyone that she had found her great, good place and that she was not leaving. Her days as a bedouin were over, she told me and my sister. Not long after she and my father had moved to Arizona, my mother told me that she had undertaken a study of the lizards that lived among the sun-blasted stones beyond the house, down by the stunted trees and shrubs.

"They keep reminding me," she said.

"Keep reminding you of what?" I said.

"They keep reminding me of how wonderful it is to simply stay put," said my mother.

My sister is also a soldier's wife, an Army officer's wife. They were stationed in Turkey when my mother checked into the Good Samaritan Hospital. They did not have a telephone. The only way to get a message to them was through the International Red Cross, which was glad to help.

My father asked me and my sister not to come to Arizona just yet. He asked us to wait. My mother's doctor wanted more tests. There was time, my father said. It would be best if we waited.

We waited.

The tests all reached the same conclusion—that there was a small cluster of tumors in my mother's brain. The tumors were cancerous. They were killing her quickly.

I finally called the hospital, talked to her doctor, a neurosurgeon. I asked him for his honest opinion about my mother.

"Come now," he said, "see your mother while she's among the living, or wait and attend the funeral."

I went. So did my sister, her children, and her husband.

Before I got to Phoenix, my mother had the first of many small brain seizures.

The first one came on the day she was supposed to get out of the hospital and go home.

"Home Sweet Home," my mother told me. She wanted what so many human beings finally long for—to die at home.

Medical science had done all it could do. Her doctor recommended ten radiation treatments. They gave my mother's face a warm, golden tan. They turned her eyes a deeper shade of blue. At first the radiation shrank the growing little galaxy of tumors in my mother's brain.

Then the tumors went back to doing what cancer does so well. They grew and grew.

I saw some of my mother's X rays, photographs of the inside of her skull. It was like looking through Dr. Raul Yarp's cracked telescope at some distant cluster of faint stars in the deep night. The tumors looked like distant stars, like tiny smears of dull, vague, milk white light.

After my mother was checked into a semiprivate room in the Good Samaritan Hospital, I called her daily—called her from Maine, from New York City, from the telephone booth in the lobby of the Hotel Querencia in the Big Bend country of west Texas

The pain in my own head was getting worse.

As I talked to my mother, made small talk, I tried to imagine a small galaxy of tumors nibbling away at my brain, feasting on my mind, my memory, my dreams and desires.

Some diet!

No wonder cancers of the brain eat so furiously, so greedily.

About the pain in my head: I did what my mother had done about the pains in her own head. I said nothing. I did not want to be a bother, cause anyone any trouble, be a burden. Meanwhile, the pain came and went, and every time it came, it got a little worse.

Finally, I did end up telling my mother about the sour goings on in my brain. She told me she had had the same pain, the same case of the blues, for years and years. So had my great-uncle Albert, she said, and her mother.

It was a family thing, my mother told me. She had hoped my sister and I would be spared.

She had never considered asking a doctor about the pains in her head, just as she never wanted to go to a doctor about the headaches and blackouts and dizzy spells.

She did not want to be any trouble, the cause of any worry. Still, she told me confidently that she was certain modern medicine could help, and that I should go and have my head looked into.

My father had his camera with him when my mother checked into the hospital. He took photographs of my mother as she did what she did not want to do, leave home, pack a bag, become a bedouin again. After my mother died, my father gave these photographs to me. There are so many, as though even then my father was trying desperately to save what he could of my mother from death, perserve images of her on film when she was healthy and rosy-cheeked, before the cancer took its toll.

I am looking at some of those photographs now as I write. It is like looking at photographs of delicate fossils, fossils of light and color and shape. There are photographs of my mother sitting on her hospital bed, sitting in the big green-vinyl chair next to her bed. She is wearing an elegant pink nightgown. Her hair is meticulous, as it always was. It was then only lightly flecked with gray. After the radiation treatments, her hair turned the color of chalk and began falling out in great wads and tangles, twists and strands.

In some of the photographs, there is a slight knowing smile on my mother's face.

It is her eyes that haunt these photographs, though. Eyes that had turned from hazel to topaz blue.

Bed No. 2, my mother's bed, was near the room's window. When I first saw my mother, she was lying in bed No. 2, which had been raised so that she could look out the window, watch the desert sun rise, watch the desert sun set.

As I bent down to hug my mother when I first saw her in the hospital, I noticed two small black marks on her forehead. The marks looked like a small black cross. I found out that the marks were the simple road map used by the radiologist.

X marks the spot.

I touched the small black cross on my mother's forehead gently.

"Careful," said my mother, smiling. "That's where they zapped me. I'm radioactive. It's not so bad. How many sixty-four-year-old women can say they've got a buzz on all the time?"

I took a damp washcloth from the bathroom, wiped the black cross off her forehead.

"Oh, leave it. The cloth, leave it right there," said my mother.

"God that feels so good. You know what takes the edge off dying? Anything cool. That's all I want from the afterlife. To feel forever cool."

As I wiped the small black cross from my mother's forehead, I remembered that I had seen a similar black cross before, on the foreheads of the gathered congregation of the Mount Hebron First Primitive Methodist Church. The Reverend Conrad Biddle had marked every gathered forehead himself, holding a small bowl of black ashes in one hand, making the sign of the cross on each waiting forehead with the thumb of his other hand. It was Ash Wednesday. It was a lovely mountain day, cool and sunny. Church services were being held outside, on the little bluff overlooking Starlight Creek.

The Reverend Biddle ordered the ashes from a Christian mail-order supply warehouse in Florida. A pound of ready-to-use palm ashes cost the church $4, plus postage and handling.

After the sermon, the gathered congregation, every forehead still marked with a black cross of palm ash, sang hymns. I was down below the bluff, in the creek, in its cold, fast water, trying to tempt trout with Elias Wonder's fly rod, when I heard them singing. Their hymns hung in the cool, spring air, mingled with the soft blues and greens of the valley, with the trill of the creek as it flowed over shallow shoals or slick, eroded limestone. The congregation broke up after the hymn singing. Many of them left the ash cross on their foreheads, a mark of their faith in God, in resurrection, in heaven, a celestial paradise that God had set aside somewhere beyond earth's miseries just for them.

As I left the cool washcloth on my mother's forehead, she whispered something to me. I bent down close. Her lips were dry and deeply cracked. She whispered again.

"Nobody gets off the planet alive," she said.

"Who would want to?"

As the tumors in my mother's brain grew and grew, as she began to drift in and out of reason, in and out of time and place, often my mother would sit straight up in her bed, a confused, bewildered look in her blue eyes.

"What's keeping death?" she would say. "I'm ready to get this show on the road.

"Death's not so bad," my mother would tell me. "Everyone gets a turn.

"Now, it's my turn.

"And it's not so bad. It's the waiting that kills you."

275

We waited together.

My mother, my father, my sister, and me, all of us.

And each day my mother would long a little more deeply not for dying, but for death.

My father fed my mother. He dressed her, put on her makeup, combed her auburn hair, which eventually turned white as chalk and began falling out in wads and knots, in clumps and strands. He kept a careful watch over the many tubes that dripped fluids out of one set of hanging plastic bags into her shrinking body and emptied fluids that dripped out of her body into another set of white plastic bags. One of the tubes gave my mother a steady stream of pure oxygen. My father made sure the tube was always in place and uncrimped, that the oxygen was on and running. He massaged the sagging, atrophied muscles of her legs, bathed her arms and sore hands with sweet-smelling lotions. Each night, my father made sure my mother slept not in one of the hospital's dull green gowns, but in one of her colorful nightgowns he brought fresh and clean to her room each day. He arranged for her hairdresser to come in once a week to do her hair. When my mother's auburn hair turned chalk white and began to fall out, he bought her an auburn wig and told the hairdresser to keep coming. My mother did not like the wig but was always glad to see her hairdresser. She would smile and pull the wig off her head and hand it to him.

"It itches," said my mother. "Take it out in the hall and beat it against a window or something. Better yet, take it with you and give it a good shampooing and vacuuming."

My father selected my mother's meals. He would read to her from the daily menu and make suggestions. Eggs for breakfast, perhaps. Orange juice. Toast and jelly. A nice salad for lunch, with iced tea. For dinner, why not try the grilled chicken and steamed mixed vegetables.

My mother would listen and always order the same thing.

"Just keep the chocolate milk shakes coming," she would say.

My father would chide her playfully and read some other choices off the menu.

My mother would roll her topaz blue eyes and smirk, whisper that it all tasted the same to her, that it all tasted like green mayonnaise and fish heads to her, all of it except the chocolate milk shakes.

"Keep them coming," she said.

Two weeks before she died, even chocolate milk shakes lost their appeal, their taste. All my mother asked for was ice. Shaved ice on her deeply cracked lips. Chips of ice on her tongue.

Early in the mornings, when the room was still thick with shadow, when the morning light coming through the room's window was soft and diffuse, the shaved ice I gently put on my mother's cracked lips looked as blue as her eyes.

For weeks and weeks, my father stayed with my mother day and night, sleeping in the big green chair by her bed. He decorated her half of the room with stuffed animals, all of them bright and colorful, with deliriously cheerful faces stitched onto their heads.

I got to my mother's room each morning by six. Visitors and doctors, social workers and therapists, floor nurses and aides, came and went. The mornings were mostly quiet, though, a quiet broken only by the sudden scream or moan or sobbing of one of the other patients on the oncology floor. My mother was always awake when I got to her room. Sometimes there were tears in her topaz blue eyes, tears not for herself, but for the woman in the bed next to hers, bed No. 1. There was a single, thin, long green curtain between them. The woman's name was Mrs. Whidby. Mrs. Whidby had cancer of the mouth. Whenever the pain came, Mrs. Whidby would open her mouth, tear at the throbbing purple veins in her throat with her hands. In trying to somehow stop or at least slow down the cancer, doctors had removed her tongue, vocal cords, chunks of her cheeks and chin. The only sound that came when Mrs. Whidby tried to scream, as she threw back her head and opened her tongueless mouth wide, was a soft gurgle deep in her lungs.

That gurgle was the most haunting scream of all.

Toxic mixtures of chemicals were being dripped into Mrs.

Whidby's blood. She had had all the surgery and radiation she could have. Now there was only chemotherapy. My mother thought herself truly lucky because her cancer was too far advanced for chemotherapy.

"No machines," said my mother.

"And no chemicals. I don't want to be sick when I die."

"There, there," said my father, turning to go into the bathroom to get more lotion with which to massage my mother's deeply wrinkled, pachydermous skin that hung from her bones in great, jiggling folds.

"Who's he?" said my mother.

"Come on, darling," said my father. "You know who I am. I'm your loving husband of more than thirty years. And you're my beloved wife."

"You're not Bishop Rawls, the upholsterer, are you?" said my mother.

"God, I didn't go and marry Bishop Rawls, the upholsterer, did I?" said my mother nervously.

"There, there," said my father. "No, darling. Come on, now, it's me," said my father, looking into my mother's blue eyes. He stroked her chalk white hair, a clump of which stuck to his fingers.

"I'm that good-looking young lieutenant you married, remember?"

"Oh, yes," said my mother. "The naval officer. Good for me. I always had a thing for sailors."

"Now, now, Donna," said my father, his voice a mix of fear and sadness, frustration and pain.

"Donna, dear, now tell me what kind of a wife are you! You're no Navy wife. Come on, now, what branch of the service have we been in for more than thirty years?" said my father.

"Coast Guard," said my mother.

"Marines.

"Air Force.

"Policeman.

"Fireman.

"Secret Service."

"No! No! . . . The ARMY, Donna. The U.S. Army. You're an Army wife!" said my father, his voice breaking, his hands trembling.

"You don't say," said my mother.

"You don't say."

I read to my mother each day.

My mother loved to read. Her library was considerable. Books had helped the years pass easily by. The tumors in her brain that had turned her hazel eyes topaz blue also gave her eyes a constant twitch. They quivered like cooled Jell-O, like a palsied hand.

So I read to her.

I would tuck three of four pillows behind her back so she could sit up in bed, look out the window, watch the cool blue desert mornings take hold as I read.

In the afternoons, when my sister and father were there, we would lift and drag and pull my mother into a wheel chair, wheel her around and around the hospital's halls. Once she saw her reflection in a floor-to-ceiling window.

"For Chrissake," said my mother, "I'm shrinking. I'm a balding rag doll.

"Roll me on, son. Roll me on."

My mother was right. She was shrinking. Dying is not so much an end as it is a change of forms. My mother's form, her body, was breaking down, shutting down, giving way, changing forms. Time was doing to my mother what it does to all of us eventually, changing her into history. The life that had been my mother would, with death's help, go back to being molecules and atoms and genes, matter and energy that would go on and on.

Ashes to ashes.

Dust to dust.

Water to water.

Carbon to carbon, calcium to calcium, and so on and so on, all of it sooner or later sinking down into the scorched red desert or rising on the cool desert winds at night, or washed away by some sudden wonder of rain, wheeling in wrinkles of light, of energy beyond annihilation.

As I read to her, my mother would stop me, ask me to put ice chips on her tongue. I was putting ice chips on my mother's tongue the morning Mrs. Whidby died.

My mother knew Mrs. Whidby was dead because she could no longer hear Mrs. Whidby's tortured, silent screams. Mrs. Whidby's tortured, silent screams were the soft, gurgling noise that rattled in her lungs.

"Today bird feeder, tomorrow birdseed," said my mother when the soft gurgle in Mrs. Whidby's lungs stopped.

"I'm right behind you, Mrs. Whidby, dear," said my mother as the nurses drew the long green curtain around Mrs. Whidby's bed, Bed No. 1.

My sister came to the hospital each afternoon. I would kiss my mother on the forehead, slip her another piece of ice, then go down to the cafeteria, where I would sip on a can of cold root beer and stare out the tinted windows at the intense orange glare of the desert sun, as my own brain went about trying to understand, make sense of what it was experiencing. Not just another death, but my mother's death, her dying. Somewhere in the spurl of chemical reactions going on ceaselessly in my own brain was my mother's smile, the sharp taste of the root beer on my tongue, all my dreams and desires and longings, all the rivers I had known and all the trout of yesteryear. In that buzzing soup of charged chemicals bubbling about in my triune brain—limbic, reptilian, and neomammalian—was not only every range of light, every press of weather and sky and time I had experienced, but the history of the earth, of life, worlds without end, even the language of stones, and my mother's blue eyes.

I would sometimes sit in the cafeteria of the Good Samaritan

Hospital for hours on end, passing the time just sipping on cans of cold root beer, staring out the windows beyond the rim of the city, out toward the sprawl of the desert, its spare beauty shimmering in the relentless sunlight.

Then I would go back to my mother's room, settle back down in the big green chair beside her bed, read to her, talk to her, laugh with her. We talked and talked, about living and dying, about heaven and hell, about the desert mornings and song birds, even about Helena, Arkansas, and the Delta blues.

I brought a cassette player and put on some Robert Johnson and Son House. The music made her smile. When she was a girl, she said, she often went to Helena and remembered how she had stood on the streets listening to bluesman playing for nickels and dimes. She later learned that among the bluesmen she had heard play outside the jook joints around Helena was Robert Johnson. His music, she remembered, made her clap her hands and tap her feet.

When I played Robert Johnson's Delta blues in her hospital room as she was dying, for a time my mother was a young girl again on the streets of Helena. She smiled. She clapped her tired, sore hands together softly, wiggled her toes, sang along. When the music stopped, she went right on singing, singing that Chicken Little was right, that the sky was falling.

"The sky is always falling," sang my mother, still clapping her hands and wiggling her toes. "Everyone gets beaned sooner or later."

My mother was glad the sky had not fallen on her until she had lost weight, finally reclaimed her figure.

My mother had been fighting weight for years, trying diet after diet after diet, always losing then regaining the same twenty or thirty pounds.

Six months before she lost her balance for good, when the pain in her head became unbearable, when she finally told my father about the blackouts and headaches and dizzy spells and asked him on Labor Day weekend to get her to the emergency room quick, she had been on another diet for six months.

She began losing weight immediately, pounds and pounds of it.

During those months, whenever I called, she would tell me proudly how much weight she had lost. And she never gained so much as a pound of it back, even when she cheated a little and had a frozen Milky Way or Snickers candy bar, both of which she dearly loved.

The weight just kept falling off. A month before a CAT scan discovered the small galaxy of tumors in her brain, my mother told me that her new diet was so successful that she had actually lost her appetite, even for her secret stash of frozen candy bars.

"Everything tastes like bad fish," my mother said.

And the pounds fell away.

Ten pounds.

Fifteen.

Twenty pounds.

More and more.

By the time she checked into the Good Samaritan Hospital, my mother had shed nearly thirty pounds.

Of course, by then she knew that it was not her diet or her dietary resolve that had slimmed her but the cancer in her brain. It had gulped down her appetite.

Death is reciprocity. Life's payback. It is tidy and thorough and settles life's accounts. It is the welcome mithridate to life's fumbling and bumbling, a change of fates, of fortune, of form. That is what I found myself thinking each evening as I left the hospital, went back to my mother's beloved house, sank myself in the cool blue waters of the pool she had insisted on and that she cleaned daily. Coming to the surface of the pool's scrubbed, blue-green surface, I would float there for hours, it seemed, watching the deep desert night go from deep purple to indigo blue.

Often, as I read to my mother, she would raise her arms out to me. She did not want a hug or kiss, or another chocolate milk shake. She wanted to be moved. I would help her roll to one side or the other, prop her up with pillows and rolled-up blankets, raise her bed or lower it. After nearly a month in the hospital, my mother could not get comfortable.

"Can I get you anything, Mom?" I would ask, feeling useless and helpless as she moaned softly while I moved her, tried to find a position that would not cause her pain.

"Yeah," she said. "Get me death. Get it here now. Get it and hurry up about it, so I can get out of this damned bed of nails. The pain of lying here is worse than whatever is growing inside my brain.

"Go on, now, see if you can find death. It's just past Mrs. Whidby's bed, just outside the door, waiting in the hall. I can smell it and hear it and feel it. What's it waiting for? I'm ready. Tell it to come on in.

"This dying all the time is going to be the death of me yet."

And then my mother would laugh.

She was always laughing. My mother loved to laugh. I made her laugh. As she lay there dying, unable to get comfortable, we laughed and laughed.

And the tumors in her brain grew and grew, and her eyes shook and twitched in their sockets and got bluer and bluer.

After the first seizure shook her brain, my mother never stood or walked again. The seizure left a hole in my mother's brain, a hole in time through which my mother kept passing, wandering in and out of normalcy and reason and sweet sanity, as periods of agnosia became more common, strangling her memory like thick gray tangles of fog. She came and went like a flame in a cold, damp wind. One moment she was a little girl in Arkansas. Then she was a young woman in Washington, D.C., working for the War Department during World War II, flirting with young officers waiting to be shipped to the front lines in France because she thought it was her patriotic duty to send them off with a clear image of what it was they would be fighting and dying for. Then,

just as suddenly, she was the shrinking lady in Bed No. 2, my
mother, with topaz blue eyes and chalk white hair that was coming out by the combful as the tumors in her brain went about
killing her. As my mother traveled in and out of time and reason,
she would complain that she was surrounded by people she had
never seen before, people she did not know. People like my father, my sister, and me.

"I'm your son," I would whisper.

"Who knew?" said my mother.

"You don't look like Nathan," she said.

"Nathan who?" I asked.

"Nathan W. Moon, your father," she said.

"No, no, mom," I said tenderly. "Pop's right here."

"Oh," said my mother, sounding more bewildered and confused than ever, "I thought he was Bishop Rawls, the upholsterer."

As she went on drifting in and out of time over the next several
days, my mother went on to tell me that Nathan W. Moon was the
only thing she had ever wanted out of World War II, a dashing
airman, a fighter pilot. She had met him in Washington. He had
just gotten his wings. He was handsome, with dark eyes and
dark, wavy hair. They went out often. They danced from club to
club, went for long walks in the sweet spring nights. They talked
and laughed. They fell in love. Nathan W. Moon finally got his orders. He was shipped off to England, then to France, where his
plane was shot down in December 1944. His family told my
mother of his death in combat. Nathan W. Moon was buried in
his home town, Richmond, Virginia.

"There, there," I said to my mother as she talked on and on
about Nathan W. Moon, about her fighter pilot and how they
danced and danced and laughed and laughed, how she lost herself in his handsome, dark eyes and wavy hair.

I kept asking my mother more and more about Lt. Nathan W.
Moon, the fighter pilot. At the time, I thought what my mother
was telling me were just stories, fantasies spawned by the growing tumors in her brain, some of dying's harmless and innocent
illusions, cancer dreams that helped the days pass easily by.

After my mother died, her sister gave me a handful of creased and cracked and crumbling pages of an old photograph album. I did not look at the pages or even think of them for months. I discovered them again in my briefcase in a hotel room in Chicago. I was in Chicago to receive an award for my first book. I had to give a speech. Even the thought of the speech made me nervous. I tried calming myself down by reading a book. When I opened the book, out fell one of the crinkled and bent and crumbling pages of the photo album that my mother's sister had given me.

The page was decorated with photographs of a young man, a fighter pilot. There were photographs of him smiling in the cockpit of his plane, photographs of him smiling in his full-dress uniform. There were yellowed newspaper clippings about his career as a fighter pilot. There was another newspaper clipping about his death in the skies over France in 1944. Lt. Nathan W. Moon and thousands of other American soldiers were trying desperately to come to the aid of thousands of other American soldiers fighting and dying and shivering to death and trying to hang on in and around the town of Bastogne. When Lieutenant Moon was shot out of the skies, he had no idea he was participating in the soon to be famous Battle of the Bulge.

Beside the small newspaper clipping announcing the death in combat of Lt. Nathan W. Moon of Richmond, Virginia, was a small black-and-white photograph of an unpretentious white marble tombstone. I could still read the inscription, which said only, LT. NATHAN W. MOON, 1920–1944. A GOOD SON. Above the inscription, whoever had cut the stone, had carved a small airplane climbing up through rafts of beautiful and peaceful white clouds.

Two weeks before she died, I asked my mother to tell me more about Lieutenant Moon.

"Who?" said my mother.

"Your handsome fighter pilot," I said.

My mother closed her blue eyes and said only this:

"What goes up must come down."

What goes up must come down.

After my mother kicked the pneumonia that had threatened her life, on and off for almost two weeks, the doctor could not come up with another reason why she could not go home to die.

Which she did. My mother died in the early morning of October 13. I was not there. I was in a room at the Best Western Hotel near the Savannah, Georgia, airport.

I had just checked in.

I had just dumped my duffel bag on the floor and flopped across the room's lonely single bed when the telephone rang. I picked up the receiver.

"Mom's dead," my sister said.

My mother kept shrinking until she died. The last of her auburn hair turned chalk white and fell out. On some mornings, when I got to her hospital room, there would be pools of soft morning sunlight on her pillow, and the hair that had fallen out during the night and was stuck to her pillow and to the shoulders of her pink night gown looked like tiny drifts of pale blue snow. Even after she lost interest, my father went on dressing my mother in nightgowns he brought clean and fresh from home, nightgowns that were red and pink and blue, any color but dull hospital green. Even after she had lost interest, my father went on putting on my mother's makeup. He painted her nails and toenails bright red.

"My toes and I are ready to go," said my mother.

Mrs. Whidby was still alive then, screaming her horrid silent screams behind the dull green curtain separating Bed No. 1 and Bed No. 2. My mother would hear the raspy gurgling coming from Mrs. Whidby's lungs and suddenly pull me close.

"Remember, no chemicals. What's the point of dying, if you can't enjoy it?"

My mother remembered every seizure she had. She told me what they felt like.

"They are warm," she said. "They are painless and peaceful and beautiful."

"Wherever they take me seems like paradise. I want to go back. I want to stay," said my mother.

"Tell me more about your headaches," said my mother.

"Just a vague pain in my head," I said.

My mother, who had become something of an accomplished amateur expert on headaches, speculated on whether the pains in my head might be signs of Bing's headaches, superficial petrosal neuralgia, or the onset of red migraines.

"You don't have to live blue," said my mother.

And the words kept sizzling and popping in my brain, tripping over failed connections, burntout relays, sour pools of disenchanted chemicals as I sat in a white lawn chair on my mother's back porch. Birds were chattering madly down in the cool, dark blue shadows of dusk as the desert beyond my mother's house went on glowing through mists of earthshine and starlight.

A chilly night wind came off distant mountains, a wind as chilly as spring rains. I remember even now how good that wind felt on my arms and throat, on my face.

So good.

As good, I think, as the ice chips I put on my mother's cracked lips and swollen tongue must have felt. I was nursing a root beer poured over a huge glass full of ice as I sat there in the deepening desert night. I let a piece of root beer–soaked ice linger against my lips, on my tongue, closed my eyes, drifted deeper into the blue-black embrace of the night.

Sweet Mother night.

And this is what I was thinking as I sat there, my eyes closed, a piece of wonderfully cold ice wedged between my tongue and teeth: I was thinking that life, like the desert at twilight, burns down, but never completely out, that it is never completely consumed. It burns down to elements and minerals, to particles and waves, the essence that is beyond essence, and flickers in the vital blue light of the glowing earth.

Things burn down to such an everlasting flame.

My mother's life burned in that wondrous and mysterious flame.

So does everything that lives, that is—blind trout and high country meadows, rising whales, even fumbling and stumbling human beings.

As the tumors in my mother's head went on gulping down her mind, eating more and more holes in her brain, sending her in and out of time, my mother told me she was sorry to have survived long enough to learn that dying could be as embarrassing and ridiculous as living. She kept saying how sorry she was to have become, so quickly, such an embarrassing old bag of bones and rubbery skin.

"When death gets here," she said, "don't expect me to have anything monumental or even interesting to say. All I can tell you is that I rather like my head better this way. Everything's so cozy and warm. All my dreams come true.

"So kiss me quick! When I'm gone, I'm gone. Smoke up Rooker's chimney, ashes among the pretty desert rocks."

Rooker's, by the way, was the funeral home in Phoenix that handled "the disposition of my mother's mortal remains." My mother was cremated there. She had decided years ago, when she was plump and healthy with rosy pink skin, that when it was her turn to die she wanted to be cremated. She decided to be cremated all those years ago because she knew even then that death was wonderfully fair and that everyone got a turn. She was simply getting ready for the time when it would be her turn.

My mother liked the idea of being quickly reduced to ash and

bone and a beautiful tendril of blue smoke drifting on a cool desert night wind.

My mother's last wish came true. She wanted to die at home so badly that she miraculously fought off the pneumonia in her lungs. Once the pneumonia set in, her doctors told us that her death was imminent. Her fever rose and rose. She had a "nonproductive" cough. She rarely closed her eyes, rarely even blinked. Her blue eyes seemed to get wider, deeper. Their nervous twitch intensified, became a silent rhythm. Her wild eyes became as blue as the light I would later see in the blind eyes of the brown trout in the deep pool along the Middle Fork of the South Platte River. Its eyes would haunt me, too. In its eyes I would rediscover the light that burned through my own dreams and memories, even the blue of my mother's eyes, that blue which is part of life's primal, coherent flame.

Sometimes, early in the mornings, as the pneumonia filled her lungs and its fever burned through her brain, I would find my mother talking loudly into her left hand, which she was certain was a telephone. She was talking loudly to my father.

"Dear! Baste the chicken or it'll burn, you hear? For Chrissake, baste the damned chicken."

Once my mother handed the telephone in her hand that was never there to me, saying, "Here, it's for you. Long-distance from the land of Oz."

I just stood there smiling helplessly, foolishly.

My mother held her tiny, bruised hand that had become a telephone close to her ear, smiled, and said, "They say to just keep following the Yellow Brick Road."

Once the fever and the pneumonia transported her back to Washington, D.C., and the last year of World War II, back to her job as a secretary at the War Department, where she flirted innocently with all the young officers headed for the front lines. My mother, at one point, lifted her arm, pointed a trembling finger toward the window. Out the window, in the distance, was a plane disappearing inside a boil of white clouds. My mother whispered to me that just such a cloud had taken Lt. Nathan W. Moon and given her another handsome soldier, my father.

"How lucky can one girl be?" said my mother.

As I say, despite the best predictions of modern medicine, my mother kicked the pneumonia. After thirty-four days in room 1221, Bed No. 2, of the Good Samaritan Hospital, the nurses disconnected the many tubes that dripped and drained fluids in and out of my mother.

It took five people to lift my mother from Bed No. 2, ease her into a wheel chair.

"Who am I today?" said my mother.

"I suppose it doesn't matter. Whoever I am, I'm still dying.

"You know, everybody gets a turn. And its my turn now."

She patted my father's hand gently, pointed toward the door, said, "Home, dear. Take me home."

My father had rented a hospital bed and a big cylinder of oxygen.

My father put the rented hospital bed not in his and my mother's room, but in one of the spare bedrooms, the one my mother liked to call my room, even though I had slept in it only twice in the ten years since she had quit being a bedouin and moved into the house she had dreamed of so long, the house in the Arizona desert, her great, good place. Home.

The third time I saw the spare bedroom that my mother kept calling my room, the rented hospital bed my mother died in was still there. So was the bottle of oxygen, which was the same color green as the heap of holly green garbage bags under which Dr. Truth would be found dead, frozen stiff.

My mother died on October 13, 1989, forty-one days after the pain in her head brought tears to her eyes and turned her hazel eyes to blue, forty-one days after she first sat on the edge of Bed No. 2 in room 1221 of the Good Samaritan Hospital, smiling tiredly as my father took what would be the last photographs of her, forty-one days after an emergency-room CAT scan took the first photographs of the amazing little galaxy of tumors in her brain. They looked like the distant stars I had looked at through Dr. Raul Yarp's cracked telescope, tiny smears of light in an infinite sprawl of darkness, like watch fires left burning in the caves of ancient man.

My mother died an hour before sunrise, as blue shadows moved like restless winds across the desert.

And the light came slowly, like measured breaths, tracing itself upon the land. It came easily through the window of the room where my mother was dying, and dripped in thick sheets down the western wall of the room, then moved on.

Moved on and on.

My father was there. He bent down over the rail of the rented hospital bed, held my mother's shrunken, bruised, swollen hands. He was crying softly. My sister was there. She was sitting at the edge of the chair that had been pulled close to the other side of the bed. She was crying softly, too.

My mother's breathing was fast and shallow.

My mother's wild blue eyes were open wide, and there were no tears.

She was not crying softly.

My mother sighed deeply and did what every human being, what everything that lives, gets a chance to do—die.

And dying is not an end or a beginning but an immersion back into life's continuum, back into life as inexplicable process, that mysterious wild dance of chance and wondrous improbability, incredible coincidence, and unbelievable possibility.

Nobody gets off the planet alive. Who would want to, my mother had told me before she died, when all we know of life and of living is here.

Here, in paradise.

There are so many, and all of them so near, Kiwi LaReaux would remind me, if she were here now as I write these words in a small notebook while waiting in the parking lot of the Piggly Wiggly supermarket, waiting for twilight, waiting to haul myself onto the back of county garbage truck No. 2.

There was an open Bible in my sister's hands as my mother died. A veil of soft red light brushed across its white pages. The Bible was open to the Twenty-third Psalm. My sister read the psalm over and over again as my mother died. My mother liked the Twenty-third Psalm. It was her favorite part of the Bible. She thought it was among the most harmlessly cheerful things that the Creator of the Universe had had to say. So my sister read it to her, again and again.

> The Lord is my shepherd; I shall not want.
> He maketh me to lie down in green pastures: he leadeth me
>   beside the still waters.
> He restoreth my soul . . .
> Yea, though I walk through the valley of the shadow of death,
>   I will fear no evil: for thou art with me; thy rod and thy staff
>   they comfort me. . . .
> Surely goodness and mercy shall follow me all the days of my
>   life: and I will dwell in the house of the Lord for ever.

And a veil of soft light brushed gently across the white pages, then moved on.

Moved on and on.

An official of the city and the county pronounced my mother dead. It took several paramedics to lift my mother's body from the rented hospital bed and slip it into a lovely plaid body bag.

What used to be my mother, what was my mother's body, what was left of it, was taken to Rooker's Funeral Home, where it was cremated, where it went up in smoke, two days later.

What was left came back to my father in a shiny bronze box. I helped pick the box from among dozens and dozens of models. So did my father and sister. My father had this simple inscription cut into the lid of the lovely bronze box:

DONNA FAY MIDDLETON

BELOVED WIFE AND MOTHER

JUNE 25, 1924–OCTOBER 13, 1989

What was in the box?

Not my mother. Not even my mother's ashes, really. The bronze box held mostly chunks and pieces of bone, which is all that cremation leaves behind, usually. Just chunks of bone that are ground into a fine gray-white powder.

My mother wanted to be cremated because she thought it was a quick and tidy way of dealing with the body's implication in death. Indeed, cremation was so quick and tidy and efficient that my mother thought it would allow her, in death, to be as she had been in life—never a bother, no trouble, never a burden.

There was something else my mother liked about cremation. She loved the idea of going up in smoke, rising on a cold, blue desert wind just at nightfall, a breath of smoke inhaled and exhaled by the good earth.

As my mother was telling me this, I was thinking that it is not that we have life, but that life has us. While it has us, we hold on tight. Death is the change of form that allows us to let go.

Let go.

Whenever a seizure would rock my mother's brain, she would say, "Wow, that one was a doozie." She told me that, while the seizures lasted, her brain was like an old church pipe organ, all the pipes open, all the peddles pressed to the floor.

"Is there anything I can do?" I would ask my mom whenever a seizure came, feeling ridiculous and awkward, helpless and foolish.

"No," my mother would say. "It's just more boat whistles and clacking trains, thunderclaps and grinding gears.

"And bells, all kinds of bells, ringing and tinkling, chiming and tolling."

My mother would tap the side of her head softly with the tip of her index finger and say, "You wouldn't believe the music going on inside!"

My mother died quietly. During the last week of her life, she came and went, was here and then gone, like a shooting star, like the soft red light against the wall of the spare bedroom where she died, that vein of desert morning light that lingered briefly and then moved on and on, widening and spreading, illuminating the room, the rim-rocked mountains in the distance, the whole desert country, the whole expanse of the dawn sky, just like the light from the tiny spark that broke the hold of Mother night, that tiny spark of light out of which has poured ten billion cubic light years of history and life. And still there is no end in sight. The light goes on and on, burns on and on, a colored flame at the edge of the expanding universe.

There are worlds within worlds.

Worlds without end.

My mother was one such world.

Kiwi LaReaux is another.

So were Lt. Nathan W. Moon and Dr. Truth.

So are Swami Bill and Woody Moos.

Life, finally, is its own consanguinity. Life is life's common ground.

There was a short memorial service for my mother on October 18.

My sister picked out the flowers, including lavender roses, which were one of my mother's favorite flowers. I took one of the lavender roses. I have it still, pressed between the pages of my dictionary.

Which is as good as place as any for pressing a lavender rose. My mother would approve, I think. She loved words. She loved books. Good books, she often said, had helped the years pass easily by.

By the time of the brief memorial service, my mother had already become what she wanted most, the last dream in her brain. She had gone up Rooker's chimney, had become a tendril of blue smoke mingling with the rising, cool desert twilight.

During the memorial service my mother's remains were back at my mother's house, in the lovely bronze box, which my father put on the coffee table in the den next to a vase of flowers and a color photograph of my mother and father taken on their thirty-eighth wedding anniversary.

Late on the night of the 18th, my father, sister, the lovely bronze box, and I boarded a plane for Washington, D.C.

The bronze box was in my father's carry-on bag. He carried it tenderly, lovingly.

Rooker's Funeral Home had given my father a letter to show to airport security. The letter was to let them know that there was nothing dangerous, deadly, menacing, or suspicious about the lovely bronze box, that all it contained were the harmless remains of a dead human being, my mother. Even so, airport security insisted on seeing the bronze box, taking it out of its soft blue velvet case and X-raying its contents.

I did not bother looking at the image of the box as it passed through the X-ray machine.

What was there to see?

We all traveled first-class, even the lovely bronze box that held some of that wondrous conglomerate of luck and happy coincidence that had turned out to be my mother.

The bronze box and its contents, tucked inside my father's

carry-on bag, were in the overhead compartment above my father's head.

As the airplane took off, my father was looking out at the deep, wide, blue-black desert night and crying softly as he held my sister's hand.

My mother's remains were buried at Arlington National Cemetery in a cold, steady rain. My mother had earned the right to be buried at Arlington National Cemetery because she was a soldier's wife.

Arlington is still an active necropolis. The burials go on and on, Monday through Friday. There are more than three thousand burials a year, as many as fifteen a day. At that rate, Arlington will be full and closed for business sometime in 2020. The hills of Arlington, though, will go on being green and shady, thanks to all that human humus and bone meal in the ground.

While the cold rain fell, there was another short memorial service for my mother at the small, quiet, lovely Fort Meyers Chapel located at the Fort Meyers gate to the cemetery. Just before the service, we met with an army chaplain who asked us about my mother so that when he spoke he could say something warm and personal about her.

Every button polished, every surface shined, the soldiers of the Old Guard watch over the Tomb of the Unknowns twenty-four hours a day, in every season, in every press of weather. During the day, depending on the season, the guard is changed every hour or half hour. At night, the guard is changed every two hours. I used to watch the changing of the guards often when my father was stationed at Fort Meyers and at the Pentagon. It is some ritual. Each guard walks exactly twenty-one paces, then turns and faces the tombs for exactly twenty-one seconds.

The army chaplain who spoke at my mother's brief memorial service at the Fort Meyer's Chapel was eloquent. He said that my mother had been a kind and caring human being. My sister had told him that. He mentioned that my mother loved to laugh, that

she had a terrific sense of humor. I told him that. And he said what my father had told him, that my mother had been a soldier's wife, his beloved for forty years.

When the chaplain finished his remarks, a soldier, every button polished, every surfaced shined, carried the lovely bronze box from the chapel to a waiting green army sedan which was parked at the front door of the chapel. There was another soldier there with an umbrella to make sure that no cold rain fell on the lovely bronze box. My father and the chaplain rode in the green army sedan. When my mother's eyes had been hazel, before the tumors in her brain began killing her and turned her eyes to blue, they had flashed with countless shades of green.

The green army sedan and the small coil of cars behind it moved slowly down Patton Drive and Marshall Drive to the entrance of the Columbarium, the bone white amphitheater where the cremated occupants of Arlington National Cemetery reside. The soldier with the umbrella appeared again, as did the soldier whose duty it was to carry the lovely bronze box carefully and respectfully. Directly behind him were the chaplain and my father.

The young soldier carrying the bronze box stopped, slowly lifted the box to a dark opening in the white wall of the Columbarium marked Court 2, Section ii, Stack 20, #4. The soldier with the umbrella no longer tried to make sure that the lovely bronze box stayed dry. Drops of cold rain spattered noisily off the lip of the box, ran down the white walls of the Columbarium. The young soldier put the box into the hole, stepped back, saluted, turned crisply, and marched back to the army sedan. I started counting.

It was exactly twenty-one paces.

The chaplain stood under the dark hole in the gleaming white wall and said a few more words, the last of which were these: "God, we commend to Your safekeeping the soul of Donna Fay Middleton, that she may now be with You in Your kingdom for ever and ever. Amen."

As the chaplain spoke, I did not have the heart to interrupt, to tell him what I had forgotten to mention to him back in the private family room of the chapel, that my mother's spirit had gone where she had wanted it to go, up Rooker's chimney, that it had drifted out over the desert she loved, a tendril of blue smoke that mingled with the cold, blue shadows of the deepening desert twilight.

The chaplain and the green army sedan left.

There were others to bury. In fact, an even dozen more that day. My father lingered there in front of that white wall in the cold October rain. My father had on his dress blues, every button polished, every surface shiny and perfect. Rows of medals hung from his chest. He handed me the camera, asked me to take pictures of him as he stood there in front of the wall where my mother's remains were buried, in that catacomb of holes and urns and boxes.

So I took photographs of my father as he turned to salute my mother. The rain came harder and colder. The last time my father saluted, he held his salute for exactly twenty-one seconds.

"I'll be along soon enough, dear," said my father in a whisper as he held his salute. His face was drawn and tired, and his skin was almost as white as the walls of the Columbarium. His brown eyes were filled with tears, with grief and love, with loneliness and loss, with bewilderment and bone-deep exhaustion.

I noticed as I looked through the camera's viewfinder that his lips and hands were trembling.

"Keep my side warm, dear," said my father.

When my father dies, he too is to be cremated. His remains are to be placed beside my mother's lovely bronze box in the same small vault inside the white marble wall of the Columbarium at Arlington National Cemetery.

I know exactly which fly I caught the blind brown trout on. It came from a waterproof matchbox in my shirt pocket where I always carry it. It was the old fly tied by my great-uncle Albert just before the tumor in his brain killed him.

After his death, after we buried him near Elias Wonder up at the cemetery next to the Mount Hebron First Primitive Methodist

Church, my grandfather went fishing. I was with him. We were fishing the dark, deep waters of Karen's Pool, just across from Elias Wonder's old shack along Starlight Creek. My grandfather was using the trout fly that Albert had tied before he died. He cast line and leader and fly with his old fly rod, letting the fly settle on the surface of the creek on the far side of the pool. The fly spiraled onto the surface of the creek like a fallen leaf and sank down into the current, alluringly, temptingly.

The fly worked. It caught a nice brown trout. It was a miracle because so few of the bizarre trout flies the old men tied ever worked, actually caught trout.

It seemed a sweet and wondrous irony, indeed, that the last two flies that Albert had tied, as the tumor in his brain was transforming him into King Lear, turned out to be irresistible temptations. Pure enticement.

We gave those last two flies names.

Albert's Delight and the Pied Piper.

I caught the blind brown trout with the Pied Piper.

And I brought it close and got lost again in the light and colors and shadows drifting across its sightless, haunting eyes, as I fumbled miserably with the hook. Finally I got it out and watched the blind trout shudder once in the dark, shallow water, then disappear.

All that was left were tiny pools of blue light that marked the trout's presence, wrinkles of blue light that were the same color as my mother's eyes when she died, a deep and wild topaz blue.

I was not in the spare bedroom, the room my mother insisted on calling my room, when she died. I was not there with my father and sister. What I know of that time, I have learned from them, pieced together in my brain with memories of my mother that drift through my brain like tendrils of blue smoke.

As I have said, I was in a room at the Best Western Hotel near the Savannah, Georgia, airport. I was still a full-time magazine writer then. I was supposed to spend the next week writing a story about the dark water magic of the Okefenokee Swamp. The pains in my own head were getting worse. I had not slept for days, ever since leaving my mother's hospital room. I had not eaten.

I had a whopping case of the meat bucket blues.

It would pass, I told myself, as it had always passed before.

It would pass.

I had not been in the room ten minutes when the telephone rang. It was my sister. My mother was dead.

I gathered up my duffel bag and went back to the lobby, explained what had happened to a lady at the desk.

"Things are tough all over," she said. "The room's still forty-nine dollars and ninety-five cents, regardless of who's dead or alive."

I was staring at her hair as I paid. It was gray-blue.

I was on the next flight out of Savannah, on another plane bound for Arizona. I spent the long hours of the flight thinking about my mother. Sometimes I disturbed my fellow passengers by laughing out loud. It was nearly midnight. People were trying to sleep. I kept looking out the window, looking for the sudden glow of the desert night, that sprawl of cold, deep blue night, radiating with earthshine and moon glow.

I turned to find one of the flight attendants bending over me. She had a warm, beautiful face, hazel eyes, skin as smooth as cream. She offered me a small white pillow, a tiny blue blanket. She said I had been laughing out loud, softly. Was everything okay? she wanted to know. Could she get me anything?

I asked for another root beer and a glass with plenty of ice.

I tucked the tiny white pillow behind my head, went back to staring out the window and dreaming and looking—looking for a tendril of blue smoke rising on a cool, desert night wind.

I remembered the last time I had seen my mother, just days before. It was like we were members of Swami Bill's church in progress, the Church of Common Decency, the Ministry of Dig-

nity, the Brotherhood of Fair Shakes, the Communion of Toleration, and the Dignity of Kindred Souls. We joked, we laughed and
laughed. We kissed. My mother wanted to give me a hug, so I
bent down close to her.

Her eyes had gotten bluer, bluer than the Gulf Stream.

As I hugged her, this is what my mother whispered sweetly,
lovingly into my ear, her last words to me.

"Thank you for caring, whoever you are."

That day in December when I caught the blind brown trout was
the last time I would fish the river, the last time I would camp in
the high meadows of South Park beyond the Front Range, in that
bowl of earth and river and mountains, of shadow and sunlight.

I had cleaned out my desk at the magazine the day before,
cleaned out my unfurnished room near the Now & Zen Restaurant, loaded up the Toyota.

The already bad economy was getting worse. Advertising was
miserable, Minzo Root told me. Every magazine and newspaper
in the country was cutting back. He had orders to tighten the
magazine's frayed economic belt. Dozens of people would have
to go, and it was only fair that the first to go should be those who
had been the last to come. So we all got the old heave-ho. It was
nothing personal. Minzo Root said he knew I would find another
job. He was smiling and laughing, trying hard to sound cheerful
and optimistic. While Minzo Root laughed and sounded cheerful,
I was praying silently, thanking the gods that I still had callused
hands and a strong back.

Minzo Root patted me on the back, told me, told everyone that
was cut loose that day, given the old heave-ho, that there was no
need to finish out the day, that we could draw our checks and
take off and hit the road anytime.

That night I ate dinner with Swami Bill and Kiwi LaReaux. We
ate, as we often did, at the Now & Zen Restaurant. Mi Oh was
there, dressed seductively, as always, in her skintight red hostess

dress. Everytime a customer came or went, everytime the door of the Now & Zen was opened or shut, the tiny bells that hung from the ceiling tingled and chimed madly in the sudden press of the night's cold wind.

Mi Oh bent down close to me, kissed me gently on the cheek, said good-bye, wished me *mushin.*

Mushin, I would later learn, was a moment free of thought, unmarred by ego, free of good and evil, of success and failure, of living and of dying, free of everything but the press of time.

Some gift!

All through dinner, I kept losing myself in the deep, heartbreaking beauty of Kiwi LaReaux's green eyes, her smooth, flawless skin, her long, thick, red hair that was pulled back off her neck, tied with a single yellow ribbon. Kiwi LaReaux's hair smelled as always of the high meadows, of cold wind and rushing water, of aspen and pine and jasmine.

Sometime during dinner, Kiwi pressed a polished moldavite stone and a Tantric mala into my hand.

"Manna from heaven," she whispered in a sigh that sent a tremble through the dim orange flame of the candle in the plastic red lantern at the center of the table.

The moldavite stone was part of a shipment Swami Bill and Kiwi LaReaux were using for their new egg-shaped flotation and meditation tanks. The secret, said Kiwi LaReaux, was plenty of Epsom salts and lots of moldavite, which, she said, were marvelous for fine-tuning one's spiritual evolution.

The moldavite stone she pressed into my hand was the color of her eyes, an incredible green, soft and deep and radiant.

When I finally took my eyes off Kiwi LaReaux, I noticed that Swami Bill had his hand over his mouth. The parrot on his shoulder was getting ready to speak, was flapping its musty, dingy green-and-blue wings. The parrot listed to the right, then to the left, as Swami Bill worked the wires in the sleeve of his apple green monk's robe.

The parrot reminded me that Bill could get me into any heaven I wanted, the heaven I dreamed of, yearned for, when the time came.

Bill squawked and the parrot squawked, and everyone, being members of Swami Bill's church in progress, laughed and laughed.

"Live and let live," said Kiwi LaReaux.

"Grin and abide," said Mi Oh.

"OLLIE-OLLIE-OXEN-FREE," squawked Swami Bill, squawked Swami Bill's parrot, its wings flopping this way and that, as the wires in Bill's sleeve snapped and the parrot toppled off Bill's shoulder and into a plate of simmering Moo Goo Gai Pan.

And we all laughed and laughed, shook hands, exchanged hugs and kisses, sang happy-go-lucky songs.

I remember the touch of Kiwi LaReaux's lips on my cheek.

Paradise.

There are so many.

The next day, as it snowed and snowed, as I drove out of Fairplay and headed south through Colorado toward northern New Mexico, I slipped one of Swami Bill's subliminal self-help tapes into my cassette player. Over the sound of waterfalls and thunderstorms, of crashing waves and chattering songbirds, was Kiwi LaReaux's lovely voice, whispering shyly.

"More grace.

"Pay as you go.

"More charity.

"More tolerance.

"More kindness.

"More laughter.

"Lots more."

I kept driving south. Even so, the snow came harder and harder. Some time during the night, I pulled off the highway near Questa, New Mexico. I crawled into the back of the Toyota, into my blue sleeping bag. Across the road was a small adobe church outlined in strings of Christmas lights, red-and-green, silver-and-gold, all of them bubbling and twinkling. The double wooden doors to the small church were open. Shadows drifted across the a stained-glass window on which the Creator of the Universe, outstretched on a great raft of billowing white clouds, extended his hand to human beings down below who were frantically reaching up, trying desperately to grab the Creator's hand and hang on.

Hang on.

Through the double wooden doors of the little church, I could see the assembled congregation, mostly women and young children and a few old men. They were standing, holding hands and singing.

They sang in Spanish. I could not understand a word of the song. Even so, it was some of the most beautiful music I have ever heard come from human beings. I watched and I listened and the snow fell harder and I fell asleep.

Morning broke clear. Thick tides of red sunlight covered the land, that whole bright country.

The doors of the church were shut, but the strings of Christmas lights outlining its doors and windows, the simple cross on its roof, were still on, blinking and twinkling wildly in the intense morning sunlight.

Already the snow below the near mountains, among the grass and earth red stones was melting, sending small, cold rivers of blue water rushing down the highway.

Water, again.

Moving water, wild water.

I smiled and headed south, let the water carry me away.

Carry me away.